Other Titles in the Jossey-Bass Nonprofit & Public Management Series

New Paradigms for Government, *Patricia W. Ingraham, Barbara S. Romzek, and Associates*

Strategic Planning for Public and Nonprofit Organizations, Revised Edition, *John M. Bryson*

Handbook of Public Administration, Second Edition, *James L. Perry*

Creating and Implementing Your Strategic Plan Workbook, *John M. Bryson, Farnum K. Alston*

Handbook of Practical Program Evaluation, *Joseph S. Wholey, Harry P. Hatry, Kathryn E. Newcomer*

Handbook of Training and Development for the Public Sector, *Montgomery Van Wart, N. Joseph Cayer, Steve Cook*

Strategic Management of Public and Third Sector Organizations, *Paul C. Nutt, Robert W. Backoff*

The Search Conference, *Merrelyn Emery, Ronald E. Purser*

Seamless Government, *Russell M. Linden*

Authentic Leadership, *Robert W. Terry*

Catalytic Leadership, *Jeffrey S. Luke*

Planners on Planning, *Bruce W. McClendon, Anthony James Catanese*

Benchmarking for Best Practices in the Public Sector, *Patricia Keehley, Steven Medlin, Sue MacBride, Laura Longmire*

Transforming Public Policy, *Nancy C. Roberts, Paula J. King*

The Spirit of Public Administration, *H. George Frederickson*

Understanding and Managing Public Organizations, Second Edition, *Hal G. Rainey*

New Strategies for Public Pay, *Howard Risher, Charles Fay*

Grassroots Leaders for a New Economy, *Douglas Henton, John Melville, Kimberly Walesh*

Human Resources Management for Public and Nonprofit Organizations, *Joan E. Pynes*

How Do Public Managers Manage? *Carolyn Ban*

Leading Without Power: Finding Hope in Serving Community, *Max De Pree*

The Leader of the Future, *Frances Hesselbein, Marshall Goldsmith, Richard Beckhard, Editors*

The Organization of the Future, *Frances Hesselbein, Marshall Goldsmith, Richard Beckhard, Editors*

Transforming Government

Lessons from the Reinvention Laboratories

Patricia W. Ingraham

James R. Thompson

Ronald P. Sanders

Editors

Jossey-Bass Publishers • San Francisco

Copyright © 1998 by Jossey-Bass Inc., Publishers, 350 Sansome Street, San Francisco, California 94104.

All rights reserved. No part of this publication may be reproduced, stored in a retrieval system, or transmitted, in any form or by any means, electronic, mechanical, photocopying, recording, or otherwise, without the prior written permission of the publisher.

Substantial discounts on bulk quantities of Jossey-Bass books are available to corporations, professional associations, and other organizations. For details and discount information, contact the special sales department at Jossey-Bass Inc., Publishers (415) 433–1740; Fax (800) 605–2665.

For sales outside the United States, please contact your local Simon & Schuster International Office.

Jossey-Bass Web address: http://www.josseybass.com

This paper is acid-free and 100 percent totally chlorine-free.

Library of Congress Cataloging-in-Publication Data

Transforming government : lessons from the reinvention laboratories / Patricia W. Ingraham, James R. Thompson, Ronald P. Sanders, editors. — 1st ed.
p. cm. — (The Jossey-Bass nonprofit & public management series)
Includes bibliographical references and index.
ISBN 0-7879-0931-9
1. Administrative agencies—United States—Management. 2. Administrative agencies—United States—Reorganization. 3. Public adminstration—United States. I. Ingraham, Patricia W. II. Thompson, James R. III. Sanders, Ronald P. IV. Series: Jossey-Bass nonprofit and public management series.
JK421.T83 1997
352.3'0973—dc21 97-33238

FIRST EDITION
HB Printing 10 9 8 7 6 5 4 3 2 1

The Jossey-Bass
Nonprofit & Public Management Series

Contents

Preface ix
The Editors xiii
The Contributors xvii

Part One: Strategic Change in Public Organizations 1

1 **Ferment on the Front Lines: Devising New Modes of Organizing** 5
James R. Thompson

2 **Heroes of the Revolution: Characteristics and Strategies of Reinvention Leaders** 29
Ronald P. Sanders

3 **The Best-Kept Secret in Government: How the NPR Translated Theory into Practice** 58
John M. Kamensky

4 **Reinventing Public Agencies: Bottom-Up Versus Top-Down Strategies** 97
James R. Thompson, Ronald P. Sanders

Part Two: The Tactics of Change in Public Organizations 123

5 **Overcoming Employee Resistance to Change** 125
David G. Frederickson, James L. Perry

6 **Ingredients for Success: Five Factors Necessary for Transforming Government** 147
Hal G. Rainey

7 **Tailoring Change Strategies: Alternative Approaches to Reform** 173
B. Guy Peters

Part Three: Lessons for Continuing Transformation 191

8 **Where the Buck Stops: Accountability in Reformed Public Organizations** 193
Barbara S. Romzek

9 **Making Government Reform Stick: Lessons Learned** 220
Donald J. Savoie

Conclusion: Transforming Management, Managing Transformation 241
Patricia W. Ingraham

Index 257

Preface

The pervasiveness of change in public organizations—at all levels of government and in virtually all nations—is undeniable. Downsizing, privatization, contracting out, reengineering, and reinvention have become the watchwords of public management. The United States, though clearly a laggard in many of the more dramatic reforms, is a leader in simple numbers. Despite the pervasive nature of change, however, the lessons drawn and/or learned from the reform efforts are surprisingly limited. This is because many public organizational changes in the United States are small and relatively hidden from view; public scrutiny is not necessarily a good partner in change. The experiences and lessons are, nonetheless, very important.

The need is growing constantly for public managers and elected officials to know of changes in other governments and other settings, and to understand the strengths and weaknesses of those changes. For managers and leaders of the various reinvention laboratories that are part of the reinvention revolution in the federal government, for state and local leaders contemplating or implementing civil service reform, and for the many public managers attempting to create performance-based organizations amid the sea of existing laws and procedures, knowing and understanding what is happening elsewhere is of enormous significance.

This need for knowledge seems somewhat odd, given the contemporary ability to communicate instantly through e-mail and the World Wide Web. The irony for those who would create and manage effective change is that increased communication does not, unfortunately, always lead to improved understanding. Indeed, there is evidence that, although management techniques and ideas are passed around quickly, evaluation of their strengths and weaknesses and their particular fit with different contexts and public settings is much slower to be developed and communicated. Policy learning and guidance, even in a time of very rapid policy information diffusion, remain elusive.

Academic analysis and insight have also been behind the curve. The presence of numerous learning laboratories and the remarkable opportunities offered for academic and theoretical analysis have not generally translated into a better ability to support future change with more rigorous theory and with better-informed policy guidance. If public managers are frequently managing "off the map" these days, academics are not far behind in venturing into the unknown.

Background of This Book

Transforming Government is an effort to sort through some of the reform and change management activities at all levels of government in the United States and to nest those activities—and the preliminary management and policy lessons they permit—in past lessons and in theory. It is not comprehensive; there are far too many management reform efforts, both large and small, to catalogue accurately, much less carefully analyze. It does, however, include reforms we have judged to be representative of the major efforts now under way.

The book's early development occurred in the fall of 1995; at that time John Palmer, dean of the Maxwell School of Citizenship and Public Affairs at Syracuse University, and Ben Ware, vice chancellor for research at the university, provided funding for a small symposium at the Syracuse University Center in Washington, D.C., the Greenberg House. The intention was to gather academics and managers of leading reinvention laboratories—a critical component of the Clinton administration's broader "reinventing government" reforms—to begin analysis of the reinvention lab experience.

The reinvention laboratories were created pursuant to a letter that Vice President Al Gore Jr. sent to all department heads on May 1, 1993. In the letter, Gore asked each department to designate two or three programs or units "to be laboratories for reinventing government." Gore's letter continued: "The point is to pick a few places where we can immediately unshackle our workers so they can reengineer their work processes to fully accomplish their missions—places where we can fully delegate authority and responsibility, replace regulations with incentives, and measure our success by customer satisfaction."

Presentations at the Maxwell Reinvention Symposium were made by selected lab managers representing the national and field offices of the Department of Agriculture (the Animal and Plant Health Inspection Service), the Department of Labor (the Occupational Safety and Health Administration), the Department of Housing and Urban Development (Public and Indian Housing), the Department of Health and Human Services (Indian Health Service), the Department of Defense (Chemical and Biological Defense Command), the General Services Administration, and the Internal Revenue Service.

The managers described changes ranging from the development of cogovernance public health structures with Native Americans in Alaska to the contracting out of real estate services in the Philadelphia regional office of the General Services Administration. The changes described had several common characteristics: they were slow, painful, and often resisted by other levels of the organization. All of the changes were cumulative; they built on a series of management and reform efforts over at least the last decade. Despite the slowness of the changes and the frequent aggravation described by the lab managers, their enthusiasm for better management and more productive public organizations was contagious.

The chapters in this book reflect the conference discussions, but also many follow-up queries and debates. They also reflect analysis of changes at other levels of government. The chapters make every effort to link the experiences described by those who are managing the changes to theory and the guidelines it would suggest. While practical lessons can and do emerge, the enormity of the lesson-drawing gap that still remains is clear.

Acknowledgments

The editors and authors of this book wish to extend our deepest thanks to the public managers and leaders who shared their experiences, their files, and their hopes for transforming government with us. We are particularly grateful to the lab managers who attended the Greenberg meeting:

Bob Albicker, Internal Revenue Service

David Gradick, Animal and Plant Health Inspection Service, U.S. Department of Agriculture

Mike Janis, Public and Indian Housing, Department of Housing and Urban Development

Bob Kulick, Occupational Safety and Health Administration, Department of Labor

Richard Mandsager, Indian Health Service, Department of Health and Human Services

Joel Sacks, Occupational Safety and Health Administration, Department of Labor

Jim Schmidt, Chemical and Biological Defense Command, Department of Defense

Jan Ziegler, Public Buildings Service, General Services Administration

Some of them have been labeled heroes of the "revolution"; they squirm at the title. As we worked on this book and came to understand the depth of commitment and talent represented by these managers, however, it became clear that no accolade can do them justice. It became equally clear that the process of change in public organizations is essentially relentless. Taking the time to step back in order to contribute to learning lessons is an added task in the complex enterprise of managing change. Our thanks. We also thank Strom Z. Kong of the Maxwell School for his assistance in assembling the final version of the book.

August 1997

PATRICIA W. INGRAHAM
Syracuse, New York

JAMES R. THOMPSON
Chicago, Illinois

RONALD P. SANDERS
Washington, D.C.

The Editors

Patricia W. Ingraham is professor of public administration and political science and director of the Alan K. Campbell Public Affairs Institute at the Maxwell School of Citizenship and Public Affairs, Syracuse University. She also directs the Government Performance Project in the Campbell Institute. She obtained her bachelor's degree in political science from Macalester College (1964), her master's degree in political science from Michigan State University (1965), and her doctorate in political science and policy science from the State University of New York at Binghamton (1979).

A former career civil servant, Ingraham has spent much of her academic career examining the issues related to reform of public management systems and structures. She has testified before both houses of Congress on reform measures and has lectured widely in the United States and abroad on the topic.

She is a Fellow of the National Academy of Public Administration, an International Fellow of the Canadian Centre for Management Development, and past president of the National Association of Schools of Public Affairs and Administration. She has also served as a staff member of the National Commission on the Public Service. She received the ASPA/NASPAA Distinguished Research Award in 1994 and the Syracuse University Chancellor's Citation for Academic Excellence, the ASPA/NASPAA Levine Award for Excellence in Teaching and Research, and the ASPA Mosher Award in 1996.

Ingraham is the author or editor of a number of books and articles. Her most recent books are *The Foundation of Merit: Public Service in American Democracy* (1995) and *Civil Service Reform: Making Government Work* (1996).

James R. Thompson is assistant professor of public administration at the University of Illinois–Chicago. He received his B.A. degree

(1973) from Swarthmore College in history, his M.P.A. degree (1976) from the State University of New York at Albany, and his Ph.D. degree (1996) from the Maxwell School of Citizenship and Public Affairs at Syracuse University in public administration.

From 1977 to 1992, Thompson held various positions in the governments of the city of Rochester and Monroe County, New York. His dissertation, titled "Organizational Politics and Innovation in the Federal Reinvention Laboratories," received an honorable mention from the National Association of Schools of Public Affairs and Administration in 1996. He has published a number of articles and book chapters on government reform and organizational change in the public sector.

Ronald P. Sanders is associate professor of public administration and director of the Center for Excellence in Municipal Management, School of Business and Public Management, George Washington University. He received a B.A. degree in business management from the University of South Florida (1973), an M.S. in human resource management and industrial relations from the University of Utah (1976), and a D.P.A. from George Washington University (1990).

Sanders serves as cochair of the District of Columbia's Council on Competitive Government and the National Performance Review's Privatization Roundtable. He has taught at China's National School of Administration and has consulted for several foreign governments, including Ukraine, Korea, and Jordan. He was awarded the presidential rank of Meritorious Executive in 1994 and has been awarded the Defense Civilian Service Medal and the Office of Personnel Management Director's Citation for Exemplary Public Service, as well as two Hammers of Reinvention from Vice President Al Gore. He has received *Government Executive* magazine's Leadership Award and was named to the International Personnel Management Association's 1994 "All Star" team.

Sanders is a coauthor of *Civil Service Reform: Building a Government That Works* (with D. Kettl, P. Ingraham, and C. Horner, 1996). He has also been published in several professional and academic journals and has contributed chapters to several books, including the Volcker Commission's final report, *Leadership for America: Rebuilding the Public Service* (1989).

From 1990 to 1995, Sanders served as the U.S. Department of Defense's senior career human resource management executive;

he founded the Defense Civilian Personnel Management Service, serving as its first director and CEO. He has been an elected member of the board of directors of the Senior Executives Association since 1990, and its secretary since 1995. Prior to his appointment in the Department of Defense, he served as deputy director of civilian personnel for the Department of the Air Force.

The Contributors

DAVID G. FREDERICKSON is a Ph.D. student in public affairs at Indiana University's School of Public and Environmental Affairs. He received his B.A. degree (1992) from Brigham Young University and his M.P.A. degree (1995) from George Mason University. His research interests are administrative reform efforts and public budgeting.

JOHN M. KAMENSKY is the deputy project director for Vice President Al Gore's National Performance Review. He received his B.A. degree (1975) from Angelo State University in government and his M.P.A. degree (1977) from the Lyndon B. Johnson School of Public Affairs.

For sixteen years, Kamensky was an assistant director with the U.S. General Accounting Office (GAO), where he was responsible for evaluating federal agency management improvement efforts. He specialized in management issues, with an emphasis on federal-state-local relations. At the GAO, Kamensky examined the experiences of several countries and states in implementing "managing for results" concepts and assisted in the development of the Government Performance and Results Act. He previously managed the GAO's work on intergovernmental programs such as block grants, regulatory reform, and grant formulas. He also served on an assignment to the U.S. House of Representatives' Ways and Means oversight subcommittee. As a captain in the U.S. Air Force Reserves, Kamensky worked for the Office of Economic Adjustment in the Office of the Secretary of Defense, assisting communities facing base closures.

JAMES L. PERRY is professor of public administration at the School of Public and Environmental Affairs, Indiana University. He received his B.A. degree (1970) in public affairs from the University of Chicago and his M.P.A. (1972) and Ph.D. (1974) degrees from Syracuse University.

Perry's research focuses on issues of public management and public personnel management. He is a leading authority on pay-for-performance systems in the public sector. He is presently conducting research on public service motivation.

Perry is the recipient of the Yoder-Heneman Award for innovative research from the Society for Human Resource Management, the Charles H. Levine Memorial Award for Excellence in Public Administration, and a National Association of Schools of Public Affairs and Administration Fellowship. He edited the *Handbook of Public Administration,* second edition (1996), and his research has appeared in such journals as the *Academy of Management Journal, Academy of Management Review, Administrative Science Quarterly, American Political Science Review,* and *Public Administration Review.*

B. Guy Peters is Maurice Falk Professor of American Government in the Department of Political Science at the University of Pittsburgh. He received his B.A. degree (1966) from the University of Richmond and his M.A. (1967) and Ph.D.(1970) degrees from Michigan State University, all in political science.

Peters is the author of eighteen books, including *The Pathology of Public Policy* (1985), *The Politics of Expert Advice* (1993), *Governance in a Changing Environment* (1995), *The Politics of Bureaucracy* (4th ed., 1995), and *American Public Policy* (4th ed., 1996); more than 120 articles in scholarly journals and edited books; and over three hundred conference papers. He is founding coeditor of *Governance* and editor of the *International Library of Public Policy* and is on the editorial boards of the *Journal of Public Policy, Public Administration Review, Journal of European Public Policy, Policy Studies Journal,* and *Journal of Public Administration Research and Theory.*

Peters was previously professor of public policy studies and political science and director of the Center for Public Policy Studies, Tulane University; associate professor of political science at the University of Delaware; and assistant professor of political science at Emory University. He has held visiting positions at the University of Strathclyde; Hochschule St. Gallen; the University of Manchester; the University of Stockholm; the University of Bergen;

El Colegio de Mexico; the University of Leiden; Erasmus University; and Carnegie-Mellon University; and is a regular academic visitor at Nuffield College, Oxford.

He has consulted with the Organization for Economic Cooperation and Development, the Canadian Centre for Management Development, the Chinese National School of Administration, and the auditor general of Canada. His principal professional interests remain comparative administration (especially administrative reform) and European politics. He is currently senior fellow at the Canadian Centre for Management Development and a adjunct faculty member at Forvaltningshogskolan, University of Gothenberg (Sweden).

HAL G. RAINEY is professor of political science at the University of Georgia. He received his B.A. degree (1968) in English from the University of North Carolina at Chapel Hill and his M.A. degree (1973) in psychology and Ph.D. degree (1977) in public administration from the Ohio State University.

His main research activities have been in management in the public sector, with an emphasis on leadership, incentives, organizational change, organizational culture and performance, and the comparison of organization and management in the public and private sectors. In 1995 Rainey received the Charles H. Levine Award for Excellence in Research, Teaching, and Service, conferred jointly by the American Society for Public Administration and the National Association of Schools of Public Affairs and Administration. He has served as chair of the Public and Nonprofit Sectors Division of the Academy of Management and as chair of the Public Administration Section of the American Political Science Association. The first edition of his book *Understanding and Managing Public Organizations* won the Best Book Award of the Public and Nonprofit Sectors Division of the Academy of Management in 1992. He also has written numerous articles on management in the public sector.

In 1991, Rainey served on the Governor's Commission on Effectiveness and Economy in Government of the State of Georgia. As a commissioner, he served on the Task Force on Privatization. In 1995 he served on the Athens–Clarke County Consolidation Charter Overview Commission of Athens–Clarke County, Georgia.

Barbara S. Romzek is professor of public administration at the University of Kansas and has served as department chair. She received her B.A. degree (1970) from Oakland University, her M.A. degree (1972) from Western Michigan University, and her Ph.D. degree (1979) from the University of Texas at Austin, all in political science.

Her research interests include public management, accountability, intergovernmental relations, and employee commitment. She consults in the area of public management and personnel administration for various federal, state, and local governments and professional management associations. She is the coauthor of *New Governance for Rural America: Creating Intergovernmental Partnerships* (1966) and *Public Administration: Politics and the Management of Expectations* (1991). She is coeditor of *New Paradigms for Government: Issues for the Changing Public Service* (1994). Her work has also been published in various social science journals.

Donald J. Savoie holds the Clément-Cormier Chair in Economic Development at the Université de Moncton, where he also teaches public administration. He earned a B.A. degree (1968) in political science and a B.S. degree (1969) in economics at the Université de Moncton, an M.A. degree (1972) in political science at the University of New Brunswick, and a Ph.D. degree (1979) in politics at Oxford University.

Savioe has extensive work experience in government and in academia. He has held senior positions with the government of Canada, including assistant secretary for corporate and public affairs with the Treasury Board (1987–1988) and deputy principal of the Canadian Centre for Management Development (1988–1990). He founded the Canadian Institute for Research on Regional Development at the Université de Moncton in 1983 and was appointed professor of public administration.

He has served as an adviser to a number of federal, provincial, and territorial government departments and agencies; the private sector; independent associations; the Organization for Economic Cooperation and Development; the World Bank; and the United Nations. His report on regional development efforts in Atlantic Canada led to the establishment of the Atlantic Canada Opportunities Agency.

Savoie was made an Officer of the Order of Canada (1993), awarded an honorary doctorate from the Université Ste.-Anne (1993), elected Fellow of the Royal Society of Canada—Canada's National Academy (1992), awarded the Canada 125 medal (1992), selected alumnus of the year at the Université de Moncton (1991), and named Honorary Patron, Order of Regents, Université de Moncton. He was also appointed *associé* of the École Nationale d'Administration Publique in 1992.

Savoie is the author of numerous books, including *Thatcher, Reagan and Mulroney: In Search of a New Bureaucracy* (1994), *Regional Economic Development: Canada's Search for Solutions* (1992), and *La Lutte pour le développement* (1988). His book *The Politics of Public Spending in Canada* was the inaugural recipient of the "Smiley Prize" (1992), awarded biennially by the Canadian Political Science Association. He was also awarded the Prix France-Acadie (1993) for the book *Les Défis de l'industrie des pêches au Nouveau-Brunswick* and the Mosher prize by the *Public Administration Review* (U.S.) for the best article in the public administration field in 1994. He has edited numerous books, contributed chapters to edited books published in Canada and abroad, and written many articles that have appeared in professional journals. He has been coeditor of the *Canadian Journal of Regional Science* and has been a member of the editorial boards of *Governance, Canadian Public Administration,* and *Optimum.*

Savoie has been a member of the advisory committee of the Order of Canada, the National Task Force on Incomes and Adjustment in the Atlantic Fishery, the steering committee of Canada's Prosperity and Competitiveness planning exercise, Canada's International Trade Advisory Committee, the Economic Council of Canada, the national executive of the Institute of Public Administration of Canada, and the advisory council of the Institute for Intergovernmental Relations at Queen's University.

Part One

Strategic Change in Public Organizations

Although "reinvention" has been a common theme of governments at all levels in recent years, attempts to assess and draw formal lessons from that activity have been limited. Basic questions remain open: Do new organizational models work? Can large government organizations change methods of doing business in fundamental ways? How viable are models that attempt to separate operations from policy? Can administrative systems be reformed independently of political systems?

Embedded in this book is the premise that an investigation of these questions and of change phenomena can be fruitfully pursued inductively, by going out into the field, observing what is happening in government organizations, and talking with the people involved in trying to bring about change.

As the contributors to this collection made the effort to connect with practitioners, some of what they found was surprising, some was not. There is much evidence to support the contention that the bureaucratic model of organizing is increasingly ill suited to the challenges of the present. Those challenges include dwindling resources, rapidly advancing technology, and public frustration with poor service delivery. One response to these pressures is simply to privatize the service delivery functions of government. The state of Texas has considered the privatization of its entire apparatus for the provision of welfare services, and private sector companies see potential for vast new markets in such proposals (Harwood, 1997). If politicians and public managers do not find more efficient and effective means of delivering service, increasingly large portions of public services may simply be turned over to the private sector.

If the bureaucratic model is inadequate, advocates of change need to identify what will replace it. In Chapter One, James Thompson identifies some elements of the emerging model, including the use of self-directed teams, partnering with other organizations to improve service delivery, and expanded use of information technology. Still, Thompson acknowledges that "no alternative as clearly defined as the bureaucratic archetype has yet emerged."

Change leaders in government have not been impeded by the lack of a clearly delineated rival to the bureaucratic model. Instead, they have employed some of the principles associated with the new approaches to organizing, such as employee empowerment and improved service to customers, in redesigning their own structures, tailored to the needs of their agency and environment. Thompson suggests that it may be precisely this flexibility that is the hallmark of this new era; rather than seeking a single organizational template, we should simply acknowledge "a move away from rigidity and permanence and toward fluidity and flexibility."

In circumstances in which the formal structure is more flexible, there is greater latitude for the exercise of leadership. In Chapter Two, Ronald Sanders cites multiple examples of public managers who have seized the opportunity afforded them by demands for change to identify and implement new modes of operation. Common attributes of these individuals, according to Sanders, include "a sense of purpose, strategic perspective, persistence, a proclivity to take risks, and a willingness to share power."

Apparent from Sanders's discussion is that change in public organizations is a highly strategic enterprise; would-be change agents have to account for the conflicting objectives of multiple stakeholders both inside and outside the organization. Often, managers embarking on a change journey do so despite disincentives, including both the risk to their own career that may be incurred by offending powerful stakeholders and the complications of imposing a change agenda on top of already-significant day-to-day managerial demands. The individuals who are willing to pursue a change agenda in such circumstances demonstrate traits and behaviors often associated with the word *leadership*. The close correlation of successful attempts at change with effective leadership is a theme that runs throughout the book.

While most would-be change agents address strategic issues in the context of a specific agency or department, John Kamensky, deputy director of the National Performance Review, had the opportunity to help devise a strategy for the federal government as a whole. In Chapter Three, Kamensky details some of the thinking that went into that strategy and discusses how the strategy shifted in response to external events. Apparent from Kamensky's discussion are both the achievements and the limitations of what has been achieved to date.

In Chapter Four, James Thompson and Ronald Sanders explore alternative strategies for reforming large bureaucratic organizations employed by the Veterans Benefits Administration and the Internal Revenue Service. They identify key dimensions along which the strategies can be explored, and they conclude that the two strategies can usefully be contrasted using engineering and gardening metaphors.

Reference

Harwood, J. "EDS and Lockheed Compete for Texas Welfare Contract." *Wall Street Journal,* Mar. 19, 1997, p. A1.

Chapter One

Ferment on the Front Lines

Devising New Modes of Organizing

James R. Thompson

As officials at all levels of government seek to "reinvent" their offices and agencies under pressure to change from budget-conscious legislatures, election-conscious executives, and service-conscious citizens, many look for guidance to the burgeoning organizational-change literature. Much of that literature is premised on the need for an alternative to the traditional, bureaucratic model of organizations. Although no alternative as clearly defined as the bureaucratic archetype has yet emerged, the outline of such a model is becoming apparent. It is grounded philosophically in Total Quality Management (TQM) and incorporates key TQM techniques and ideas, such as teaming, employee empowerment, and a customer focus, but it goes beyond TQM in a number of respects. It emphasizes the use of technology to expedite the transfer of information, learning as a means of maintaining organizational flexibility, and networking with other organizations as a means of achieving objectives.

As this new model emerges and as organizations attempt to test its various features, a central problem becomes that of implementation or, in the words of Kanter, Stein, and Jick (1992, p. 5), how to get "from here to there." The would-be change agent is likely to encounter many obstacles; some, identified by Herbert Kaufman (1971), are the "collective benefits of stability," people who stand to lose status or pay, the psychic costs of change, resource limitations, sunk costs, and official and unofficial constraints on behavior. The problem of implementation is exacerbated in the public sector by features of our political system that tend to reinforce hierarchical approaches to organizing, most prominently the desire of political overseers for clear lines of accountability.

This chapter examines some of the key elements of the new organizational model and includes a discussion of the problems some agencies have encountered as they have attempted to implement these elements. The discussion is placed in the context of what Nadler, Gerstein, Shaw, and Associates (1992, p. 4) describe as organizational "architecture." Architecture includes "the formal structure, the design of work practices, the nature of the informal organization or operating style, and the processes for selection, socialization, and development of people." Features of the new architecture that are discussed here include the use of teams, the reengineering of work processes, the use of information technology, networking, "virtual" organizations, and learning as a feature of organizational life. Each of these elements is discussed in the context of one or more case studies of change or attempted change by a public agency.

Moving to Team-Based Structures

Due in large part to the quality management movement, teams have become one of the central elements of the new organizational "architecture." Teams provide a basis for incorporating many of the "organic" features identified by Burns and Stalker (1994) into day-to-day organizational functioning: horizontal communication, the capacity for self-direction, and the displacement of narrow technical concerns by a concern for overall organizational performance. Nadler, Gerstein, Shaw, and Associates (1992, p. 5) identify autonomous work teams as a key element of the new organizational architecture. They comment that such teams "provide their own supervision, cross train and change roles, and in many ways are empowered to take responsibility for their own processes and results."

Government agencies as well as private sector organizations are making increased use of teams as a means of enhancing performance while complying with restrictive budgets. Factors that have encouraged the use of teams in the federal government are the endorsement of quality management techniques by Presidents Ronald Reagan and George Bush and a memorandum sent by

President Bill Clinton to all department heads requesting a reduction in the supervisor-employee ratio from 1:7 to 1:15 as part of an effort to reduce the overall civilian workforce in the executive branch by 12 percent as part of the National Performance Review (NPR). In fact, the *Report of the National Performance Review,* issued in September 1993 to kick off President Clinton's "reinventing government" initiative, explicitly endorses the use of teaming: "In a rapidly changing world, the best solution is not to keep redesigning the organizational chart; it is to melt the rigid boundaries between organizations. The federal government should organize work according to customers' needs and anticipated outcomes, not bureaucratic turf. It should learn from America's best-run companies, in which employees no longer work in separate, isolated divisions, but in project- or product-oriented teams" (U.S. National Performance Review, 1993, p. 48).

Teaming at the Animal and Plant Health Inspection Service: The Field Servicing Office

The creation of self-directed teams of employees has been a key element in efforts by the Field Servicing Office (FSO) of the Animal and Plant Health Inspection Service (APHIS) in the U.S. Department of Agriculture to transform the way it does business. The FSO is a small, 150–person office located in Minneapolis that provides administrative services such as procurement, personnel, and budgeting to the agency's far-flung and numerous field offices. The director, David Gradick, initiated a quality improvement project at the office in the late 1980s. The FSO had long been an object of controversy within APHIS; high-ranking individuals in the two largest units, Plant Protection and Quarantine (PPQ) and Veterinary Services, had sought to dismantle the FSO and have its functions transferred to their own regional offices. For Gradick and his staff, quality management techniques provided an opportunity for improved performance that could serve to preserve the unit's existence.

Gradick took advantage of an offer from the 3M Corporation to pilot its quality management techniques at the FSO. The 3M training in quality management was supplemented by training in teaming techniques, which was contracted for separately. Although Gradick, as unit head, staked considerable capital, both financial and personal, on the program, he did not mandate the use of quality management techniques within the organization. Individual units were given discretion about whether or not to move to team-based structures. It was two years before the first of the various functional units, the Realty unit, opted to organize as a team. Over the next two years, eleven other teams were created. According to Gradick, "There was peer pressure to join teams. The people moving in that direction had privileges, control over budget; they could assign work, schedule vacations, do performance evaluations."

The last of the teams to be created was the Leadership Team, comprised of former supervisors. Of the twenty supervisors present when the project started in 1987, only nine were left in 1994, and according to Gradick, "there is not enough work for them to do." Members of the Leadership Team serve as facilitators for the other teams on an as-needed basis and have begun marketing the FSO's services outside the organization.

When President Clinton's management reform initiative began, there was a call for "reinvention laboratories" to experiment with new modes of organization and service delivery. Gradick and his staff applied and two of the teams, the Realty Team and the Procurement Team, were included as part of the lab. The reinvention lab status encouraged team members to think "outside the box"; instead of looking at incremental improvements to existing processes, the two teams looked for ways to make dramatic improvements in cycle times by attempting to change factors that they had previously assumed were beyond their control. Says Gradick, "The lab opened people's horizons. We had been muddling on our own to improve processes. The lab got people to look at regulations that we thought were in stone but weren't."

In order to expedite their work processes and improve service to their customers, the two teams requested waivers from a number of government-wide rules and regulations. For example, the Realty Team sought and obtained the authority to issue waivers from the Americans with Disabilities Act (ADA). When the Veterinary Services unit had to house an inspector at a livestock market, the ADA would ordinarily have required that the entire livestock market be made accessible to persons with disabilities. In these situations, a waiver would be requested. Where previously it would take as long as 120 days to get a waiver from the departmental Office of Operations, with the delegation of the waiver authority, the cycle time was reduced to one day.

Changes such as the delegation of ADA waiver authority have allowed dramatic improvements in service even though manpower has been cut. The Realty Team reduced the average number of days to process a lease from 186 days before 1993 to 127 days in 1994. The Purchasing Team is able to process purchase orders in an average of 1.7 days compared to 11.6 days for other organizations that the FSO was benchmarked against. Its cost per transaction was $28.25 in 1994 compared to $160.77 for other government procurement offices. The Purchasing Team claims to have saved its customers over $800,000 from the budgeted amounts in fiscal year 1994 by seeking out cheaper alternatives. Critical to the organization's success in making these changes has been a change in culture. Says Gradick, "The FSO had been a regulatory organization. People saw their job as getting in requests, making a determination, asking if it could be done. They switched to becoming consultative, helpful, to helping users get what they wanted."

Teaming at the Animal and Plant Health Inspection Service: Miami Plant Protection and Quarantine

Although a multiplicity of forces are moving federal agencies toward the use of teams, shifting from a traditional, hierarchical structure to one in which teams predominate is difficult; employees have to learn new communication and interpersonal skills, managers need to learn to be facilitative instead of directive, and leadership has to cede some of its power to employees. The Miami office of PPQ, also within APHIS, has attempted to shift to a team-based structure, and an examination of that unit's experience is edifying as to the kind of problems and issues that can arise in the course of implementation. Generally, collateral changes in other organizational elements must accompany this type of shift if it is to succeed. Such changes include ensuring that employees and supervisors acquire new skills, gaining the cooperation of all stakeholders, and decentralizing power.

PPQ is responsible for preventing the importation of plants that present a threat of disease or infection to American crops. At the Miami International Airport, PPQ employees examine the belongings of up to twenty-five thousand passengers per day to make sure that no prohibited fruits or vegetables are brought into the country. The baggage area, known as "the purple dungeon," has been one of the least desirable places to work within PPQ. When employees were queried as to what could be done to make the workplace more tolerable, they suggested the creation of self-directed teams, and PPQ management endorsed the suggestion.

In the first phase, about thirty employees were organized into teams. Although the teaming arrangement seemed to work at first, after a while enthusiasm trailed off and the workers became frustrated. One problem was that neither the workers nor the supervisors had the appropriate skills to work as a team. For example, the members of a team were expected to assess each other's performance but hadn't been trained in how to do it; supervisors were expected to facilitate rather than direct but hadn't been provided with facilitation skills.

There was also a feeling that agency leadership was only paying lip service to the concept of employee empowerment. PPQ headquarters produced a strategic plan that included a "vision" of how the agency would be performing work in the year 2000, but line employees weren't consulted in the drafting of the plan, nor did teaming figure prominently in the agency's plans. According to William Manning, state plant health director for Florida and head of the Miami PPQ office, "That document, contrary to self-management, did not allow for contributions from the field level; it was developed in a vacuum at headquarters." Morale among the workers dropped until headquarters convened a "search conference" in which workers from all levels of PPQ participated in devising a new strategic plan.

Shifting to a team-based structure had implications for the role of the union that represented most of PPQ's employees, the National Agriculture Association. Traditionally, when an employee had been charged with an infraction, the union would intervene on the employee's behalf. With a team-based structure in which the employees were expected to police themselves, the union's advocacy role was no longer appropriate. One management official commented that the union "suspected a hidden agenda" and was reluctant to cooperate with the initiative. A manifestation of the union's apprehension about the new arrangement was its refusal to agree with management's suggestion that members of the first teams to be created should be selected based on which employees had the skills to work in a team environment; instead, the union insisted that the selection be based on seniority.

Another issue that has arisen is what to do with workers who do not want to perform as team members. Current plans call for a phase-in period in which those who prefer not to function as part of a team will be given a chance to find other work. Meanwhile, the job announcement for entry-level positions has been changed to state that applicants must be willing to work in a team environment.

Despite the problems, both the employees and the agency leadership have persisted with the new approach. Additional resources have been committed in the form of a dedicated organization development (OD) specialist. According to Ruth Lewis, who works in the personnel office at APHIS and who has been assigned to devise an approach for making the rewards system compatible with the new structure, the attitude at PPQ headquarters is: "Work teams are the way of the future. Let's get Miami back on track so we can say that this organization has successfully done it."

Reengineering Organizational Processes

Another contribution of quality management to the new architecture of organizations is a focus on what can be described as the "horizontal" dynamics of organizations, to which the concept of "process" is central. In contrast to functional divisions, which predominate in traditional structures, many innovative organizations are adopting more of a process orientation that directs attention to the customer or product recipient rather than to the functional unit.

This process orientation is a central tenet of reengineering dogma as set forth by Hammer and Champy (1993) and Davenport (1993); both highlight the advantages of cross-functional teams as a means of maintaining a process focus. Cross-functional teams can be structured to incorporate entire processes, thereby reducing the incidence of errors and the delays that occur when each functional unit acts independently of the others.

Reengineering Processes at the Veterans Benefits Administration

Among the organizations that have successfully experimented with reengineering principles by designing processes that enhance service to the customer has been the New York regional office of the Veterans Benefits Administration (VBA). The emphasis that this office has placed on both improving service to the customer and enhancing the quality of worklife for employees illustrates the extent to which the intangibles of stakeholder support become an integral element of the new organizational architecture.

The New York office is one of fifty-eight regional offices of the VBA that, along with the Veterans Health Administration and the National Cemetery System, comprise the Department of Veterans Affairs (VA). The primary function of the regional offices is the processing of veterans' claims for benefits. The heart of each regional office is the Adjudication division, in which the claims examiners who make the determinations about each compensation and pension claim are located. The New York office, with 340 employees and an operating budget of seventeen million dollars, is one of the larger offices in the system.

In many respects the VBA fits the definition of an "industrial-era bureaucracy" described in the *Report of the National Performance Review* (U.S. National Performance Review, 1993) as "the root problem" with government. In these organizations "tasks [are] broken into simple parts, each the responsibility of a different layer of employees, each defined by specific rules and regulations." The report identifies the problem with these organizations as follows: "With their rigid preoccupation with standard operating procedure, their vertical chains of command, and their standardized services, these bureaucracies were steady, but slow and cumbersome" (p. 3). Consistent with that description, the VBA has been characterized by multiple levels of management, functional silos, narrowly defined tasks, and an assembly-line approach to processing claims.

If the way the VBA has traditionally operated represents the root problem with government as outlined by the National Performance Review, what New York regional office director Joe Thompson and his staff have done to change it embodies the NPR's recommended solutions. One theme of the report was "putting customers first." The paramount objective of Thompson and his staff in designing their new organizational structure was improved service to veterans. Soon after embarking on the changes, they convened two focus groups comprised of veterans who had received service from their office. According to Thompson's assistant director, Patricia Amberg-Blyskal, the clearest message from the focus groups was the extreme frustration veterans felt when dealing with the New York office. The veterans felt that too often the workers couldn't help them because their jobs were too narrowly defined. Upon viewing the tapes made of the focus group discussion, Amberg-Blyskal's reaction was: "How can you not change this?" The tapes have subsequently been shown to all the employees. According to Amberg-Blyskal, it was the best way of conveying to employees the need to change: "It was not Joe telling them, but their customers."

One reason for the veterans' frustration was the way the VA has traditionally been structured and the way claims have traditionally been processed (see Figure 1.1). All person-to-person contact with veterans was handled by counselors in the Veterans Services division while the actual processing of cases was handled by the claims examiners in the Adjudication division. When veterans called in with questions about a claim, the call would go to a counselor in the Veterans Services division. Since the counselors did not actually work the cases, they would have to call the veterans back after the file was retrieved from the Adjudication division, and even then they were unable to respond to many of the questions that were posed. Each time the veterans would call, they would get a different counselor and would have to explain their circumstances all over again. Says Thompson, "The VA was sending messages we didn't intend to send. The sense that the veterans had was that the process was designed for our efficiencies rather than to provide service to them."

The solution that Thompson and his staff devised was to merge the two divisions and to combine the jobs of counselor and examiner into the single position of case manager. Each case manager is assigned a range of claim and social security numbers and handles all claims from that set of clients. Furthermore, the case manager takes each claim from start to finish. The system not only provides the veterans with a single point of contact but allows them to talk with the workers who are actually making decisions on their

Figure 1.1. Old Work Flow.

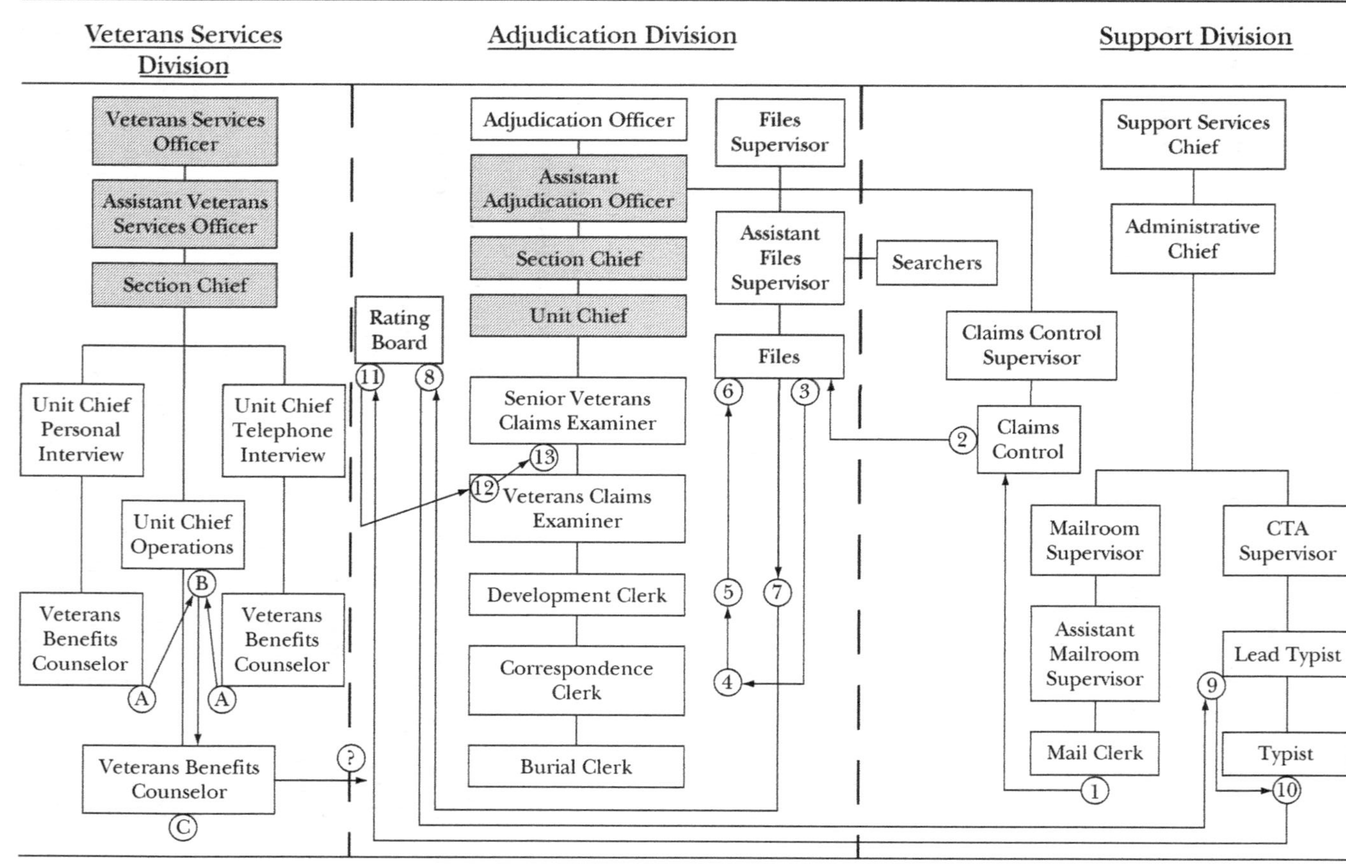

claims. The new structure allows a vastly simplified flow of work consonant with the latest reengineering techniques. Instead of a process with as many as thirty steps and multiple handoffs between workers and divisions, there are now only four steps with a single handoff between workers (see Figure 1.2). Among the advantages are clear accountability for work and fewer chances for mistakes as cases are passed between workers.

The creation of the case manager position and the reengineering of the claims adjudication process have been coupled with the establishment of work teams. The team structure complements the job changes by amplifying the extent to which employees control their work environment. A total of sixteen teams have been created, each with twelve members. Although the teams are intended to be self-directing, each is assigned a "coach," most of whom previously held supervisory positions.

A major objective of the redesign was to make the jobs more fulfilling for the employees. Thompson himself started his career as a claims examiner in the office he now directs. He describes the job as "mind-numbing and dispiriting." The consolidation of divisions

Figure 1.2. New Work Flow.

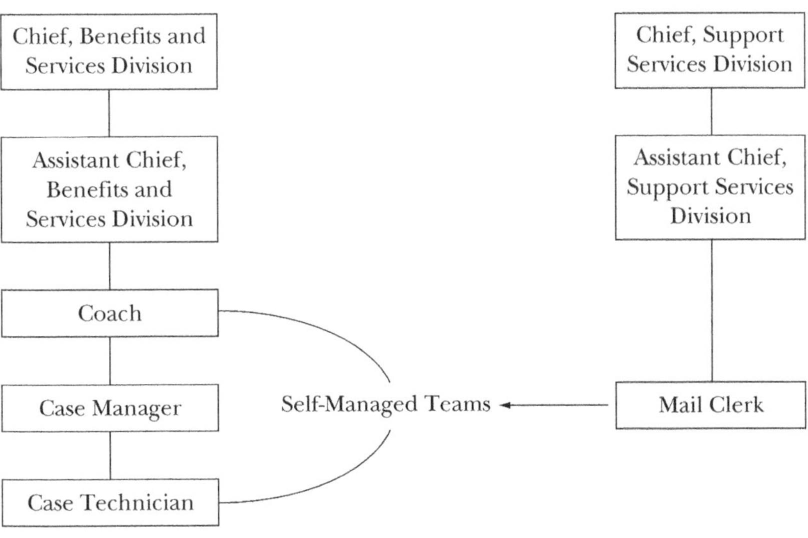

and the replacement of the claims examiners and counselors with the case manager position allows each employee to perform a greatly expanded range of functions.

For the claims examiners, who had not previously had direct contact with clients, the work is more fulfilling. Herman Wright, who has worked in the office for thirteen years, says, "It is more work but more gratifying. I have more control. I am assigned a range of claim numbers; these are my people. I like the personal contact and the fact that if I tell the veteran I'm going to do something, I can do it." Steven Hughes, with the office for four years, says, "Combining the divisions has made the job more interesting. There is more scope for intelligence, and it is a more satisfying job. There is more feedback from veterans. We can develop a personal relationship with our clients." Hughes adds, "It puts pressure on you to perform. Before it was just a folder, now it's a name and a face. You feel a compulsion to get it done." Veterans' groups are pleased as well. Mark Winn of the Disabled American Veterans says of the new structure, "It's tremendous. I have received no service complaints in two and a half years."

Reengineering the New York City Department of Probation

The adoption of new principles for organizing and the application of reengineering techniques is not restricted to the federal government. The New York City Department of Probation has utilized reengineering techniques to revamp its process for supervising adult probationers. The experience of that agency suggests that the new principles can provide a means for enhancing performance under the threat of dramatic budget cuts.

In 1992, due to severe budget cuts, the Department of Probation was faced with a loss of one-third of its probation officers. Had the department continued to do business in a traditional manner, caseloads would have risen from 150 to 350 offenders per officer, a level that, according to the department, would have "made meaningless any notion of protecting public safety" (New York City Department of Probation, 1994, p. 10). Instead, the department set up a task force to completely revise the way it did business. Utilizing reengineering techniques, the task force decided to distinguish between offenders based on the degree of risk that they presented and to focus resources on those who posed the greatest risk to public safety. Separate processes were established for violent and nonviolent probationers. Potentially violent probationers were assigned to an "enforcement" track, which incorporates more frequent contact and more intensive treatment methods than does the "nonenforcement" track. Using modern information technology, automated kiosks were set up around the city where low-risk, nonviolent offenders could report, so that the probation officers could be freed from the more mundane monitoring tasks. Information technology was also used to collect extensive data on each probationer by, for example, tracking how he or she responded to different treatment methods. This allowed an adjustment of supervisory methods as needed and provided a database for evaluating the effectiveness of the different treatments.

Leveraging Change Through the Use of Information Technology

As evidenced by the use of automated kiosks by the New York City Department of Probation, technology that facilitates the transmission and storage of data can be used effectively in support of reengineered structures. Information technology is described by Davenport (1993) as an "enabler" of process reengineering. Moving toward more automated methods for gathering and processing information can both simplify and expedite processes by eliminating the human intervention that would otherwise be necessary.

The extent to which information technology can change and expedite operations is apparent from efforts by the U.S. Bureau of the Census to reengineer its data collection processes. The Bureau's two thousand field interviewers have been equipped with laptop computers to allow the immediate entry of response data. The computers automatically edit the information for consistency and to ensure that each question has been answered. When the interviewers have completed their surveys, they go home and plug the computer into a modem; the data are transmitted to the central office during the night. Unemployment data collected in this manner are now forwarded to the Bureau of Labor Statistics two to three days earlier than previously, providing additional, valuable time for analysis prior to their presentation to Congress.

Merced County, California, undertook a radical reengineering of its welfare application processes, with information technology as a prominent contributor. The agency used expert systems and artificial intelligence to encode the vastly complex eligibility determination procedures. Eligibility information that was previously captured on paper is now entered directly into the computer, allowing the elimination of over four hundred hard-copy forms. Once it has been captured electronically, the information can be processed much more expeditiously than previously, allowing a reduction in personnel. According to the Merced County Human Services Agency, among the advantages of the new approach are the following (Kidd, 1994):

- Clients only have to complete a single-page application rather than thirty pages as they did previously.
- Recipients receive benefits in one to three days instead of thirty to forty-five days.
- Eligibility determination is made in one to two hours instead of five hours.
- Production rates for workers have increased 148 percent.

The Veterans Administration Medical Center in Baltimore has used information technology to greatly expedite processes for taking X-ray photos and for laboratory testing. The hospital acquired a filmless radiology technology called the Picture Archiving Communication System, which digitizes X-ray photos. Among the advantages of the new approach are these:

- The image is available within minutes.
- The image can be manipulated on the screen.
- People at different locations, for example, the radiologist and the primary care physician, can see the image at the same time.
- The image can also be transmitted from satellite locations elsewhere in Maryland to Baltimore for analysis. As a result, smaller outlying hospitals are able to avoid the cost of hiring a radiologist for the purpose of analyzing the photos.

The hospital also created the position of multifunction technician to perform a number of laboratory tests at the bedside, using miniaturized equipment. This equipment makes critical information on a patient's condition available much more quickly than previously. For example, it used to take a half-hour to determine how much oxygen was in a patient's blood; it now takes ninety seconds. Lives are being saved as a result.

The U.S. Department of Justice is using advanced information technology to develop an automated system that will greatly simplify the booking process for five of its component law enforcement agencies—the Federal Bureau of Investigation (FBI), the Bureau of Prisons, the Drug Enforcement Administration, the Immigration and Naturalization Service, and the U.S. Marshals Service. Justice has set up a pilot project in Miami whereby booking information is shared by the different agencies. Traditionally, when a detainee is arrested and booked by one agency and then transferred to another, booking information, such as fingerprints and a mug shot, is captured all over again. It takes months for some of the information that is now captured on paper, such as fingerprints, to be digitized and entered into the FBI's master database. Under the newly automated procedures, the data are captured electronically, made available to all the other agencies so that they don't have to repeat them, and entered immediately into the FBI's database without the normal three- to four-month lag. Ralph Zurita of the U.S. Marshals Service in Miami says that booking procedures that formerly took forty minutes can now be completed in about twelve minutes.

Networking Information and Organizations

In *Organizational Architecture: Designs for Changing Organizations,* Nadler, Gerstein, Shaw, and Associates (1992) describe what they term the "network" organization, which incorporates a number of features of the other models, including teams, a process orientation, and a pattern of organization whereby "pools of assets, knowledge and competence are 'distributed'; that is, they reside in multiple locations [and] resources are neither solely concentrated in the center nor disbursed to business units" (p. 32).

Some government organizations have begun to take advantage of networking features. One approach to doing this is to create "centers of expertise" throughout the organization. In most federal agencies, headquarters has been the traditional repository of knowledge and expertise. At the General Services Administration

(GSA), this has begun to change. The GSA has ten regional offices. The Philadelphia regional office, named a reinvention lab by the NPR, took advantage of that status to procure an automated personnel system from the U.S. Navy. As a laboratory, the Philadelphia office was able to waive some internal rules and regulations that previously had deterred such "off-the-shelf" acquisitions. The automated personnel system was a success, and when the other regions heard about it, they sought authorization to purchase this system as well. Employees from the Philadelphia office have been assisting other regional offices with installation of the system.

In setting a precedent for a region to take the lead on a major project like the automated personnel system, the Philadelphia office has given rise to the concept of developing centers of expertise in the regions. The Philadelphia region is the logical office to take the lead in automated personnel systems; other regions may become expert in retirement benefits or some other aspect of personnel work. The result would be a substantial shift in organizational culture: instead of looking to Washington as the font of all wisdom, the regions could network among themselves for specialty services. Cost savings would be likely to result to the extent that only one of the ten offices would have to staff up in each area of expertise.

The "centers of expertise" approach would have the advantage of providing increased flexibility and improved service. The relationship between offices would be contractual rather than hierarchical, providing an incentive for each office to provide good service. Further, innovation and initiative would be rewarded to the extent that offices able to provide such services could justify higher levels of funding and staffing.

Internal franchising of services is another form of networking. Some agencies in the federal government have begun to provide service to units outside their own agency. The sale of the automated personnel system to the GSA represented a form of franchising by the Navy. Another office within the GSA employed a similar approach in acquiring an automated time-and-attendance system from the Federal Aviation Administration. The FSO in APHIS, discussed above, now provides administrative services to two other units within the Department of Agriculture, the Agricultural Marketing Service and the Grain Inspection, Stockyards and Packers Administration. This relationship paid off in an important way for the FSO; at a point when serious consideration was being given to a proposal to shut the FSO down and distribute its functions to two newly created regional hubs, it was lobbying by these external units that convinced APHIS leadership to leave the FSO intact.

Partnering

Networking can work externally as well as internally as agencies partner with unions and other stakeholders to improve service delivery. In the context of the NPR, much emphasis has been placed on partnering with employee unions, and a number of agencies have employed this approach with promising results. For example, the Debt Collection Service (DCS) in the Department of Education is responsible for collecting on defaulted student loans. The DCS has only 260 employees, down from over 1,200 a few years ago. Many of its operations, such as collection, have been privatized; twelve collection agencies that retain a portion of what they collect are now under contract. As a reinvention laboratory and consistent with the recommendations coming from the NPR, the head of the DCS, John Haines, established a partnership agreement with the union. Demonstrating his strong commitment to quality management principles, Haines allowed the union to have a much more prominent role than exists at most agencies, even those that have their own partnership agreements.

Haines brought the union in as a full partner with management in devising a new organizational structure; it even allowed the union to have a role in hiring management personnel. Traditionally, directors of the unit's four regional offices had been selected by Haines in consultation with his deputy, Tom Pestka. Under the new approach, a six- or seven-member team, including peer managers, line employees, union representatives, and Pestka, makes the decision. The team operates by consensus so that any member, including Pestka, has veto power over the selection. To date, that veto power has not been invoked. In fact, when a regional director was selected for the Atlanta office, both Haines and Pestka said that the new process resulted in a better selection than the one they would have made on their own.

The changes have been particularly revealing for Pestka, who initially was skeptical. Pestka describes himself as a "rapid-strike manager," adding, "If there is a change in mission, I want to implement it right away, without discussion." He says, "Managers tell me from time to time that what we're doing is crazy, radical. I think so too, but it is working." He adds, "The union shocked the hell out of me; I've been a battler of the union. With the partnership approach, we've been able to talk and exchange ideas. It's been good because tension between management and the union has been reduced. I prefer to do business this way."

In some agencies, networking has extended beyond labor organizations. The Health Care Financing Administration (HCFA) in the Department of Health and Human Services experimented with "reg-neg" (regulation negotiation), an approach to developing regulations in which those affected by the regulation have a chance to participate in its promulgation. Reg-neg was used in the development of a regulation on hospice wages. As a result of the new approach, the HCFA is expecting a "positive reaction to the rule," according to Maryanne Troanovich, executive for regulation management.

The Mission to Planet Earth (MPE) project at the National Aeronautics and Space Administration (NASA) brought users in to participate in its effort to develop an earth science data system. Those users have included scientists from within NASA as well as representatives from academia, state and local government, and private industry. Robert Price, MPE director, says, "We involved users in all phases of design, development, and evaluation. The basic principle was putting the customer first; the customer was intimately involved in all parts of the process." He adds, "The process has worked very well. The users were very pleased with the first version; it meets their requirements."

The Bureau of Customs engaged the airline companies as partners in seeking to improve the service being provided to air passengers. In order to expedite the processing of passengers through customs, the Bureau asked the airlines to provide advance information on passengers. Customs also created the position of passenger service representative (PSR) at fourteen major ports of entry. The PSRs have established customer service standards and serve as ombudsmen for dissatisfied travelers.

The Virtual Organization

Agencies on the cutting edge of innovation like APHIS are starting to go beyond teaming and networking to innovations such as the *virtual organization.* APHIS is attempting to institute a virtual Information Technology Service (ITS), whereby information resource management (IRM) units located throughout the organization will report and take direction centrally while remaining physically and budgetarily dispersed.

There are 250 information resource specialists in APHIS, broken up into pockets of anywhere from two to thirty people and reporting up multiple chains of command. The Information Systems Planning Team was created to investigate how the agency's IRM needs could best be met. The team's report, according to the agency newsletter, "described an agency in which each unit was developing its own information systems; many had similar functions, duplication was common and most could not share information with each other" (U.S. Department of Agriculture, 1995, p. 4).

One option considered by the Agency Management Team—the agency's executive committee, consisting of the director, deputy director, and unit heads—was to consolidate all IRM personnel in a single unit at headquarters. The divisions with the most sophisticated IRM operations opposed that approach, however, and as a compromise, it was agreed that IRM personnel would remain where they were organizationally but would receive direction centrally, thereby creating a virtual organization.

The ITS has only two management layers, the chief information officer and five "coaches"; the employees are organized into twenty-five self-directed teams. The teams choose their leader, analyze customer needs, and make assignments based on need and availability. A Business Advisory Team (BAT), composed of a senior-level manager from each program unit, serves as a board of directors and helps to ensure that the ITS remains responsive to its customers. The BAT has prioritized hundreds of projects needed to create a state-of-the-art IRM program. According to the agency's internal newsletter, "ITS managers will create virtual project teams, which will exist long enough to accomplish these projects. After the projects are complete, team members will return to their home-based teams" (U.S. Department of Agriculture, 1995, p. 5).

Although this arrangement has been a boon for a number of previously isolated IRM personnel who now have the opportunity to interact with their peers and to develop new skills, it has presented a difficult challenge for top management. David Gradick, the chief information officer and head of ITS, directly controls only about three million dollars of the thirty-million-dollar ITS budget. ITS employees are budgeted in their home unit. When Gradick wants to assign an employee to a project in a geographic location other than the one where the employee is based, he or his coaches have to convince the host unit to pay travel costs. There is also a temptation for the program units to cut positions that they no longer fully control. Gradick says, "We need to make a paradigm shift away from the attitude that if I don't control that money, I can't influence how it is used. It requires bridges, collegial relationships."

A Learning Organization

Some theorists who are seeking new ways of organizing have identified characteristics of what they call a learning organization, one that shows a capacity to adjust to a changing environment or changing circumstances (Senge, 1990). Key to becoming a learning organization is the establishment of new channels of communication that cut across those that the organizational structure would dictate. APHIS exhibits many of the characteristics of a learning organization. At APHIS, a culture has developed in which employees are encouraged to take the initiative in finding ways to make the organization more effective. A group of mostly younger, midlevel employees who share a belief in the need for a fundamental change in how public agencies do business organized themselves into a group of "reinvention advocates." The advocates serve as internal consultants to other units that need assistance in dealing with issues related to change. A pair of advocates helped in reengineering the process for reaching cooperative agreements with other countries, reducing the average cycle time from over three years to forty-two days.

In most agencies, having workers circulating through the organization and stirring things up outside their formal roles would make the higher-ups uncomfortable. At APHIS, the agency head, Lonnie King, allocated fifty thousand dollars to the advocates' group to be used in support of innovative projects. Says King, "The informal organization is where things happen. If we don't do something there, things won't change."

Richard Kelly, one of the advocates, cites the absence of an attempt by leadership to keep all the change initiatives tightly structured as key to the generation of all the activity. Kelly says, "There is self-selection by individuals about what they think is important to improve the agency. Everybody is on at least three or four teams; the teams are highly redundant. There are at least four teams planning the future of APHIS. There is not one clearinghouse for reinvention, innovation, visioning. Multiple processes are under way. There is a lack of effort to channel and control visionary activities, which is why we are a hotbed. If you had to register an idea and put it on the agenda, you wouldn't be seeing as much."

One indicator of the receptivity to innovation at APHIS is the high incidence of reinvention laboratories, units that have been given some freedom from internal constraints in order to experiment with new forms of service delivery. APHIS, with only 6,000 of the Department of Agriculture's 108,000 employees, has eight of the department's fourteen reinvention laboratories. Richard Kelly's regulatory analysis unit is one of the reinvention labs.

Kelly's objective in seeking designation as a lab was to expedite the review of regulations by reducing the number of offices that had to sign off on them. By persuading the Office of General Counsel, the Office of Budget and Program Analysis, and the Assistant Secretary's Office to waive their approval rights, Kelly and his staff are now able to get some regulations cleared in as few as thirty days compared to the ninety days it often took previously. Other units within APHIS, such as the Veterinary Services and PPQ divisions, like the new approach because it allows their regulations to take effect sooner.

APHIS leadership has endorsed other learning tools. One was a reinvention forum to which representatives of all the reinvention labs and the central staff units were invited. The purpose of the forum was to identify obstacles to the changes being undertaken at the labs and to get different units and individuals to commit to overcoming them, including the obstacles that were dubbed "the undiscussables," such as the issues of turf that crop up so often in the context of change. Lonnie King says, "I'm pleased people will put that on the table. It is real progress. If you don't reward taking risks and do something about the undiscussables, the employees won't bring them forward." King also sponsored a strategic planning initiative called a future search conference at the suggestion of the OD unit. According to OD unit head Dan Stone, strategic planning efforts can take a year, and "the world is different by the time you are done." In contrast, the future search process took four days. Stone describes the purpose as "to set a vision and a strategy for the organization." He adds, "We tried to include all relevant perspectives, different levels, functions, external stakeholders." One hundred people from both within and outside the agency spent a week developing a new vision for the agency. The first conference was followed by a second, in which specific strategies to achieve the vision were developed.

The future search process helped to provide a context for all the agency's various change initiatives. Lonnie King calls it "connecting the dots." King says that for some people, all the changes were overwhelming: "They didn't want to face a new initiative." The purpose of the future search process was to say, "What you're doing does make a difference. Things you did last year are aligned to this strategy. Here's how they fit."

Conclusion

Relying on the metaphor of architecture to describe alternative organizational configurations, while valuable for conceptualizing the need to rearrange the structural elements of organizations, has some major liabilities. The dictionary defines architecture as "the art or practice of designing and building structures." Structure, in turn, conveys a sense of rigidity and permanence. What is perhaps most notable about the elements described above is the extent to which they represent a move away from rigidity and permanence and toward fluidity and flexibility.

Bureaucracy is rigid in that it has clearly defined reporting structures, has formalized rules of operation, and segregates individuals according to function and task. It is precisely the capacity to penetrate the barriers presented by these formal elements of organization that distinguishes the new organizational practices. Teams and a process orientation serve as useful vehicles for surmounting functional divisions; partnering, franchising, and "virtuality"—the use of virtual organizations—all serve to reduce the reliance of organizational units on headquarters for service and information; and information technology provides a substitute for hierarchy as a means of coordination and control.

Fluidity is a characteristic not only of the new organizational configurations themselves but of the era. The evidence presented above makes apparent the extent to which we are witnessing a period of experimentation as the old bureaucratic mold is broken and new approaches to organizing are tested. Accordingly, the following key questions that this discussion raises may be answered only with the passage of time:

1. Will one or a few new organizational configurations prevail or will the new era be characterized by a high degree of heterogeneity?
2. Will these new forms be sufficiently congruent with the values of political overseers to permit their perpetuation and expansion?
3. Will a critical mass of internal and external support for change, which is necessary to overcome natural inertia and overt opposition from some stakeholders, be developed?
4. Will the rigidities of current structures cause policy makers to simply abandon government if alternative means of service delivery cannot be devised?

How these questions are answered will have profound implications for our system of governance in the years to come. The chapters that follow explore these and other issues and provide insights into what might be ahead.

References

Burns, T., and Stalker, G. M. *The Management of Innovation.* Oxford: Oxford University Press, 1994.

Davenport, T. H. *Process Innovation: Reengineering Work Through Information Technology.* Boston: Harvard Business School Press, 1993.

Hammer, M., and Champy, J. *Reengineering the Corporation: A Manifesto for Business Revolution.* New York: HarperBusiness, 1993.

Kanter, R. M., Stein, B. A., and Jick, T. D. *The Challenge of Organizational Change: How Companies Experience It and Leaders Guide It.* New York: Free Press, 1992.

Kaufman, H. *The Limits of Organizational Change.* Tuscaloosa: University of Alabama Press, 1971.

Kidd, R. "A Case Study in Change Management: The Impact of Change on Organizational Performance and Human Behavior." Manuscript prepared for the Office of Functional Process Improvement. Washington, D.C.: U.S. Department of Defense, 1994.

Nadler, D. A., Gerstein, M. S., Shaw, R. B., and Associates. *Organizational Architecture: Designs for Changing Organizations.* San Francisco: Jossey-Bass, 1992.

New York City Department of Probation. *Adult Supervision Restructuring: A Model for Reengineering City Government.* New York: New York City Department of Probation, 1994.

Senge, P. *The Fifth Discipline: The Art and Practice of the Learning Organization.* New York: Doubleday/Currency, 1990.

U.S. Department of Agriculture, Animal and Plant Health Inspection Service. *Inside APHIS,* 1995, *15*(5).

U.S. National Performance Review. *Report of the National Performance Review.* Washington, D.C.: U.S. Government Printing Office, 1993.

Chapter Two

Heroes of the Revolution

Characteristics and Strategies of Reinvention Leaders

Ronald P. Sanders

> *There is nothing more difficult to arrange, more doubtful of success, and more dangerous to carry through than to bring about changes in the constitution of the State. The innovator makes enemies of all those who prospered under the old order, and only lukewarm support is forthcoming from those who would prosper under the new.*
> Niccolò Machiavelli, *THE PRINCE* (1513)

When he wrote nearly five hundred years ago about the leadership challenges involved in changing the "constitution of the State," Machiavelli must have had the reinvention of government in mind. First popularized by Osborne and Gaebler in their book *Reinventing Government* (1992), reinvention has become the battle cry in the latest war against government bureaucracy, a war that promises one more time to make government "work better and cost less" (U.S. National Performance Review, 1993). But unlike its many

Note: I wish to acknowledge the contributions to this chapter of Dr. James R. Thompson of the University of Illinois—Chicago. Many of the quotations and anecdotal data contained herein come from his extensive dissertation research on federal reinvention laboratories, and while I take full responsibility for the interpretation of those data, the chapter would be far less interesting and informative without his fine work.

venerable progenitors, this war has elements of reinvention that resemble a guerrilla war, one that is being waged—at least in part—from the bottom up and the inside out, by bureaucrats themselves.

These are bureaucrats who know firsthand just where Machiavelli was coming from. They are the change agents (one wag calls them "termites," for reasons that will become clear later) who are chipping away at government bureaucracy piece by piece, in relative and often self-imposed obscurity. These bureaucrats are leaders, a word not often associated with government, at least according to conventional wisdom. Indeed, many would argue that "bureaucratic leadership" is an oxymoron. However, as the transformation of government continues, it is becoming increasingly clear that it is just this kind of leadership—from career civil servants down at the "street level" of government—that may be the key to successful reinvention.

Our purpose here is to examine several examples of such successes, paying particular attention to those who led them. Our aim is to document the styles and strategies of these bureaucrat-leaders, in order to determine how they made a difference. In so doing, it becomes apparent that the transformation of government requires a different breed of leadership, one that does not (indeed, cannot) rely on classic notions of power, hierarchical authority, and technical expertise to bring about change. Indeed, Heifitz (1994) argues that these elements are dysfunctional in a dynamic and disorderly environment, where one cannot simply say, "Make it so." Instead, he offers an "adaptive" model of leadership, one in which leaders rely on confrontation and consensus as catalysts for change; this model seems to be borne out in the reinvented (or reinventing) public organizations that we have studied.

In this regard, we have identified five characteristics, attitudes as well as aptitudes, that typify the leaders of those transformed organizations. These characteristics—a sense of purpose, a strategic perspective, persistence, a proclivity to take risks, and a willingness to share power—are described in detail below. Note that while we have generalized our findings, our sample of such leaders is relatively small, drawn from federal reinvention laboratories as well as from other innovative government organizations and agencies at the federal level. Moreover, the evidence presented here, based largely on interviews with members of organizations, is primarily anecdotal. However, these findings are consistent with published research on organizational change, and they provide a useful starting point for further investigation. More important, they begin to capture some of the qualities envisioned by Machiavelli when he first contemplated the reinvention of government five centuries ago.

Reinvention and the Devaluation of Leadership

Does It Matter Anymore?

Is leadership (at least in its traditional form) all that important in an age of increasingly flattened public organizations and empowered employees, or does it just get in the way, the natural guardian of a potentially obsolete status quo? If one listens to the rhetoric of reinvention, especially in the federal government, it is easy to get the impression that leadership—specifically from career executives and managers—is at best unnecessary and at worst organizational drag.

For example, as an early and explicit part of its reinvention strategy, the Clinton administration went out of its way to embrace federal labor unions, under the theory that employee support was essential to organizational transformation. To be sure, there is ample evidence, both anecdotal and empirical (for example, see National Partnership Council, 1994; Kochan and Useem, 1992), to support this strategy, but at least in the beginning of its campaign to reinvent the federal government, the White House applied it at the expense of federal career executives and managers (Ban, 1995), with much of its early rhetoric focusing on empowering front-line employees and cutting the ranks of midlevel officials. Indeed, the National Performance Review (NPR) specifically called for doubling the average supervisor-to-employee ratio across the federal government, from 1:7 to about 1:15, thereby potentially halving the number of managers.

Change Happens

There are many who subscribe to the view that leadership, especially traditional managerial leadership, is less critical to government reinvention than the inevitable and inexorable forces that are external to its various institutions. In part, the devaluation of leadership is an artifact of systems theory and the notion that organizations behave biologically, adapting naturally to the demands of their environment. In this view, the contribution of individual leaders to organizational change is minimized; if such change is a function of environment and of such impersonal processes as homeostasis, integration, and adaptation, individuals are less important than the system as a whole.

In this deterministic view of the world (Astley and Van de Ven, 1983), the engine of organizational change is external, fueled by trends outside the organization that force it to adapt or die. Leadership takes a back seat to larger historical and environmental forces, exogenous conditions and events too compelling to be influenced by individual initiative alone; instead, change takes place because the larger system reaches some new equilibrium with its environment. Kaufman (1991) goes even further, asserting that organizational change is less a matter of adaptation than it is a matter of chance, a random occurrence that has little to do with the abilities and aspirations of its leaders. Thus, organizational determinism is passive, positing that "change happens" (a variation on the infamous bumper sticker). As a consequence, it leaves little room for the purposive actions of the individual.

However, the reality of reinventing government suggests otherwise. In that reality, almost all federal agencies and organizational units are subjected to the same severe environmental stresses, but regrettably few public organizations have successfully reinvented themselves in the face of those stresses. We argue that one of the things that distinguishes these few success stories from the rest of government is leadership—the ability of an individual or group of individuals to *make* change happen. Organizational determinism fails to adequately account for this, the "agency of choice," especially "by those who have the power to direct the organization" (Child, 1972, p. 2).

Don't Reinvent Without One

Thus, according to Doig and Hargrove (1987), external environmental conditions, such as crisis, threat, turbulence, and uncertainty, only set the stage for leadership. Organizational innovation still requires someone with a unique set of qualities and competencies (for example, the courage and capacity to lead without authority) to take advantage of it. Doig and Hargrove found that "entrepreneurial leaders" in the public sector often employed similar change strategies—for example, most were able to envision and articulate a new goal for their organization, develop internal and external constituencies and coalitions in support of that goal, and redefine their organization's culture and value system to reinforce the behaviors necessary to achieve it.

These researchers suggest that such entrepreneurial public sector leaders possess an "uncommon rationality" when it comes to organizational change, which enables them to adeptly discern opportunity in an emerging organizational situation and then to effectively link their own initiatives to the larger political or historical trends that create this opportunity. Our inquiry suggests that the transformation of government is not likely to occur without this rationality. Indeed, this type of leadership, particularly on the organization's front lines, may be the single most important ingredient in the reinvention recipe, where organizational adaptation becomes deliberate and purposive, a function (indeed, a responsibility) of the leader.

In studying change in a number of private sector organizations, Beer, Eisenstat, and Spector (1990, p. 224) found that organizational "revitalization . . . began with unit leaders who were willing to risk being pioneers"; such a pathfinder is not at the top or the bottom of the larger organization, but in its middle, typically an "insider, a localite whose forte is that he knows the system" (Rogers and Shoemaker, 1971, p. 278). There is no reason to believe that government is any different in this regard, and in fact, our own examination of federal reinvention efforts strongly supports such a conclusion. In almost every case we studied, successful organization-level change could be traced to the actions of one or more entrepreneurial leaders, catalysts who actually sparked the change process; effectively linked it to some larger, exogenous agenda; and then managed the transformation to its conclusion. And while they did many of the things that leaders are traditionally expected to do—articulate a vision, establish coalitions, align employees, and take risks—they also practiced their art in nontraditional (or at least nonbureaucratic) ways.

Back to the Future: The Paradox of Purpose

A Sense of History

The philosopher Friedrich Wilhelm Nietzsche once said, "He who has a 'why' can live with almost any 'how.'" Like Machiavelli, Nietzsche could have been writing about the transformation of government, for this is a maxim adeptly applied by many of the successful reinvention leaders we observed. Almost by definition, public organizations have lofty purposes, often rooted in a storied historical context (the Depression-era origins of many federal agencies come to mind), and these leaders were able to instill or, in some cases, rekindle that sense of history and purpose in their managers and employees, using the energy of their commitment to the "why" of the organization to improve its "how." However, there is a downside: this "back to the future" strategy takes purpose and mission for granted. Indeed, as we discuss below, it may deliberately aggrandize them as a way of leveraging change. It thus risks overwhelming resistance to any initiative perceived as inconsistent with those organizational bedrocks.

A sense of purpose and mission provided leverage for Air Force major general Philip Nuber, director of the Defense Mapping Agency (DMA), a U.S. Department of Defense reinvention lab employing over twelve thousand military and civilian employees. Nuber says that regaining a sense of purpose, whether this is defined in terms of customer or mission, was critical to his successful organizational transformation: "You've got to remind everyone why they're here; it's how you get everybody to refocus and change." In the DMA's case this was critical; in an age of electronic satellite imaging, mapmaking (at least in the traditional sense) was in danger of becoming obsolete. Threatened by technology, the organization had lost its sense of purpose, and Nuber seized upon this to bring about a dramatic turnaround. He had an advantage: "I was a fighter pilot; I knew how important maps—not photos, but real maps—were to warriors." So everywhere Nuber went in the DMA, he told war stories (in effect, stories about the DMA's customers) to employees, reemphasizing the importance of their core mission, their raison d'être: providing soldiers with the very best maps. This was why people, especially cartographers, came to work for the DMA, and Nuber used that motive to drive reinvention, even teaching employees "how to brag like fighter pilots" about their mission and their maps.

Then Air Force captain Scott Brady was shot down over Bosnia. When he was safely rescued, he gave much of the credit to his map—a standard-issue, made-by-DMA map. Nuber was quick to use that event to reinforce the lessons he was trying to teach, and in the process, he helped the DMA to regain its sense of purpose. Although he is quick to deny the credit, much of this can be traced back to his "remind them why they're here" approach to reinvention; that constant refrain (now taken up by his senior civilian staff) has helped the organization to reinvent itself. The DMA has since established a reputation for excellent customer service. It has been recognized by the Joint Chiefs of Staff (after all, they read maps too), and it was a finalist for a President's Award for Quality and Productivity Improvement in 1995; its nomination package even included an autographed copy of Scott Brady's map, inscribed with a thank-you from the pilot.

One Step Back, Two Steps Forward

As the DMA case suggests, purpose is often rooted in an organization's past, and there is considerable irony in the notion of looking back in order to start forward. There is also irony in the fact that a public organization's sense of purpose—the very thing that may have appealed to its employees in the first place—is usually one of the first things its members forget. According to Nuber, it is the leader's job to help employees remember. Capturing and communicating this sense of purpose was not difficult for the reinvention leaders we studied, probably because they themselves already had it; almost all of them tended to describe their organizational missions with missionary-like zeal, and the most successful of them seemed to be able to leverage that sense of purpose to convince sometimes skeptical subordinates that organizational transformation was a way for dedicated employees to better serve their respective publics and constituencies, without disturbing their faith in the overarching purpose of the agency.

In effect, these reinvention leaders were able to bifurcate the organizational status quo into the "why" and the "how" of their agency's mission, using their employees' commitment to the former as the platform for transforming the latter. In this regard, these leaders typically offered a vision that was bounded, incremental, and instrumental rather than the radical, paradigm-shifting kind usually associated with "true" transformation. They tended to take their organization's core mission—collecting student loans, inspecting meat, processing veterans claims, making maps—as a given, usually codified in statute and thus assumed to be beyond the reach of reinvention. Accordingly, their visions had a narrow focus on improving the various means to that end.

Consider the Field Servicing Office (FSO) of the Animal and Plant Health Inspection Service (APHIS), where then director Dave Gradick provided the impetus for reorganizing the operation around self-managed work teams. That initiative had less to do with the substantive aspects of the agency's mission or structure than it did with its implicit "work technology," that is, with the organizational relationships between and among line units and staff support functions. This was an instrumental and incremental initiative if there ever was one; nevertheless, the teams have dramatically reduced the cost of providing internal support services to other APHIS units. In doing so, they have also engendered subtle but far-reaching changes to the organization's culture. At first blush, these changes do not seem dramatic; however, to a bureaucracy steeped in a culture of compliance, they may represent a microshift, and the employees acknowledge Gradick as "the force behind" the changes, their spark. In his own words, he just "tried to give people a vision of how things can be," with emphasis on the word "how."

Ends and Means

This example is typical of reinvention, at least at the federal level. What can only be characterized as instrumental, incremental initiatives predominate in its inventory of interventions: staff (as opposed to business) process reengineering, self-managed teams, quality and customer service initiatives, and reorganizations (centralizing as well as decentralizing). These all deal with the "how" of administration, rather than the more fundamental—and much more intractable—"why" of a particular agency. However, this is not to minimize their impact; indeed, over the long run, these changes to process and culture may have a more lasting effect on the public's confidence, perceived and otherwise, in government institutions and government performance. And that may be the best we can hope for in reinvention.

Thus, while the literature on leadership and organizational change typically centers on those who successfully challenge organizational orthodoxy, that orthodoxy, in the form of an agency's core purpose and mission, can actually facilitate reinvention in government. In this regard, purpose and mission seem to serve as a framework, a way to bound change and make it less threatening to employees and those who lead them. In many of the cases we observed, reinvention leaders were able to leverage strong employee commitment to mission, using that commitment as a means of catalyzing organizational change. Indeed, in focus groups and interviews, employees of reinventing organizations exhibited an almost evangelical allegiance to their agency's mission, commonly using phrases like "our program" or "our initiative" to assert personal ownership of both their organization's basic purposes and the improvements they were helping to engender.

But there can be a downside to this "back to the future" approach to change. While a reinvention leader may be able to employ history, purpose, and mission to mobilize a workforce, those elements can also become a source of bureaucratic inertia, engendering organizational tunnel vision (pun intended) and resistance to anything that employees may perceive as a threat to that mission, including reinvention itself. And as we have noted, even when reinvention leaders have employed mission as a positive catalyst for change, it can narrowly focus reinvention efforts on the instrumental and the incremental, on simply improving the means to a taken-for-granted end. Much of federal reinvention fits this category.

Thus, at its worst, too strong a sense of mission can result in an opposition to more radical change in which people can't see the forest for the trees, such as that envisioned by some of the NPR's more ambitious follow-on efforts. For example, "ReGo II" asks agency heads to consider privatizing traditionally governmental functions, and it has caused many organizations—even such hotbeds of leadership and change as the various federal reinvention laboratories—to raise the red flag of resistance (Gore, 1995). One reinvention leader, who had instituted significant administrative changes in her unit, went so far as to characterize these more radical proposals, which included the potential privatization of her agency, as a "double cross" on the part of the NPR.

Permission, Partnerships, and Power Sharing

Reinvention License

In a bureaucracy as large and imposing as the federal government, reinvention leaders seem to require at least tacit permission (perhaps sanction is a better word) to start their work. And once they receive it, the most successful of those leaders are quick to pass it on, in the form of partnerships and other participatory, power-sharing arrangements, to subordinates, stakeholders, and customers, involving them extensively in the transformation process. In this context, the term *permission* should not be construed to mean that reinvention leaders need or want some superior's consent for each and every change they seek, although it has taken on this complexity in some especially change-resistant agencies. Instead, we intend the term to convey something more contextual and climatic, a shift in the organization's cultural value system that signals that "change is OK." Thus, permission means leverage, even if it is little more than rhetorical, something that gives reinvention leaders an official license to pursue their strategic agendas.

As a characteristic of reinvention leadership, permission has two dimensions: getting and giving. Most of the organizational-change literature speaks to this notion of permission in one form or another. For example, in their study of change in several private sector companies, Beer, Eisenstat, and Spector (1990, pp. 179–180) observed: "At the corporate level, top management had to develop a climate that encouraged revitalization in all units. It did this by enabling innovative approaches to organizing and managing to take root in a few model organizations, then spreading them." Substitute the words *president and vice president* for *corporate* and you've just described the NPR. By putting the not inconsiderable force of his own office behind the federal effort, Vice President Al Gore has sent a signal to reinvention leaders throughout the bureaucracy, both present and potential; as much as anything else, the NPR represents permission, and many change agents feel that it is now safe to come out of the closet. Thus, while the reaction of many inside and outside of the federal establishment has been a cynical "Here we go again," the reinventors we studied had a much different response. The words gave them license to start—or in many cases to continue—the process of transforming their own little piece of the bureaucracy.

State Sanction

Permission and an institutional climate conducive to change seem to be a requirement for reinvention at the state level as well. In many cases, state and local reinvention has been driven from the top down, by governors and mayors, city managers and county administrators, with varying degrees of success, but a few innovative chief executives have experimented with a more permissive, bottom-up approach. For example, during and after his successful 1992 gubernatorial run, Florida governor Lawton Chiles was a vocal champion of reinvention as a way of curing some of the state's financial woes. Like President Clinton, he even commissioned his second-in-command, the lieutenant governor, to lead the effort, and Florida's inventory of initiatives reads like a textbook on government reform. In just over three years, Chiles and the state legislature have tackled personnel and procurement reform, privatization, deregulation, financial management reform, strategic planning, performance-based budgeting, and Total Quality Management, to name just a few of the initiatives (Berry, Chackerian, and Wechsler, 1996).

However, although most of these efforts originate from the governor's office, Chiles has also granted several of his cabinet heads license to conduct experiments in personnel and budget flexibility in their state agencies, experiments that look for all the world like federal reinvention labs, and preliminary results are encouraging. For example, the state's Department of Labor and Employment Security has developed a simplified job classification scheme, and positive results have also been reported by the state's Division of Workers Compensation, which tested its own streamlined classification system, as well as a performance-based compensation scheme (U.S. General Accounting Office, 1994). To be sure, these successes are due in part to innovative agency-level leadership, but that leadership would not have emerged without sanction from the statehouse.

A "Trickle-Down" Model

Thus, in the cases we studied, successful transformation began not with prescription but with permission. At the top of government, that sanction is often symbolic at best—the words of Vice President Gore or Governor Chiles may open the door of reinvention, but plenty of bureaucrats lurk behind it—and it must somehow be "trickled down" to the front lines. Here is where permission takes on a more tangible form, and top agency leaders, typically subcabinet political appointees, have employed a variety of methods to reinforce the signals from the chief executive. Dan Beard, former head of the Bureau of Reclamation, handed out "forgiveness slips" (other agency leaders have employed "permission slips," but Beard says that he wanted to send the message that "it is better to ask forgiveness than permission") to employees and their managers, entitling—indeed, encouraging—them to try something risky and new.

Similarly, former General Services Administration (GSA) head Roger Johnson granted two of his several regional directors "reinvention charters" that empowered them to unilaterally waive internal agency regulations and operating procedures that were not based in statute. Jan Ziegler, an official from one of the chartered regions, says, "It was a masterstroke," but adds, "I don't think they [headquarters] knew what they were doing." Maybe headquarters didn't, but Johnson surely did. The importance of a permissive climate to reinvention in government—or in any private enterprise for that matter—cannot be overstated, and it is clear that that climate must be constantly communicated and consistently reinforced if the bureaucracy's inherent inertia is to be overcome.

Indeed, that necessity is underscored by one of the most interesting findings in our study of reinvention. Our reinvention leaders expect some measure of bureaucratic resistance, and as savvy bureaucrats themselves, they know how to deal with it. What has surprised many of them is the lack of support, and the sometimes outright opposition, from the political leadership in their agencies—that is, from the administration's own appointees, principally at the middle and lower levels of the political hierarchy. This was one of the most common complaints voiced at a March 1996 conference of over 550 government reinventors sponsored by the

NPR and the Maxwell School of Citizenship and Public Affairs, among other groups.

Throughout the conference, reinvention leaders from a variety of federal agencies lamented this antipathy among appointees, particularly among those in headquarters staff positions who have the power to grant regulatory waivers (and thus provide added flexibility) to innovative agency subunits. One recounted how her political boss had characterized the NPR as "so much fluff," while others noted how quickly supposedly loyal appointees "go native" over classic bureaucratic issues of turf and control. Conference delegates identified this issue as their number one concern (interestingly, resistance from senior career executives came in second), telling members of the vice president's NPR staff and the President's Management Council who attended on the final day of the conference: "They're your people; do something about them!"

Shared Power

As we have suggested, the successful reinvention leaders we encountered also gave as much permission as they got, through partnerships and participatory, power-sharing relationships with their organization's various stakeholders and constituents; however, these relationships can sometimes be problematic, particularly in rigid, compartmentalized bureaucracies where authority is position-based. Heifitz (1994) posits that such structures can become pathologically authority-dependent, and he argues that effective, adaptive leadership often means "giving back" authority (and personal responsibility) to organization members, literally forcing them to deal with change themselves. It is a style that places an almost hackneyed emphasis on teams and empowered employees, but one that should not be taken to mean that managerial leadership is superfluous. On the contrary, it may be even more important in crafting, guiding, and maintaining these partnership relationships.

This participatory approach to organizational change is nothing new; it is something that has long been studied, and often advocated, by the change literature, and it seemed to be characteristic of almost every effective reinvention leader we examined. Jan Ziegler, who involved customers, suppliers, and subordinates in her reinvention efforts at the GSA, talks about achieving what she calls "synergistic inclusivity" through such involvement, with all of the organization's stakeholders aligned and focused on improving performance. Phil Nuber would concur. When he took over the DMA with its twelve thousand employees, he found an organization that delegated all of the tough decisions upward. "Sometimes you have to make people make decisions," he says, "so I told [my direct reports,] 'If you ask me to make your decisions for you, I will—but it may get ugly.' If they still insist that I do their jobs for them, I'm not above deliberately doing something dumb, just to remind my managers and employees of what can happen if they don't take personal responsibility."

The Veterans Administration's Joe Thompson took a slightly different approach, but with the same end result; he too "gave back" authority to his subordinates, in his case, through the discipline of reengineering, establishing and empowering (and then guiding) teams of employees to analyze and redesign the region's benefit claim process. Just like Nuber, he did it deliberately, establishing the climate for change by sharing his traditional, hierarchical power with those teams of subordinates. So did Bill Murphy, who heads up the Cincinnati office of the Occupational Safety and Health Administration (OSHA). He organized his employees into teams and announced that he would no longer review their work. He told them, "It's your work; you decide if it's good enough to send out; I am willing to take the risk of sending it out without review. . . . I have confidence in you. Some [of the employees] said, 'I'll have to look at my work more closely before I turn it in.'" As expected, there were some growing pains as employees learned to accept and internalize this responsibility, but they did, and Murphy's office is now one of the most productive in OSHA (Thompson, 1996, p. 158).

Détente

This power-sharing approach to organizational transformation also applies to relationships with those above the reinvention leader, his or her immediate political superiors. Clearly, a strong working partnership with the middle political levels of the bureaucracy is crucial to reinvention, especially if it is to become institutionalized beyond individual units. Indeed, where such a relationship exists, it represents a formidable engine of change. Michael Janis, a senior career executive in the Department of Housing and Urban Development's Public and Indian Housing Administration, talks about the potential power of the political appointee to facilitate organizational transformation: "You have to have career buy-in [but] political appointees make a difference. [Our reinvention efforts] couldn't have been accomplished without the assistant secretary's buy-in." Janis also describes the political-career relationship that developed over time: "We became a team, the assistant secretary and his staff dealing with the agency's political leadership, we career executives focusing on our staff counterparts, both groups focused on our long-term goals; our reinvention efforts would not have been so successful without that team approach—it was a very powerful combination."

These same lessons apply to public employee unions. Traditionally, management has kept these unions at arm's length, the result of a statutory and policy framework in both private and public sectors that assumes conflicting interests. However, that assumption often evaporates in the face of threats to organizational survival, and perhaps out of sheer necessity, cooperative partnerships between management and organized labor have become an important element of reinvention at all levels of government.

While a detailed discussion of these partnerships is beyond the scope of this chapter (see Ban, 1995; National Partnership Council, 1994; for a more general discussion, see Kochan and Useem, 1992), it is sufficient to note that they too are a key part of the successful reinvention leader's participatory repertoire, and among the most challenging to develop. Remember the Department of Education's Tom Pestka, the converted "union battler" from Chapter One? His boss, Debt Collection Service director John Haines, another of our reinvention leaders, took on that challenge, allowing employees and union officials to sit on selection committees for management positions and giving them a veto over selections for those positions. That risky move paid off in better relations and better performance, but it took a leader strong enough to give up authority, to permit others (sometimes even old organizational enemies) to share in the power of her or his position.

Aspiring reinvention leaders take note: this permissive, participatory approach is hard for managers and members alike. It is difficult for employees who are used to being told what to do, but it is just as problematic for managers of the "old school" to cede the power and authority traditionally vested in their office—power that many feel they've (finally) earned. Take the case of Norman Morse, chief of nursing services at the Department of Veterans Affairs' Baltimore Medical Center (Thompson, 1996), who gave his nurses the discretion to decide how best to provide their services: "I designed a system where I decentralized my power and decision-making[,] . . . delegating authority to other people. The feelings that come out are something you have to live through [and] I found it difficult. Before you had control of things yourself, and you give it all away. You have to learn how to become a transformational leader and coach [but] doing it is one thing and feeling it is another" (p. 159).

Persistence and Strategic Perspective

The Long View

Patient tenacity, persistent focus, personal commitment. Almost every reinvention leader we studied exhibited these qualities, and they are all characteristic of what can only be called the long view: these leaders share a strategic perspective that realizes that organizational change is a years-long process, a personal crusade that requires an extraordinary commitment if it is to be successful. Beer, Eisenstat, and Spector (1990, p. 184) call this a "persistence of belief," and they found that effective organizational renewal required leaders who were willing to make that kind of long-term investment, even at some personal risk and sacrifice (discussed in the next section). And make no mistake about it; there is vision behind that commitment. These leaders do have an idea of the changes they want to bring about, a plan (sometimes public, but more often than not private) typically born out of years of frustration in their own bureaucracies. As the GSA's Jan Ziegler puts it: "I've waited twenty-one years for the opportunity to make changes."

As we have noted, many of these changes are purely administrative, involving such seemingly mundane things as eliminating reports and levels of review, but their intended effects are anything but. Indeed, it is clear that many of these innovators employ what we have called "strategic incrementalism" (Thompson, Sanders, and Ingraham, 1994)—that is, the deliberate use of a series of subtle, seemingly small-scale steps that are intended to lead to some grander vision over the longer term. According to Wheatley (1992), dynamic systems that are under great stress, like the government organizations we studied, are particularly sensitive (and susceptible) to what one of our reinvention leaders calls "small changes that seem insignificant" (for example, delegating signature authority). Nancy Carr, a Hammer Award–winning leader who reinvented the National Acquisition Center in the Department of Veterans Affairs describes this approach as a way of achieving "major systems change, but in bite-sized pieces, so people could get a taste of it."

These administrative increments can provide the reinvention leader, especially one who has a long view, with a "creative lever" (Briggs and Peat, 1989). In this regard, it is apparent that the leaders we studied all had some generalized notion of where they wanted to take their organization, but they had the patience to get there in "bite-sized pieces." They also had the patience to let participation and stakeholder consensus determine the substance of those pieces; most seemed to focus on a grander, more expansive view, leaving the details to be worked out by the organization's members themselves. For example, in the DMA, Phil Nuber's vision was simple—"Remember the soldiers"—but he forced his senior managers to develop a strategic plan to actually realize it. (Yes, sometimes participation must be made mandatory!)

This patience may be tested by the larger organization's demand for more immediate and dramatic gratification. Joe Thompson's reengineering effort at the Veterans Benefits Administration is a classic case in point: his attempt to create a cadre of generalist "case workers" out of once–rigidly compartmentalized technical specialists promises a substantial improvement in customer satisfaction and, over time, greater efficiency. However, it takes time for employees to acquire new competencies. As a consequence, short-term results have been predictably disappointing: quality and timeliness (both key agency performance measures) are down, and although customer satisfaction is improving, the increasing impatience of Veterans Administration headquarters—its need for a "quick win"—could eventually threaten the project's agency-wide viability (Thompson, 1996; see also Chapter Four). This organizational impatience is not at all uncommon; Beer, Eisenstat, and Spector (1990, p. 185) observed that an "inevitable variability" in results "is likely to occur during the long revitalization process," and it takes a special kind of leader—one with no lack of faith in his or her agenda (like Nancy Carr and Joe Thompson)—to transform an organization.

The Pony Express Strategy

Reinvention may require special strategies and tactics. One of the reasons that public organizations become so impatient with efforts like reinvention is that most of them have already "seen it all" when it comes to management improvement campaigns. Like many private concerns, the federal government has long suffered from a penchant for "flavor-of-the-month" solutions to its management ills. That penchant has given us the acronyms PPBS, MBO, ZBB, TQM, BPR, and now, at least for some cynics, NPR, each with a relatively short popularity half-life; however, for many of the successful reinvention leaders whom we studied, this alphabet soup of acronyms spells O-P-P-O-R-T-U-N-I-T-Y, and they have taken advantage of it in some interesting ways.

Remember how the old Pony Express riders were able to cover great distances in relatively short periods of time? Their secret was fresh horses. They traveled from way station to way station along their route, picking up a fresh horse whenever the one they were riding began to tire. With the new horse came a burst of energy, and further progress in their long journey (Sanders and Thompson, 1996). In the same spirit, many of the reinvention leaders we studied view the latest in the federal government's seemingly endless parade of management fads as nothing more than another fresh horse. In almost every case, each leader had his or her own private long-term agenda for organizational change, but in contrast to some of their more cynical colleagues, these leaders embraced each new fashion statement, harnessing it to revalidate and reenergize their efforts.

And few fads have been as accommodating as the NPR to the strategic perspective of the reinvention leader; indeed, its broad "motherhood and apple pie" principles are ambiguous enough to encompass just about any initiative. For example, in APHIS, Dave Gradick's journey began in 1988 with a pilot Total Quality Management (TQM) program, and when the NPR arrived on the scene, he was one of the first to seek designation as a reinvention laboratory. Armed with that designation, his Field Servicing Office has continued a number of initiatives that grew out of the original TQM effort (such as self-managed work teams). Though Joe Thompson in the Veterans Administration has taken a similar approach, he seems to be riding several horses at once. He has pursued a whole host of special designations that would facilitate his change agenda. Like the FSO, Thompson's office began as a TQM pilot in the Bush administration and later was a reinvention laboratory under the NPR. Thompson and his staff have also applied to become a personnel demonstration project under the 1978 Civil Service Reform Act, which would allow them to modify or waive various government-wide personnel laws and regulations, as well as a pilot project—with comparable waiver authority—under the 1993 Government Performance and Results Act.

Another reinvention leader, who asked to remain anonymous, summarized the long view implicit in the Pony Express strategy this way: "I started out by calling what I wanted to do TQM. Then it was reengineering. Today it's reinvention. But it's still the same changes that I wanted to make all along." Another admitted, "I wanted the new administration to continue what I had done in the old administration. We started this years ago as a quality circle initiative." Today it is a reinvention laboratory. Clearly the label doesn't matter as much to reinvention leaders as the changes they champion; however, to be fair, their choice of "horse" is not entirely tactical (especially with regard to TQM); rather, most of the long-range goals articulated by the leaders we studied were substantively compatible with at least some of the tenets of the particular management improvement program they were riding at the time.

Nevertheless, even when they saddle themselves to the *technique du jour,* these leaders know that they will encounter formidable bureaucratic resistance (indeed, this resistance is often directed both at the technique itself and at anyone who embraces it). Thus, there is a downside to the Pony Express strategy, and as a consequence, many of the leaders we studied end up keeping their true objectives and accomplishments to themselves; theirs can be a very private vision, often out of bureaucratic necessity. As one of our reinvention leaders put it, "There is a huge motivation not to share [what we're doing] because somebody will tell us to stop." In part, this too is just tactical, a facet of the guerrilla war waged by organizational change agents everywhere, but some of it is also driven by fear—for the reinvention leaders' agendas, and sometimes for the reinvention leaders themselves. Because for all of the rhetorical support from the White House or the statehouse, reinvention remains a risky business in government.

Risk, Proclivity, and Pyrrhic Victories

Risky Business

Permission and participation notwithstanding, reinvention is not for the risk-averse; just ask Machiavelli. Beer, Eisenstat, and Spector (1990, p. 182) note that "while having the top corporate officer on board the revitalization effort was useful," successful renewal required committed division- and plant-level managers who were willing to "break traditions." But there is a price associated with doing this, and many of the reinvention leaders we studied bear the scars, administrative and otherwise, that come with championing change—from small bureaucratic headaches and hassles to time served in that infamous organizational Gulag, the "turkey farm," where employees who have offended their superiors are sent, in dead-end jobs with few or no responsibilities. They bear witness to the fact that the successful reinvention leader must have a proclivity for taking risks, sometimes very personal ones, when participating in the transformation of government.

In this regard, reinvention still struggles against government's culture of compliance, a culture manifested and perpetuated by all sorts of rule-based accountability mechanisms (internal auditors, inspectors general, General Accounting Office evaluators, congressional and other legislative oversight committees, ombudsmen and media watchdogs, and dozens of complaint avenues and "hot lines") that stand ready to question the slightest variation from the norm. These can intimidate and inhibit reinvention, and the capacity to face them is something that sets our reinvention leaders apart. The view of one federal manager is typical, and entirely understandable: "I'm scared of these authorities myself. . . . You get audited; the Inspector General comes in two or three years later, the people involved aren't there anymore, and it causes a lot of red faces" (Thompson, 1996, p. 157).

This manager's fear is not of being caught doing something wrong; rather, it is of being perpetually second-guessed in matters of judgment and discretion, and the experience can be quite intimidating for the fainthearted. One of Joe Thompson's fellow Veterans Benefits Administration executives tells of such an encounter. His actions are characteristic of the successful reinvention leader: "I had the inspector general in here doing a review of financial processes for benefits. They tried to enforce things in our manuals from ten years ago that haven't been updated. They said, 'You've given too much authority to your employees in these areas; you're not in compliance with the master control system.' I asked them if they had found any waste, fraud, or abuse. They said no. So I said that we would keep doing it the way we've been doing it!" (Thompson, 1996, p. 157).

The GSA's Jan Ziegler also exemplifies the risk-taking proclivity of the effective reinvention leader. As the head of one of two major GSA regional reinvention labs, she tried to streamline the process of approving major building renovation and construction contracts, all in the name of better customer service. She found that a good bit of the contract-approval cycle time was spent worrying about very small differences in overhead charges, charges that were more than offset by the expense of further delay (the phrase "penny wise and pound foolish" comes to mind). Concluding that the monetary "risk level was very small, perhaps $2,000 on a $700,000 contract," Ziegler implemented a "class deviation," setting a flat overhead rate. The small financial risk made good business sense, but the bureaucratic risks are another matter. According to Ziegler, "Someone will come in and say, 'You could have gotten the contract for $1,500 less,'" triggering all sorts of audits and reviews and justifications that do little more than second-guess what are clearly matters of judgment. Ziegler's response? "I tell the auditor to get out" (Thompson, 1996, p. 154). Just another day at the office for a reinvention leader.

Pyrrhic Victories

However, even these small victories can be Pyrrhic (Sanders and Thompson, 1996), and the "unreinvented" have ways of extracting bureaucratic revenge. One reinvention leader reported, "After we got a waiver to streamline the contract-approval process, every one of our contracts got audited by headquarters." A reinvention leader in another agency had the same experience: "We requested authority to set up our own supply system; we immediately got resistance from our regional headquarters, and supply system reviews went up. And after we received authority to approve our own [supply] contracts, 100 percent of our contracts were audited." Some reinventors have taken extraordinary (and in relative terms, risky) steps to avoid this kind of bureaucratic retribution; one revealed, "We keep two sets of books so we can give our headquarters our numbers back on their form—in effect, we're telling them, 'This is what you want to see, now go away.' Until we can get rid of them, we'll play their silly game." Silly, but still serious. One reinvention leader, complaining about his headquarters' refusal to approve regulatory waivers, would only agree to an interview on a "not for attribution" basis, for fear of incurring the wrath of higher-ups as they considered critical resource decisions involving his organization (Sanders and Thompson, 1996).

There is a good reason why many reinvention efforts are clandestine. Where they are not, some reinvention leaders pay the ultimate organizational price. That was the case with John Bucelato, a navy captain (now retired) who ran a large aircraft-maintenance depot employing some forty-five hundred civilians, most represented by unions. When he first arrived in 1991, the facility was quite literally in danger: quality and productivity were poor, costs were high, relations between labor and management were hostile, and the installation was rumored to be a candidate for closure. That rumor came true—the Department of Defense decided to shut down the depot in three years—and Bucelato was faced with perhaps the most daunting of reinvention challenges: keeping a doomed organization productive even while closing its doors. He responded in the same way as the other reinvention leaders we have studied, with vision, strategic perspective, persistence, and participation, as well as with a willingness to take some risks.

Bucelato "knew that the chances of reversing the closure decision were slim; the only hope was to keep people focused on their jobs as a way of dealing with the denial and anger." And if that didn't work, he told employees, being part of a high-performing organization would at least help them find other jobs. Bucelato enlisted and involved the facility's unions, a process that took several months—and outside professional assistance—to overcome their "Why should we?" attitude. With their eventual help, he instituted an aggressive quality management program that brought costs down and quality up. At the same time, he guided the creation of an innovative, employee-run retraining and outplacement program that eventually became almost too successful, finding job opportunities for workers before they were displaced. Employees even published their own brochure showcasing their technical skills and productivity.

The ironic results: the facility closed on September 30, 1996, but before it did, it received productivity, safety, and environmental awards from the state of Virginia, the secretary of the navy, and the Environmental Protection Agency; it was a semifinalist for the Department of Defense's Installation Excellence Award; its labor-management partnership was cited as a model by the president's National Partnership Council; over 80 percent of its workers found jobs through its outplacement program; and Captain John Bucelato lost his job. You see, what Bucelato did just wasn't done. Bases that are being closed are supposed to go away quietly; they most assuredly are not supposed to reinvent themselves and thereby implicitly call into question the wisdom of their closure. The message to Bucelato from his headquarters was: "Don't make waves."

That was never his intention; rather, his focus was on mission. "Remember," he says, "we had three years between the [closure] announcement and the closure itself. So we had two options: we either could get very good, or we could get very bad—and the consequences of a bad aircraft-maintenance facility can be fatal." Their choice was reflected in the facility's performance indicators; they kept going up, and the awards and recognition kept coming, despite counseling from Bucelato's superiors telling him to "keep a low profile." As performance grew, so too did the suspicions of higher headquarters. A major inspection by the inspector general, even in the midst of closure, finally brought the situation to a head. After weeks of frenetic preparation, the depot passed with flying colors, and Bucelato gave everybody involved the next workday off as a reward—coincidentally, the day after Thanksgiving. Although his action was entirely consistent with administrative rules, Bucelato was told to cancel the leave "because it just didn't look right" for a base that was about to close. He refused and was reassigned to a headquarters position shortly thereafter; he has since retired.

This too is part of reinvention, and the leaders we talked to were realistic about the risks they had incurred when they signed up. Some of those risks are purely bureaucratic—audits, inspections, the dreaded "turkey farm"—but some are also very personal. A reinvention leader from a domestic agency told us, "My name has become associated with reinvention, and it's as if everyone assumes I'm doing all of this for Gore. I'm not, but that doesn't matter. As long as it's 'politically correct,' I'm OK, but if we get a new administration, I'm dead!" Does that possibility deter her? She says it doesn't: "I've waited too long for this." Any regrets for Bucelato? He responds in the same unequivocal way: "I would do what I did again in a minute." They and their peers all display this same proclivity for risk taking, an attitude best summed up by Dave Gradick of APHIS: "I told my employees, if you see something that doesn't make sense, ignore it; we'll deal with the repercussions together."

Teacher and Talk Show Host: New Metaphors for Leadership

At the beginning of this chapter, we argued that leadership makes a difference in the transformation of government, which is why only some public organizations have been able to reinvent themselves to meet the challenges of today's turbulent public sector environment. Those challenges require a sense of purpose, a proclivity for risk and power sharing, a strategic perspective, and, above all, persistence—all characteristic of the successful reinvention leaders we studied. At first blush, there are no real surprises here. For the most part, these are the kinds of qualities that are traditionally used to describe leaders of all stripes, and one could conclude that reinvention is just another variation on that more general theme. These are transformational leaders in the classic sense (Burns, 1978; Bass, 1985), engaged in the incremental transformation of government.

Nevertheless, some aspects of reinvention leadership may be unique. For example, we were struck by the extraordinary patience and tenacity demonstrated by the leaders we studied, qualities that are needed to deal with the extreme intractability of government bureaucracy. In more than one case, we encountered leaders who had decades-long perspectives and were unswervingly focused on incrementally improving institutional performance over the long term, with little or no prospect of reward or recognition for their efforts (indeed, many have faced just the opposite). Their patience was tested often by changing administrations, appointees, and reform agendas, but they were able to devise effective strategies—like the Pony Express—to sustain their efforts over time. Consider the fact that in almost every reinvention success we encountered, those who led it could trace its history over the "life cycle" of two or three government- or agency-wide management improvement campaigns, such as quality circles, TQM, or reengineering.

In addition, we were struck by the isolation involved in the transformation of government. Beset by resistance from below and above, the leaders we studied took some comfort in the reinvention rhetoric, but for the most part, they were left to struggle alone, often in the face of a hostile headquarters, suspicious peers, and intransigent employees. To be sure, many of these leaders were recognized—some even by the vice president himself—but sometimes these awards are like a scarlet letter; after the ceremony is over and the dignitaries are gone, the leaders are still left alone to tilt at the bureaucratic windmill. Such resistance is hardly unique to government, except perhaps in degree, but the antipathy (or just plain apathy) of midlevel political appointees that we found seemed especially problematic; after all, these are the officials charged with giving life to the political rhetoric. In the face of this lack of support, it is remarkable that so much bottom-up progress has been made.

In this regard, we were also struck by the apparent applicability of private sector organizational-change models—particularly the one posited by Beer, Eisenstat, and Spector (1990)—to the reinvention of government. Certainly, the "corporate" climates established by Vice President Gore and Governor Chiles are consistent with their model, as is the NPR's emphasis on bottom-up change, in the form of reinvention laboratories and unit-level change agents (see Chapter Four). However, a government setting adds some unique challenges to the mix: politics, bureaucratic and otherwise (the corporate version pales in comparison), and the turnover of political appointees; the statutory basis for many governmental processes and procedures; multiple stakeholders; and, last but not least, the legislature and separation of powers. These institutional variables require reinvention leaders to employ a different, more difficult, set of strategies and tactics to transform government. That transformation may also require a different, more difficult, set of leadership competencies.

Learning and Teaching

According to Senge (1990), an organization's chances of surviving in a chaotic, uncertain environment depend on its capacity to continually adapt and innovate—in other words, to learn (see also Vaill, 1996; Kettl, 1994). In this context, reinvention is nothing more or less than organizational learning, and these authors would all suggest that it is the leader's responsibility to make that happen. If so, it is a responsibility that is clearly met by the reinvention leaders we studied. However, examined in this light, learning and adaptation seem too passive an explanation for the profound influence that these leaders have had on their public organizations. They are not just learners; they are teachers.

The kind of leadership we observed in our study involves more than just "sitting in the classroom" with the rest of the organization. The leader must also collect, synthesize, interpret, and then impart to the organization's members what he or she has learned, the values as well as the experiences, from his or her unique vantage point. If successful reinvention represents effective organizational learning, then successful reinvention leadership represents effective organizational teaching. After all, as we have just argued, reinvention (and learning) don't "just happen." They are the result of planned, purposeful, and determined action. If an organization is to reinvent itself, its members must first be taught why and how.

The ability to do just that emerges as a subtle but essential leadership competency among those we studied. Joe Thompson taught his employees how to reengineer their work and, in the process, how to question some of the traditional ways of processing claims and dealing with customers. Phil Nuber taught his employees how (and when) to make decisions, and also how to brag. Dave Gradick and Jan Ziegler taught their employees how to take risks and exercise judgment; Bill Murphy taught his how to work together as a team. And they all taught their organizations a little about their own history and purpose. Note the distinction here: these leaders did not *tell* people what the problems were or how to solve them; they *taught* them how to define and deal with them themselves, and then they guided them as they began to apply what they had learned to the reinvention of their organizations.

This suggests another, more colorful metaphor for reinvention leadership: that of the television talk show host. If you've ever watched talk shows, they appear to be barely controlled chaos. That is the point of their popularity—and their relationship to reinvention. Like talk show hosts, in addition to being teachers, reinvention leaders must be able to keep their employees focused on broader organizational objectives even while they are trying to cope with the everyday uncertainty and chaos of change.

A talk show host starts each broadcast by setting the broad theme for the day and then introducing (or, in some cases, turning loose) purposely provocative guests. Then the fun begins, with the host left to manage the sometimes raucous interaction between the guests and the studio audience, while staying within the initial thematic framework. Nothing is scripted except that theme, and the entertainment value of the show is entirely up to the host's skill as an interpersonal referee. Similarly, almost all of our leaders described an episode or series of incidents in their reinvention journey that resembled the talk show scenario: long, agonizing, but ultimately crucial problem-solving or problem-defining sessions with employees, midlevel managers, union officials, headquarters and congressional staff, external stakeholders, and others. All the leaders demonstrated talk show host–like skill in staying "on message" while reconciling the conflicting interests in play.

This is reinvention leadership at its (somewhat facetious) best, and the key ingredients in this recipe are relatively straightforward: combine single-minded purpose and a strategic perspective with a proclivity for risk, add a heavy dose of participation and persistence, bake (or broil) in the crucible of organizational change, and voilà—you've got a reinvention leader, a potential hero of a potential revolution. This is obviously easier said than done, but one thing is certain: don't try to reinvent government without one.

References

Uncredited quotes are from personal interviews and from comments made at the Maxwell Reinvention Symposium, held Sept. 26, 1995.

Astley, W. G., and Van de Ven, A. H. "Central Perspectives and Debates in Organization Theory." *Administrative Science Quarterly,* 1983, *28,* 245.

Ban, C. "Unions, Management, and the NPR." In D. F. Kettl and J. J. Di Iulio Jr. (eds.), *Inside the Reinvention Machine: Appraising Governmental Reform.* Washington, D.C.: Brookings Institution, 1995.

Bass, B. M. *Leadership and Performance Beyond Expectations.* New York: Free Press, 1985.

Beer, M., Eisenstat, R. A., and Spector, B. *The Critical Path to Organizational Renewal.* Boston: Harvard Business School Press, 1990.

Berry, F. S., Chackerian, R., and Wechsler, B. "Administrative Reform: Lessons from a State Capital." Paper presented at the American Society for Public Administration National Conference, Atlanta, July 2, 1996.

Briggs, J., and Peat, F. D. *Turbulent Mirror: An Illustrated Guide to Chaos Theory and the Science of Wholeness.* New York: HarperCollins, 1989.

Burns, J. M. *Leadership.* New York: HarperCollins, 1978.

Child, J. "Organization Structure, Environment, and Performance: The Role of Strategic Choice." *Sociology,* 1972, *6,* 1.

Doig, J. W., and Hargrove, E. C. *Leadership and Innovation: A Biographical Perspective on Entrepreneurs in Government.* Baltimore: Johns Hopkins University Press, 1987.

Gore, A., Jr. "National Performance Review, Phase II: Putting It Together—Objectives, Working Principles, and Approach." Memorandum sent to agency heads, Feb. 1, 1995.

Heifitz, R. *Leadership Without Easy Answers.* Cambridge, Mass.: Harvard University Press, 1994.

Kaufman, H. *Time, Chance, and Organizations: Natural Selection in a Perilous Environment.* Chatham, N.J.: Chatham House, 1991.

Kettl, D. F. "Managing on the Frontiers of Knowledge: The Learning Organization." In P. W. Ingraham and B. S. Romzek (eds.), *New Paradigms for Government: Issues for the Changing Public Service.* San Francisco: Jossey-Bass, 1994.

Kochan, T. A., and Useem, M. *Transforming Organizations.* New York: Oxford University Press, 1992.

Machiavelli, N. *The Prince* (L. Ricci, trans.; E.R.P. Vincent, ed.). New York: Random House, 1940. (Originally published 1513.)

National Partnership Council. *National Partnership Council Report to the President on Implementing Recommendations of the National Performance Review.* Washington, D.C.: U.S. Office of Personnel Management, 1994.

Osborne, D., and Gaebler, T. *Reinventing Government: How the Entrepreneurial Spirit Is Transforming the Public Sector.* Reading, Mass.: Addison Wesley Longman, 1992.

Rogers, E. M., and Shoemaker, F. F. *Communication of Innovation: A Cross-Cultural Approach.* New York: Free Press, 1971.

Sanders, R. F., and Thompson, J. R. "Laboratories of Reinvention: A Special Report." *Government Executive* (Special Supplement), Mar. 1996, pp. 1–12.

Senge, P. *The Fifth Discipline: The Art and Practice of the Learning Organization.* New York: Doubleday/Currency, 1990.

Thompson, J. R. "Organizational Politics and Innovation in Federal Reinvention Laboratories." Unpublished doctoral dissertation, Syracuse University, 1996.

Thompson, J. R., Sanders, R. P., and Ingraham, P. W. "Implementing Change in the Federal Government: Two Models." Paper presented at the Annual Research Conference of the Association for Public Policy Analysis and Management, Chicago, Oct. 1994.

U.S. General Accounting Office. *Managing for Results: State Experiences Provide Insights for Federal Management Reform.* Report no. GAO/GGD-95–22. Washington, D.C.: U.S. Government Printing Office, 1994.

U.S. National Performance Review. *Report of the National Performance Review.* Washington, D.C.: U.S. Government Printing Office, 1993.

Vaill, P. B. *Learning as a Way of Being: Strategies for Survival in a World of Permanent Chaos.* San Francisco: Jossey-Bass, 1996.

Wheatley, M. *Leadership and the New Science.* San Francisco: Berrett-Koehler, 1992.

Chapter Three

The Best-Kept Secret in Government

How the NPR Translated Theory into Practice

John M. Kamensky

Like nearly all of his predecessors, President Bill Clinton vowed to fix the government after he took office in January 1993. At about the same time, the General Accounting Office (GAO) offered its assessment of the challenge he faced: "The state of management in the federal government is not good. Too many principles, structures, and processes that may have worked well years ago no longer allow the government to respond quickly and effectively to a rapidly changing world" (U.S. General Accounting Office, 1992, p. 4).

Studies by congressional committees, the National Academy of Public Administration, and others offered similar assessments (U.S. House of Representatives, Committee on the Budget, 1991; U.S. House of Representatives, Committee on Government Operations, 1992; National Academy of Public Administration, 1983; Barrett and Greene, 1992). These assessments, however, were more apt to point out problems than offer concrete solutions.

None of this was new. Ten major efforts to reform the federal government had been conducted since Teddy Roosevelt's 1905 Keep Commission (Moe, 1992, p. 16). However, past reform efforts often foundered on the Achilles' heel of reform: weak or nonexistent implementation efforts (U.S. General Accounting Office, 1981; Szanton, 1981). Again, like many of his predecessors, President Clinton vowed that his effort to reform the federal government would not be "a report sitting on a shelf" (Clinton, 1994c, p. 364). Still, skeptics inside and outside of government scoffed at the effort. They had seen it all before: it was too radical, it was too disjointed, it was not focused on the right issues, it was the "flavor of the month" that would soon fade (Goodsell, 1993; Jasper and Alpern, 1994; Moe, 1994). Yet, after four years, the Clinton administration's reform efforts, led by Vice President Al Gore, continue to be vigorously implemented and are achieving measurable results even in the midst of continuing political challenges to the scope and role of the federal government in today's society.

This chapter focuses on some of the strategic approaches undertaken by the National Performance Review (NPR) after the initial recommendations were announced in 1993, and on the evolution of its implementation efforts over the following four years.

What Is the National Performance Review?

President Clinton launched the NPR as a major government reform initiative in early 1993. It was quickly dubbed "reinventing government" after a popular book by that name (Osborne and Gaebler, 1992). President Clinton asked Vice President Gore to lead the effort and gave him a six-month deadline to report back to him with a blueprint of changes that would create "a government that works better on less money and that is more responsive" (Clinton, 1993b, p. 352). Vice President Gore plunged into the effort. He created a clear focus from the beginning: concentrate on how the government works, not on what government should be doing. He strongly believed that the lack of consensus on the role of government during the previous decade among Americans and their representatives could not be solved by such a reform effort. He was subsequently criticized for taking this path by private sector management guru Peter Drucker (1995), among others. However, events during the following years have validated his pragmatic decision to focus on fixing the day-to-day management of government and not to imitate the demise of previous reform efforts that had focused on organizational structure or policy issues related to the role of government in society.

Vice President Gore became personally involved in every aspect of the NPR. Within weeks after Clinton's announcement, he led a series of "town hall" meetings of federal employees across the government to learn about their problems firsthand. He met with leaders of private sector corporations that had undergone major changes, in order to learn about their use of quality management and reengineering techniques; he also met with reform leaders from other countries. And, unlike leaders of previous federal reform efforts, he turned to career federal employees to run and staff this initiative. His interagency task force of 250 federal employees was supplemented by teams in each agency. He met individually with each agency head to cement her or his support for his recommendations. But he didn't wait for recommendations; he immediately asked agencies to create "reinvention laboratories" to pilot new innovations, and nearly one hundred were created in the months while the NPR was under way. By the time he presented his recommendations to President Clinton in September 1993, there was already a large degree of commitment to future action.

In contrast, the 1984 Grace Commission had comprised some two thousand volunteer businesspeople. It had compiled its 2,478 recommendations largely in secret and proposed savings of $424 billion over three years. A large number were rejected outright by the president, and a GAO and Congressional Budget Office study showed the savings to be wildly inflated (Moe, 1992, p. 44).[1]

The vice president's NPR reported back to President Clinton in six months, on time, with a wide range of proposals that would dramatically change the culture of the government to make it more results-oriented. The NPR estimated that these measures would save $108 billion during the following five years. The biggest cost savings would come from proposals to substantially cut "overhead costs"—supervisors, auditors, and personnel, budget, and financial specialists—while preserving the jobs of people on the front line who deliver services.

The NPR's efforts largely fell from public view after the initial release of the report. However, this was no measure of top-level commitment or of the progress that was being made. Six months later, at a ceremony commemorating his initial announcement of the creation of the NPR, President Clinton contrasted the work of the vice president with the previous reform efforts that had been attempted in this century: "Here's the most important reason why this report is different from earlier ones on government reform. When Herbert Hoover finished the Hoover Commission, he went back to Stanford. When Peter Grace finished the Grace Commission, he went back to New York City. But when the Vice President finished his report, he had to go back to his office—20 feet from mine—and go back to working to turn the recommendations into reality" (Clinton, 1994c, p. 365).

The more than twelve hundred recommendations in the NPR's 1993 summary report and its more than two thousand pages of technical accompanying reports proposed a series of actions at many different levels. Some were very broad (require agencies to "provide customer service equal to the best in business"), while others were quite discrete ("reduce by 11 the number of Marine Guard detachments" at embassies) (Gore, 1993, pp. 47, 97). In addition, the NPR offered a series of guiding principles for agency reinventors, based on the characteristics of some of the successful public organizations it examined: (1) put customers first, (2) empower employees, (3) cut red tape, and (4) cut back to basics (p. 6). These principles for action created a framework that many employees adopted as their own and ultimately helped to foster grass-roots action by thousands of federal employees, including many who never read the NPR report but heard about what it set out to do.

What happened after the initial report was released with fanfare at the White House? Vice President Gore's first caution was: "With this report, then, we begin a decade-long process of reinvention" (Gore, 1993, p. 9). And in his first status report a year later, he remarked, "Those who have been working on this issue harbor no illusions about how difficult this transformation will be. They will need all the help they can get" (Gore, 1994a, p. 73). Don Kettl, a researcher at the Brookings Institution who assessed the NPR's first year of progress, observed: "In its first year, the NPR has proven one of the most lively management reforms in American history" (Kettl, 1995c, p. 9). And by the NPR's 1995 status report, Vice President Gore was saying, "Reinventing the federal government isn't an event. . . . [It's] becoming a way of life for employees in agencies and the customers they serve across the nation" (Gore, 1995a, p. 7). He also declared, "If you haven't felt a difference yet, you will. This year" (p. 92).

In the four years since the NPR's initial report, academicians have still debated the efficacy of its recommendations. In addition, Congress is still debating the role of government and how to reshape its functions. Meanwhile, federal agencies have been actively implementing the principles and recommendations of the NPR. Vice President Gore refers to this process as the "Cal Ripkin approach" to reform, after the record-breaking baseball player who spent a quiet career plugging away until he was a legend (Gore, 1995c, p. 3). Although there has been much activity following the initial and subsequent NPR reports, describing the implementation of the NPR is very much like the story of the blind men describing an elephant. It all depends on who's touching what part; none of them is wrong but none is entirely right, either. Probably the closest of all NPR observers is Don Kettl, who discerned at least three different NPRs (Kettl, 1995c, p. 14). His description is an accurate one and the implementation story from each of these three NPRs differs from the others. For example, the progress on implementation can be viewed from (1) the point of view of the White House and the NPR task force, (2) the point of view of the agencies and the initiatives they have taken beyond those recommended in the NPR's reports, and (3) the point of view of the front-line work teams within agencies. The view from each vantage point tells a different story.

The NPR Task Force: A Catalyst for Change

After the initial NPR report in September 1993, nearly all the members of the original task force returned to their agencies, and Vice President Gore charged a smaller group of career federal employees with leading the implementation of key recommendations and tracking the overall progress of the effort. The NPR's role evolved over the following four years, adapting to the changing reform environment. It initially sponsored a series of cross-agency activities and led the implementation of several key initiatives outlined in the initial report. After the 1994 congressional election, a second phase of the NPR was launched at the request of President Clinton. Then, in early 1996, Vice President Gore charged the NPR with developing strategies to help agencies improve services to the public in a world of constantly declining resources as a result of the balanced-budget agreement. In response to these events, the NPR continually adjusted its strategies in pursuing Gore's vision of "creating a government that works better and costs less."

Keeper of the Torch

Upon the release of Vice President Gore's September 1993 report, the remaining life span of the task force was uncertain, so the NPR quickly moved to jump-start as many recommendations as possible. In the weeks following the release of the initial report, it helped to coordinate the development of over two dozen initial presidential directives, such as those putting into place recommendations to streamline the federal workforce by 252,000 over a five-year period (subsequently raised to 272,900 by law) and to create customer service standards.

The NPR also quickly helped to create several policy-level networks, such as the President's Management Council, which was comprised of the chief operating officers of the major agencies—normally the deputy secretaries. It also advocated the creation of the union-management National Partnership Council as well as the Government Information Technology Services Working Group, which sponsored cross-agency applications of technology. These policy-level networks helped to create a government-wide focus on selected areas of reinvention. And, as will be discussed later, the NPR created a communication network among reinventors using the Internet and encouraged the development of informal groups among federal employees such as the Consortium for Culture Change.

In the following months, it became clear to the White House that the NPR would need to have a longer, yet still indefinite, life span to ensure that the vice president's recommendations would be acted upon. It became the "keeper of the torch of reinvention." The NPR undertook several initiatives in areas where it was clear that no other group was providing leadership. These included identifying early reinvention successes and using them to teach others the principles of the NPR. It also included ensuring that agencies created customer service standards as required by a presidential executive order that was one of the NPR's key recommendations.[2] Working closely with over 150 agencies to help them create more than one thousand customer service standards was a key accomplishment in the NPR's first year of implementation (Clinton, 1994a; Clinton and Gore, 1994).

The NPR defined its role as being a catalyst for action, a convener and sponsor of cross-agency activities, and a champion of its principles. As it found external champions for its initiatives, the NPR withdrew its efforts in those areas. For example, Steve Kelman at the Office of Management and Budget (OMB) followed through on its procurement recommendations, the Chief Financial Officers Council implemented its financial management recommendations, and the Department of the Treasury's information technology expert James Flyzik carried out its electronic technology recommendations; this allowed the NPR's task force to shift its attention to other initiatives that lacked obvious champions.

The OMB also played a key role in implementing a series of NPR recommendations. It acted quickly on the recently adopted Government Performance and Results Act, creating over seventy pilots for performance measurement. The law required only ten (U.S. Senate, 1992). The OMB also led in drafting a major piece of legislation containing over fifty of the NPR's recommendations that needed legislative approval (Clinton, 1993a). The House of Representatives passed the proposal in less than a month, but it died in the Senate. Most of the provisions were ultimately adopted in separate bills. In fact, Congress passed over thirty-four bills containing many NPR provisions in the following year (Gore, 1994b, p. 125).

As he did during the development of the initial report, Vice President Gore took an active role in implementing the recommendations. In early 1994 he observed that many federal workers did not seem to understand what reinvention was about. He spent time teaching them by recognizing the teams of employees who were successfully reinventing their workplaces.[3] He began giving out his coveted Hammer Awards—a real six-dollar hammer framed and festooned with red, white, and blue ribbon—to teams that put their customers first, empowered their employees, and cut red tape. Ultimately, many of the vice president's "tutorial awards" were videotaped and turned into a government training film. He also made a series of speeches, such as his lecture on "the new role of the federal executive" (Gore, 1994b), and participated in different forums, including an electronic forum on the Internet with federal employees.

A year after Vice President Gore's initial report, there was a flurry of assessments of the NPR's progress. Gore issued a status report in September 1994 that cataloged agencies' progress in implementing specific recommendations. However, he also found that many agencies were not only acting on the recommendations in his report but also undertaking their own initiatives, based on the NPR's principles, that had not been proposed originally in the recommendations. For example, the Department of Defense decided to reengineer its travel process and developed a strategy that would save nearly one billion dollars a year (Koonce, 1995). The Federal Communications Commission began auctioning its broadcasting licenses in late 1993, and by mid-1996 it had netted the government more than twenty-one billion dollars (Gore, 1996a, p. 2). The Small Business Administration streamlined its loan process for small businesses from four weeks to three days (Gore, 1994a, p. 57). None of these actions were recommended by the NPR, but they all reflected its basic principles. They seem to suggest that there was more to the NPR than just the report or the specific recommendations it contained.

Adapting Reform to a Changing Environment

In late 1994, the world of government reform changed with the turnover of Congress to the Republicans. Suddenly, improving government operations took a back seat to a new set of questions centered around what the government should be doing in the first place. Although these questions were raised in early 1993, the environment was not right to resolve them. Vice President Gore was committed to making recommendations that had some chance of success and felt that, after more than a decade of Republican presidencies that attempted to redefine the role of government in society, making another attempt at addressing these questions would result in an academic report destined for a bookshelf. He was unwilling to pursue this course. But with a Republican Congress willing to raise this question, President Clinton asked Vice President Gore to undertake a second phase of reinvention targeted at such questions (Clinton, 1994b). The NPR was also charged with reassessing the federal government's approach to regulating the private sector (Clinton, 1995a, 1995b).

The NPR created a series of teams with the OMB and the 24 major agencies. This second NPR also assessed the operations of the 132 small and independent agencies. The NPR's objectives expanded on the scope of the 1993 NPR. They included increasing customer choices, terminating obsolete programs, and identifying opportunities to consolidate or privatize functions or devolve them to states or localities (Gore, 1995b). Some of the changes went beyond what had been politically possible just a year earlier, for example, creating housing vouchers for those living in public housing projects and allowing them to choose where they would live. Others were just common sense, such as staggering the payment dates for new social security beneficiaries throughout the month to eventually eliminate the "peaks and valleys" workloads of Social Security Administration offices (Gore, 1995a, p. 136).

The NPR also focused on reforms to the regulatory system. The public debate had historically centered on the creation of new regulations. Vice President Gore held more than a dozen meetings with regulatory experts and the heads of key regulatory agencies in different policy arenas. From this series of meetings, he concluded that the root cause of many of the problems with the existing regulatory system that were identified by most businesses was not the goals of the regulations but rather the enforcement process. So President Clinton and he convened the heads of all the major regulatory agencies and asked them to cut obsolete regulations and pointless paperwork and to change the regulatory enforcement culture from a confrontational culture to one of partnership. Some results were immediate. For example, the Health Care Financing Administration stopped requiring physicians to fill out an "attestation form" for each government-insured patient. This ended the preparation of eleven million forms a year that were useless in preventing fraud. This simple action saved doctors two hundred thousand hours a year that they could then spend on health care instead of paperwork (Gore, 1995a, p. 44). Other results took more time, for instance, changing the performance appraisal systems that agencies used in assessing their enforcement staff so that they focused on achieving program results, such as increasing worker safety, not just on assessing their levels of citations or fines levied.

By September 1995, the NPR task force had compiled a second report card on its progress. This report concluded that the "reinventing government" initiative had completed 30 percent of its original recommendations, saving fifty-eight billion dollars.[4] It also included a series of new recommendations stemming from its second-phase NPR that totaled another seventy billion dollars in savings to taxpayers over the following five years, cutting more than sixteen thousand pages of obsolete regulations, and reducing regulatory burdens on the private sector by twenty-eight billion dollars a year (Gore, 1995a, pp. 3, 6).

In addition to the NPR, many other groups worked behind the scenes to ensure that concrete action was taking place. The Chief Financial Officers Council led changes in the financial management arena. The Government Information Technology Services Working Group sponsored innovative cross-agency computer projects. The President's Management Council provided leadership in streamlining agency field operations. The National Partnership Council created a labor-management forum that led to better workplace communication. In addition, other groups also contributed to the quiet successes of the NPR.

Adapting to a Changing Environment—Again

By 1996, the federal reform landscape had begun to change once again. As a result of the ongoing budget debate, it became clear to most domestic agencies that they would face declining fiscal resources for the foreseeable future. The president's fiscal year 1997 budget projected a balanced budget by the year 2002, which would require domestic agencies to reduce their spending by an average of more than 20 percent, without adjusting for the effects of inflation. The Republican-led Congress proposed even greater cuts (U.S. Office of Management and Budget, 1996).

Vice President Gore recognized that agencies needed a blueprint for approaching these cuts and proposed a series of new initiatives intended to show how the administration would responsibly govern in a balanced-budget world. He observed that agencies needed to increase their focus on the ends, not the means, of what government does and to delegate more authority to managers on the front line. He also believed that information technology would allow a shift away from the traditional "one size fits all" approach to a more custom-fitted approach tailored to the missions of individual agencies. He crafted a set of initiatives based on expanding partnerships between federal agencies, states, localities, and the private sector and advocated interagency efforts to provide an integrated approach to service delivery.

Building on the successes of the NPR's reinvention labs and other initiatives, he proposed (Gore, 1996b) that agencies expand existing initiatives on customer service, regulatory partnerships, and transformation of the culture in the federal workplace. He offered several new initiatives:

- *Convert to performance-based organizations.* Agencies would take functions that deliver measurable services and grant them greater autonomy from government-wide rules in exchange for greater accountability for results.
- *Create performance-based partnership grants.* The existing grant system would be converted to federal-state-local partnerships based on results rather than process.
- *Establish single points of contact for communities.* One person would be designated as the single point of contact in each of the nation's larger communities to create integrated accountability for the federal government.[5]

These initiatives were elaborated upon in the president's fiscal year 1997 budget, which was presented to Congress in the weeks after the vice president's speech (U.S. Office of Management and Budget, 1996), and again in the fiscal year 1998 budget (U.S. Office of Management and Budget, 1997).

Where to Next?: The Second Clinton-Gore Administration

As the first Clinton-Gore administration came to a close, the NPR reassessed its approach to implementation. In March 1996, the NPR cosponsored a conference that convened participants from its reinvention labs. This meeting and others like it in the following months allowed information to be shared among the participants about the successes of their peers, but it also identified challenges that still needed to be addressed. The participants pointed to the need for three sets of actions: (1) better understanding of reinvention and better support from their agencies' political appointees and senior career executives; (2) a clearinghouse of information across agencies on how teams successfully obtained waivers, delegations of authority, and other changes; and (3) some support for those who take risks. The NPR committed to developing strategies to address each of these challenges (Thompson, 1996).

By early 1997, the NPR began to outline a strategy, based in large part on the feedback it received from reinventors on the front line. It consciously chose not to launch a series of new initiatives but rather to focus on integrating existing initiatives into the fabric of the government. The second-term goal began as an effort to take the many hundreds of small successes identified in the first four years to be the norm across agencies.

The NPR continues to lead initiatives to expand implementation of its basic principles. However, while it plays a visible role in shaping the direction of reinvention and encouraging public recognition of the changes that are occurring, the NPR interagency task force's work isn't what really defines and sustains the progress of the broader reinvention effort. The real progress is occurring in many agencies and hundreds of places on the front lines.

The NPR in the Agencies: Leadership Counts

When Vice President Gore reviewed the drafts of the original NPR recommendations, he met individually with the heads of all the major agencies to gain their personal commitment to implementing the proposed actions. Many agency heads not only agreed but committed to go further. Gore strongly believed that leadership in agencies was the key to successful reinvention (Shoop, 1994). Each agency created internal reinvention teams that not only took on implementation of the recommendations in the vice president's report, but also launched major cultural shifts within their own agencies. In many cases, dramatic changes were led by top political leaders in these agencies. For example, George Weise at the Customs Service, Dan Beard at the Bureau of Reclamation, and Joe Dear at the

Occupational Safety and Health Administration (OSHA) all instituted and led remarkable changes in their agencies.

George Weise, Commissioner of the Customs Service in the Department of the Treasury, led the transformation of an agency where some staff once proudly claimed that it had a "204-year tradition unhampered by progress." By mid-1993, he convinced Congress to pass the Customs Modernization Act, which, among other things, lifted the ban that prevented Customs from studying any reorganization. It quickly did a study and replaced its seven regions and forty-four districts with twenty management centers. It cut its headquarters staff by one-third and shifted these resources to the front lines (Gore, 1994a, p. 21). It reengineered its cargo- and passenger-handling processes to facilitate access into the country and at the same time increased its seizures of illegal drugs and other banned imports. In one case, an importer had previously been required to file 700,000 forms a year; this was changed to one form a month (Singleton, 1995).

Dan Beard, commissioner of the Bureau of Reclamation in the Department of the Interior, took an unpopular and moribund agency that was responsible for building dams in the West and converted it into a first-class natural resources management agency. He told employees that they were going to have fewer dollars, fewer people, and more work. He shifted authority to the thirty-five field offices and turned the two-thousand-person headquarters operation into a service center; the field offices could turn to the center for advice or buy services from it. He cut staff by one thousand, lowered the supervisor-to-employee ratio from 1:5 to 1:15, and streamlined approval processes significantly (Gore, 1994a, p. 13). He encouraged innovation and risk by issuing "forgiveness coupons" to his managers and telling them that they had to redeem at least one during the course of the year if they went out on a limb too far when they were testing new approaches. He felt that real innovations cannot happen unless some mistakes are made (Beard, 1995). By the time he left government in late 1995, the bureau had been selected by the Ford Foundation for its Innovation in Government Award (Corbin, 1995).

OSHA, in the Department of Labor, was under political attack when Joe Dear became its assistant secretary in 1993. The attacks increased with the Republican takeover of the Congress in 1994.

Dear asked OSHA to reexamine its approach to enforcing its regulations and to focus more on improving safety in the workplace. For years, the old OSHA would sweep into a company; write up violations of its regulations, big ones as well as petty ones; and leave behind a bill. This policy infuriated businesses, especially small businesses, and contributed to public dislike of the agency. It also did not lead to significant improvements in health or safety. Dear led in eliminating silly rules. For example, inspectors used to levy an automatic four-hundred-dollar fine if workplaces did not have an OSHA compliance poster on the wall; now inspectors carry the posters with them and help employers to put them up. He also encouraged the agency to increase OSHA's consulting services to employers and work with them in partnerships to improve safety (Gore, 1995b, p. 32). In Maine, a test site for this approach, safety teams of employers and workers found fourteen times more hazards than OSHA had, injury rates dropped 35 percent, and productivity increased 25 percent (Gore, 1995a, p. 26; Behn, 1995). In subsequent years, this approach was expanded to other states with similar results. For example, in 1996, after it had been instituted in Kansas, fatalities in the oil industry dropped to zero for the first time.

Remarkable stories like these were occurring across the government, but changes were not driven solely by the political leadership. More difficult to see, but more profound, were the changes that occurred within the career service. The depth of these changes is difficult to plumb because of their diffuse nature and the conflicting signals that employees on the front line have received from Washington. They faintly hear the "works better" message, but they are vividly confronted with the "costs less" refrain. The NPR's message is beginning to be heard by employees on the front line. They are the ones making changes on their own initiative, and they will be the ones who sustain the progress toward meeting the challenges first outlined by Vice President Gore in 1993.

The NPR on the Front Line: Empowerment Works

Across the government, mostly outside of Washington, individuals who never saw the detailed recommendations of the NPR still found themselves personally challenged by its vision and principles. They became personally committed to "creating a government that works better and costs less." These people agreed with the vice president's assessment that "the problem is not lazy or incompetent people; it is red tape and regulation so suffocating that they stifle every ounce of creativity" (Gore, 1993, p. 2). They saw a shift in attitude in Washington and they wanted to believe in Gore's empowerment message. To them, it was not an administration initiative; it was a movement. For example, in addition to Dan Beard's forgiveness coupons, Education secretary Richard Riley and the late Commerce secretary Ron Brown gave "permission slips" to their employees, encouraging them to use their commonsense judgment without having to constantly ask permission (Gore, 1994a, p. 15).

Other observers, such as David Osborne and Christopher Hood, see this new approach to governing—decentralization, customer focus, and employee empowerment—as a shift in the basic paradigm of public administration (Osborne and Gaebler, 1992; Hood, 1994; Kamensky, 1996). This shift is a global phenomenon, part of the transition from industrial-era bureaucracies to the information age. For example, the governments in Belgium, Portugal, and the United Kingdom have all issued customer service standards much like those proposed by the NPR. Likewise, these governments and others have moved more authority down within their systems to front-line managers (Organization for Economic Cooperation and Development, 1995).

To encourage this shift, the NPR encouraged action by individuals and front-line workers. It used several mechanisms to try to communicate directly with front-line workers. First, it used traditional approaches such as training videos and newsletters. Second, it focused on trying to identify successful operations and hold them up as models for others to emulate. Third, it tried to create innovation "hothouses" by encouraging agencies to designate selected units as reinvention laboratories that would be granted waivers from internal agency rules, allowing them to try new approaches, which were often variations of strategies used in the private sector to bring about organizational transformations. And fourth, it encouraged the creation of a series of informal networks among individuals to stimulate the diffusion of innovations, such as the Consortium for Culture Change.

Recognition as a Tool for Transformation

In early 1994, Vice President Gore concluded that the word wasn't getting out to the front lines. He wanted to identify unsung heroes and showcase successes that were happening around the country so that others could emulate these pioneers. To do this he wanted to personally recognize these teams by giving them awards and sending them congratulatory letters. He understood that traditionally little or no recognition had been given to good work within the government. He also understood that recognition was a much better motivator than the fear of sanctions.

Gore's Hammer Awards played an important role. They were different from most other awards because there was no artificial annual limit on how many could be awarded. The agencies nominate teams. In the four years after the initial NPR report, over eight hundred Hammer Awards were presented around the country, and they seemed to have an enormous impact on the pride and morale of affected employees ("Highlights of '95 Hammer Award Winners," 1996).

The first award was given to a team of employees in the New York City regional benefits office of the Department of Veterans Affairs. There, regional manager Joe Thompson had his staff step back from their existing benefit-award process and look at its effect (Thompson, 1995b). Each employee toiled in anonymity, performing a task in classic assembly-line fashion. No one ensured that veterans would receive start-to-finish satisfaction. Thompson said, "The results of our efforts frequently frustrated if not angered our customers, and the processes that we used in the office to do business sucked the life out of our employees. Other than that, everything was going pretty good" (Gore, 1994a, p. 3). He led a redesign that shifted from an assembly-line to a team process. This cut the claims process from twenty-five steps to eight, cut processing costs, reduced backlogs, and improved customer satisfaction. The employees were happier because they worked more with veterans and were not solely focused on processing paper. As befits the government's organizational culture, this award was immediately subjected to a congressional audit, but it passed with flying colors (U.S. General Accounting Office, 1994b). This team exemplified all of the NPR's basic principles: providing customer service, cutting red tape, and empowering employees.

Other Hammer Awards recognized similar achievements, some of which had begun as quality management efforts in earlier years. For example, an Internal Revenue Service team in Ogden, Utah, allowed employees to respond to correspondence rather than use computerized form letters that generated nonsense. The team also created partnerships with its union (Gore, 1994a). In the Department of Defense, a team redesigned the administrative portion of the travel process, identifying a potential billion dollars a year in savings (Gore, 1994a, p. 50). At the Railroad Retirement Board, employees reengineered their transaction-posting process for tax statements. They increased payment accuracy to 99.8 percent, cut per-case costs from twenty-one dollars to two dollars, and cut a backlog of over 50,000 cases to under 650 in under twenty-four months (U.S. National Performance Review, 1997). In each of these cases, career employees took on reinvention as their own personal challenge and solved problems that, in many cases, had festered for years.

These awards stimulated significant interest among federal employees and conveyed the message that change was possible. In many cases, local press coverage of these awards helped to spread the message to other federal workers that change would be rewarded, as well as showing the public that government could work.

Permission to Be Different

In one of his first acts as "reinvention czar"—even before he had finished recruiting the NPR team—Vice President Gore participated in a cabinet meeting where he asked all agency heads to sponsor reinvention laboratories that could pilot new approaches and sanction innovation. Traditionally, pioneers were sacrificed by agencies on the altar of internal regulations and inspections. Gore wanted to signal that it is OK to try new approaches. Many of the laboratories have been in operation for more than four years. They vary widely in their constructs; for example, the entire four-thousand-person Agency for International Development designated itself as a laboratory; the eight-person evaluation office in the National Park Service is also a laboratory (U.S. National Performance Review, 1997; Thompson, 1995a).

By March 1997, more than three hundred individual labs had been sanctioned by agencies. The GAO surveyed the labs to determine what they were doing and to see if they had produced any constructive results. It concluded that the labs were addressing the goals of the NPR and that their initial results "suggest a number of promising approaches to improving existing agency work processes," but that it was too early to tell if these results would be more widely adopted (U.S. General Accounting Office, 1996c, p. 3).

The GAO found that some agencies permitted some of their units to be established as labs while other agencies—most notably the Department of the Interior—used labs as part of their strategy for changing the culture of their agencies. It also found that the need for waivers from agency regulations, once thought to be a major reason for the labs, was not a major factor in making internal changes possible. Most units found that being designated as a lab raised their visibility and that this was more important to their innovation efforts. The GAO also found that most labs had no performance data measures in place but planned to institute them. Nevertheless, the GAO did identify clear results being generated by the labs and encouraged their continuation.

The significance of the experiences of the labs, however, was a greater recognition by the NPR that, even when changes are successfully made to the processes and systems that give managers more discretion and flexibility, the managers may not willingly adopt these changes because they are personally risk-averse. The remaining challenge is even greater than that of changing the systems: it is the challenge of changing the culture and values of the managers themselves.

Spiderwebs

Because the NPR viewed its role as primarily one of catalyst and convener, it quickly created a series of networks in late 1993 to lead the actual implementation of its work. The NPR believed that the staff within the agencies had to be committed to the changes it advocated, and that it could not make the proposed changes itself.

A key strategy was the creation of a series of networks across agencies. The organizational culture in most agencies is insular; the staff rarely reach beyond their agency's boundaries for ideas or support. Some jokingly called this the "not invented here" syndrome. The NPR encouraged breaking down these boundaries and working collaboratively to solve problems, both within the government and with the public. Gore often referred to this approach to problem solving and program operation as creating "virtual" organizations.

As noted earlier, Gore's 1993 report recommended a series of top-level networks such as the President's Management Council, but the NPR also encouraged the formation of a series of working-level networks, collectively dubbed "NetResults"; they were often computer-based, but some were less technologically focused (Shoop, 1993). These networks were largely targeted to selected groups of related professionals. The one that grew the fastest was FinanceNet, which focused on improving financial management. It was sponsored by the existing Chief Financial Officers Council, formed in 1991. Other networks included the Consortium for Culture Change (for change agents within agencies), ARNet (for acquisition reformers), IGNet (for inspectors general), the Budget Officers Advisory Council, and BenchNet (for benchmarking champions across agencies).

Some of these networks were responsible for significant NPR accomplishments. For example, the Chief Financial Officers Council tracked and ensured the implementation of each of the dozens of financial management recommendations in the NPR's report. Likewise, the information technology group promoted the recommendations targeted to their community and issued periodic status reports. Some groups, such as the Consortium for Culture Change, sponsored seminars, workshops, and conferences around NPR themes. A benchmarking consortium sponsored a series of studies regarding the benchmarking of specific services (Johnson and Stern, 1995).

In addition, the Federal Executive Boards (FEBs) around the country—the front-line managers of agencies in communities with a large federal presence—are undertaking cross-agency projects. For example, the Houston FEB created a "U.S. General Store" that provides a one-stop business assistance center. Business customers who visit deal with one person who has been cross-trained in the services and regulations of all fourteen participating agencies (Gore, 1995a, p. 58). Similar general stores are being opened in other places around the country.

In summary, these and related networks served as one of the key grass-roots implementation strategies for the NPR and created cross-agency alliances for action that were new approaches to acting on change in the federal government. They were comprised of people who voluntarily wanted to improve government; they were not created by some official act from a higher authority. They epitomized Gore's vision of good leadership, where leaders serve as facilitators, not controllers. Although these actions are affecting the operating cultures in individual units, the cumulative effect across the government has not yet been assessed.

Assessing the Results

As Don Kettl noted, there has been a swirl of NPR activity. But after the initial rush of praise in 1993, the negative perspectives began to flow. As one critic noted, "It contains both good and bad ideas, and a lot of overblown rhetoric which is mostly irrelevant to solving federal management problems" (Jasper and Alpern, 1994, p. 27). By the end of the first year, however, Kettl noted that "the negative perspective had found many more adherents than the positive one" (Kettl, 1995c, p. 4). For example, Ronald Moe, a chronicler of past presidential reform efforts, concluded that the Gore report "constitutes a major attack on the administrative management paradigm with its reliance upon public law and the President as Chief Manager" (Moe, 1994, p. 117). He saw the NPR's actions as being "based on a profound misunderstanding of the role of law in the administration of the executive branch" (p. 115). But assessments by orthodox public administration scholars were generally conceptual critiques of the premises, not of the actual results being achieved by the NPR and the agencies.

Although the NPR task force issues an annual self-assessment of its progress in implementing its recommendations, the savings achieved, and the reduction in management overhead positions in agencies, it has yet to evaluate the impact of its results on either public service or the public. This is not unusual when it is compared with reform efforts in other countries. The Australians also did periodic assessments of the reforms they implemented during the 1980s. However, almost a decade passed before they conducted an in-depth evaluation of the impact of their changes. They believed that it was not worthwhile to conduct in-depth evaluations until the processes had been in place for several years (Australian Task Force on Management Improvement, 1992). Even though it may be too early to undertake a comprehensive impact evaluation, the key measure for the success of the NPR was set early on by President Clinton: can government win back the faith of the people? (Clinton, 1993c). This is a high standard that will take time before showing results.

In addition to the NPR's self-assessments, three sets of studies on the NPR had been made as of September 1996. First, the GAO issued a series of assessments of the NPR's implementation progress (U.S. General Accounting Office, 1993, 1994a, 1996a, 1996b, 1996c, 1996d). These reports basically verified the progress being made and cautioned that more needs to be done. In 1993, shortly after the NPR report was released, the GAO examined in detail the NPR's recommendations and disagreed with only one of the 384 major recommendations (U.S. General Accounting Office, 1993).[6] It also assessed the NPR's progress after the first year and concluded in a report of more than five hundred pages: "Some progress has been made in implementing many of the NPR recommendations since September 1993, but few have been fully implemented. . . . We generally agree with the thrust of most of the recommendations and support their continued implementation" (U.S. General Accounting Office, 1994a, p. 2). In 1996, it assessed the NPR's 1995 claims of completed recommendations and concluded that, in fact, it could independently verify that most of those that had been declared completed had in fact been fully implemented (U.S. General Accounting Office, 1996b). However, it could not verify the NPR's savings claims (U.S. General Accounting Office, 1996d), and it found that agencies were not streamlining in accordance with the NPR's objective that overhead positions should be reduced before front-line positions (U.S. General Accounting Office, 1996a).

Second, a subcommittee of the House Government Reform and Oversight Committee, chaired by Congressman Steven Horn, conducted a series of eight hearings on the NPR in 1995 and issued a report that claimed that the administration had not gone far enough in its recommendations and that the NPR was too ephemeral. The committee's majority concluded that management of the federal government needed more improvements. It offered a series of recommendations that embraced the ideas of the traditional public administration community: central control agencies should be strengthened; an office of management, reporting directly to the president, should be created; and a reorganization commission should be appointed. The subcommittee's minority members, however, observed, "No administration can make the necessary changes overnight[;] . . . improved service does not come from reinventing the bureaucracy—or by creating a new office—but by changing the culture of how the work gets done" (U.S. House of Representatives, 1995, p. 47).

Third, the Brookings Institution issued a study in 1995 that assessed the NPR and concluded that its progress was real but that there was no assurance that changes would be sustained. Researchers at the Brookings Institution observed, "The first year of the NPR generated more progress than almost anyone—indeed, perhaps more than the reinventors themselves—imagined possible" (Kettl, 1995c, p. 11; see also Kettl, 1995a).

A series of other observers were likewise impressed. A team of journalists preparing a report card on the management of the federal government for *Financial World* magazine observed in an open letter to President Clinton: "You've been working behind the scene to improve governmental financial controls, contract oversight, performance measurement, strategic planning, training, procurement, and a host of other . . . procedures. . . . And we think you're making real progress" (Barrett and Greene, 1994, p. 42). Max De Pree, author of the popular *Leadership Is an Art* (1990), called Gore's 1993 report "the best book on management available in America" ("Reinvention Roundtable," 1994, p. 6). Tom Peters offered a similar assessment in his foreword to the Penguin Books version of the 1993 Gore report (Gore, 1993b). Joseph Juran, in a letter to the NPR in 1995, also praised the effort.

This range of assessments of the NPR focused on different dimensions of progress. Some observers, such as the GAO, focused on the implementation of specific recommendations. Others, such as De Pree, focused on the potential influences on operating culture. It makes sense to look at progress across the "three NPRs" mentioned earlier, but much of this is anecdotal. Following is a brief description of several additional dimensions by which the NPR's success might be assessed.

Effects on the Public and Customers

The NPR's ultimate goal is to increase the level of trust Americans have in their federal government. It hopes to do this by creating better customer service, a less intrusive regulatory presence, and better value for tax dollars. Changing this perception will take years. President Clinton points out that the way for government to win back the faith of the people is "one customer at a time" (Gore, 1995a, p. 92). Information on the effects so far is anecdotal. For example, the number of thank-you letters to federal agencies seems to be on the rise. Gore's 1995 and 1996 status reports include a summary of a small sample of them. The nexus between public trust in government and improvements in government services is not clear, but there is a presumption that a connection exists.[7] Possibly the evolution of the Government Performance and Results Act will provide additional information in coming years.

Federal agencies are beginning to assess their progress toward meeting the customer service standards they set in more systematic ways. In 1996, they surveyed over one million customers in order to target improvements in their services, but results will not be available until mid-1997.[8] However, in the United Kingdom, efforts to measure customer service became a driving factor for internal improvements in agencies. Progress in meeting the standards and the public accountability associated with sustaining high-quality service have been a factor for the continued public support for reform in the United Kingdom.

Emphasizing customer service in any reform agenda seems to be a crucial factor for long-range public support for continued administrative reform. It addresses the "So what? What's in it for me?" issue. Yet the customer service component is only one dimension of any multifaceted assessment of changes to the underlying operational culture of the federal government.

Effects on the Systems of Government

Exhibit 3.1 summarizes some of the key accomplishments of Vice President Gore's reform effort in its first four years. The most visible of the NPR's changes are those related to the specific recommendations it made in its series of reports. The NPR tracks more than 1,500 individual recommendations and reports annually on progress toward completing them. As of September 1996, when it finished its most current status report, 43 percent of the 1,250 original recommendations had been completed, and sixty-two laws had been enacted containing more than one-third of the recommendations requiring legislative action.

The NPR claimed savings of more than $97 billion out of the $178 billion recommended, billions more in reinvention-inspired actions by agencies, and a reduction of over 214,000 in federal employment, out of the 252,000 originally proposed to be eliminated over five years. New laws included two that repealed or revised hundreds of previous procurement laws and streamlined the procurement process to the tune of $12.3 billion in savings. Also, the president signed bills to authorize a line-item veto of congressional appropriations, to abolish wool and mohair subsidies dating from the Korean War, and to eliminate hundreds of obsolete congressionally mandated reports. He also approved measures to privatize the Naval Petroleum Reserve and to abolish the Interstate Commerce Commission.

The new recommendations targeted to agencies and the regulatory system in the NPR's second phase in 1995 were also being actively implemented. By September 1996, some 19 percent of these recommendations had been completed and twelve thousand pages of obsolete regulations had been eliminated. Another thirteen thousand pages of regulations had been rewritten into plain English and agencies were creating a series of partnerships with the private sector as well as with states and localities. A number of actions had been taken to shift the culture of the federal government to be more results- and customer-oriented, including the OMB's leadership in the rapid implementation of the Government Performance and Results Act, the voluntary participation of about half the cabinet in signing performance agreements with the president, and, most important, creation of more than three thousand customer

Exhibit 3.1. Reinvention at a Glance.

Government Is Working Better

Over 200 agencies have publicly committed to more than 3,500 customer service standards and are in the process of measuring their compliance with them as part of their measures under the Government Performance and Results Act.

The public is seeing the difference: the Internal Revenue Service allows taxes to be filed over the phone; many agencies provide services via the Internet; the Social Security Administration stunned the business world in 1995 when it was recognized as having the best toll-free phone service; the Blue Pages in the phone directory are beginning to list services like the Yellow Pages instead of listing agencies organizationally. Confidence in federal agencies rose 9 percent.

More than 45 percent of the National Performance Review's recommendations have been fully implemented; as of March 1997, about sixty-two laws containing more than one-third of the recommendations requiring legislative action have been signed into law, including significant reforms in procurement, information technology, debt management, and the reorganization of Customs and Agriculture.

Regulatory partnerships and streamlining have led to the elimination of nearly 16,000 pages of regulations, the rewriting of 31,000 pages of rules, a major Plain English campaign, the use of partnerships in achieving regulatory compliance, and $28 billion a year in reduced regulatory burdens.

Government Is Costing Less

The NPR identified $177 billion in savings over five years. As of September 1996, it determined that $97 billion of these savings proposals had been locked into place.

In addition, agencies identified an additional $24 billion in savings that they said were directly related to their own internal reinvention efforts, on top of the savings identified in the NPR's reports.

More than 200 programs and 2,000 field offices have been eliminated or privatized in the past four years, including the helium reserve, the Naval Petroleum Reserve, the Bureau of Mines, and the Board of Tea Tasters.

The NPR surpassed the proposed goal of cutting 272,900 positions by 1999. As of early 1997, the workforce had been reduced by 291,000 positions. Thirteen of the fourteen cabinet departments had cut staff (the exception being Justice, because of crime reduction initiatives). However,

Exhibit 3.1. Reinvention at a Glance, cont'd.

the NPR recommended that many of these cuts be in "overhead" positions, and agencies reduced these positions by less than half the recommended amounts.

Reinvention Is Happening on the Front Lines

Entire agencies are being reinvented: the Agency for International Development, the Federal Emergency Management Agency, the Energy Department, and the Department of Housing and Urban Development, among others.

Agencies are shifting resources to the front lines: customs eliminated its regional offices and moved one-third of its headquarters staff to the field; the Park Service moved one-quarter of its headquarters staff to the front lines. The Federal Bureau of Investigation moved 600 agents from behind desks to the front lines. Other agencies are doing the same.

Agencies have created more than 850 labor-management partnership councils.

Agencies have cut 625,000 pages of internal regulations.

Agencies are sponsoring more than 300 reinvention labs and more than 800 teams have been recognized with a Hammer Award.

service standards by which 214 agencies publicly committed to having their performance judged (Clinton and Gore, 1995).[9]

Action was also taken to empower employees to do their jobs better. Increased attention to reengineering processes such as travel processing and time-and-attendance systems, along with smarter investments in information technology, have resulted in less worker time spent in processing mindless paperwork and more time doing an effective job. For instance, the Department of Defense is converting its medical records to electronic files and believes that it will ultimately save one billion dollars a year in unproductive time previously spent searching for lost paper medical records. In addition, agencies substantially cut their internal rules. Major agencies cut theirs by more than 625,000 pages.[10] For example, the Office of Personnel Management eliminated the ten-thousand-page *Federal Personnel Manual.* Agencies also issued procurement cards to their employees to ease the purchase of supplies and revised their personnel procedures to encourage labor-management partnerships. By February 1997, over 850 labor-management partnerships had been created in agencies, and they made a positive difference. For example, the Denver Mint found that its litigation costs dropped by millions of dollars after its union and managers began to work cooperatively (National Partnership Council, 1996, p. 9). Nevertheless, even with these successes, much remains of the NPR's original agenda, and the public is only beginning to perceive a change. The initiative is still fragile.

Where to Next?

Vice President Gore has chosen to rely on an interagency task force rather than create a permanent agency or turn over the effort to the President's Management Council or the OMB. The staff consists of about fifty people who are representatives of their agency on this interagency task force. Most stay from three to six months; the work is heavily project-based. In the first four years, over eight hundred people worked on the task force. The team's strength is the constant influx of new ideas and the fact that they carry the spirit of the NPR back to their home agency when they return. In some cases, this strength might be considered a challenge, because it makes it difficult to ensure sustained attention to longer-term initiatives.

Creating Sustainability

Some outside observers, including several in Congress, have called for a more permanent institution to manage the change in government performance. They believe that permanence will enhance the effort because it will be a clear signal that the administration is serious about its initiative. For example, a House oversight subcommittee recommended the creation of a separate Office of Management reporting to the president (U.S. House of Representatives, 1995, p. 8). Likewise, the National Academy of Public Administration (Fosler, 1995, p. 10) and Brookings Institution scholar Don Kettl (1995c, p. 5) made similar observations.

Others, however, believe that institutionalizing the initiative would divorce reform from the fact that its existence and success must be tied to the personal interests of the president and vice president in reforming government. Once it was institutionalized, the president and vice president would no longer have a personal stake in its success. The experience of other countries offers no clear guide. For example, the British reform effort under the Conservatives was directed by the deputy prime minister for more than a dozen years. There was no permanent office, but the government did not change political parties for nearly two decades (1978–1997). In Australia, the reform effort has been guided by its equivalent of the OMB, a statute-created board somewhat similar to the President's Management Council, and an interagency cadre of staff similar to the NPR that reports to the board. There, the government has changed hands politically and the reform effort has been sustained.

The NPR has been working more closely with the traditional lead in federal management issues, the OMB. The OMB's current leadership is strongly committed to improving management. The strongest signal on this front is its effort to integrate the implementation of the Government Performance and Results Act into its normal budget reviews; its work with agencies on ensuring that this happens is taken seriously (Koskinen, 1997). Also, the NPR and the OMB worked jointly on the NPR's Phase II teams as well as in the development of the NPR's agenda for the second administration. These efforts are indirect ways of gaining institutionalization of the NPR's efforts, but the second-administration agenda may be the most important one because the NPR is gradually integrating its reforms into the existing operations of the government rather than remaining a separate effort.

The debate over institutionalization, however, may be a side issue to the reform effort. The real issue is identifying the key levers of change in organizations. Osborne and Plastrik (1997) identified five: ensuring a clear mission, creating a customer focus, empowering employees on the front line, ensuring that there are clear consequences for actions, and creating an entrepreneurial culture. Each of these has been a part of the NPR's agenda. However, in the next few years, three sets of issues probably will be more significant challenges to the future of reinvention than the mode in which the NPR is constituted: the challenge of changing the behavior of individual employees on the front line, the need for some strategy to take the NPR's successful innovative pilots to a larger scale, and the eventual need to address structural changes in the broader institutions of the federal government.

The Challenge of Unleashing Human Potential

After four years of effort, it is possible to see the effects on the internal cultures of the agencies of good or indifferent leadership. Good leadership, such as that occurring in the Bureau of Customs, the Bureau of Reclamation, and OSHA, has unleashed the latent human potential in these agencies. The most immediate challenge facing the NPR is to expand these changes across all agencies. To do this, the NPR plans a three-pronged approach.

First, the NPR is expanding the attention it pays to the role of senior managers as change agents. It hopes to assess how managers are chosen to lead within agencies, ensure that they are given clear expectations for management, and have a say in how they are trained and rewarded. Vice President Gore began this step in early 1997 at a cabinet retreat where he laid out the "rules of the road" for reinvention during the second term. They were based on concrete successes in the first administration in the areas of customer service, partnerships, and untapping human potential in the workforce. These rules—called the Blair House Papers for the location of the retreat—were sent to every senior manager in the government in the following weeks and training courses were designed around them (Clinton and Gore, 1997).

Second, the NPR is examining the waiver and delegation processes agencies use to convey the flexibilities being granted statutorily or by central agencies. For example, it has found substantial anecdotal evidence from front-line employees that the flexibilities being granted by law and by the central control agencies are not consistently being delegated to front-line teams in large organizations. This is where leadership in the agencies and by senior front-line managers becomes crucial to changing an organization's culture. The NPR hopes to pinpoint these instances, create acceptable alternative tools to ensure accountability, and encourage senior agency leaders to take on these challenges.

Third, the NPR is developing additional strategies to convey changes and is involving the workforce directly, for example, by creating networks among senior executives and ensuring that its Internet website has useful management tools for front-line employees. In the future, culture surveys and related assessment tools will be used to help in pinpointing areas where additional attention is warranted. Changing the culture of the federal workforce to be more customer-oriented, results-focused, and performance-based will take years, but the framework has been put in place as a result of the NPR's early initiatives.

Crafting a Strategy to Build on the NPR's Successes

The NPR piloted a number of innovative approaches to creating better customer focus and making agencies more results-oriented. Vice President Gore's vision is to have agencies work across their organizational boundaries and concentrate on the needs of the customer, not the bureaucracy.

The NPR has piloted innovations through its three hundred reinvention labs. The GAO lauded this initiative, but cautioned that some mechanism is needed to take the successes of these labs and diffuse them across the government (U.S. General Accounting Office, 1996c, p. 59). For example, the idea of multiagency U.S. "general stores," such as the ones piloted in Houston and Atlanta, seem to have great merit, but they require much coordination to begin operation and need some central government support and sponsors. The NPR can handle a small number, but dozens would require a different approach. Likewise, other NPR initiatives—performance-based organizations, state partnerships, and local community partnerships—can all be developed on a small scale but will require a different organizational approach if they are successful and expand from a handful to hundreds.

The NPR's initial step in its effort to go from examples to reinvented agencies is to shift its attention from its past work with departments, where its involvement was broad but shallow, to a small handful of bureaus that have a significant impact on the public, on business, or on other agencies, where it will have the opportunity to provide more in-depth assistance. These include agencies such as the Internal Revenue Service, the National Park Service, and the Food and Drug Administration. It will work closely with these bureau-level agencies to ensure that their leadership can use the tools of reinvention and that their strategic plans, prepared as part of the Government Performance and Results Act, set challenging goals. It is probable that an increased focus on the use of information technology may provide the leverage needed for dramatic changes in these agencies.

In the first four years, the NPR successfully spun off the leadership of some of its specific initiatives to other groups such as financial management, franchising, information technology, and procurement reform. The challenge remains to find logical homes for some of the other cross-agency partnership initiatives it is piloting.

Restructuring the Government

For more than a decade, House and Senate committees that have jurisdiction over government reform issues have promoted the creation of a bipartisan commission to examine the structure and role of government. For example, one bill would arbitrarily require reducing the number of cabinet departments from fourteen to ten, among other actions. This proposal, however, may be premature and does not address the root causes of many of the problems that drive behavior and create some existing management problems in the executive branch today. There is a serious need for reformers to examine the existing budget development and implementation structures as well as the structure of congressional committees if they want to fundamentally change the incentives that drive current behavior in government. These two systems create many of the existing incentives and serve as the "rules of the game" at the macro level.

Past experience has shown that "moving organizational boxes" is politically very difficult and, even when successful, does not result in significant changes in organizational behavior. While reexamining organizational structures may be an appropriate step in the long term, agencies cannot wait for further studies. They need to begin changing immediately to survive the impact of the existing and impending budget cuts imposed by the balanced-budget agreement. The administration's commitment to the creation of performance-based organizations is its strategy for addressing these challenges. President Clinton said, "We want hundreds of organizations to become performance-based, to be trailblazers in increasing productivity and making their customers happy" (Clinton, 1996). Only after these budget-driven reinventions of existing operations have been digested can Congress reasonably attempt the next step of "reorganizing the boxes." This may be years down the road.

The Brookings Institution's federal management expert, Don Kettl, in testimony before the Senate committee considering legislation proposing restructuring, concluded that "restructuring is the last step in launching reform, not the first. Structure is a tool, not a goal in itself. To begin with structure in an effort to achieve a symbolic victory is to risk sacrificing that symbol for long-run disappointment. . . . Real reform has to be driven by the search for performance" (Kettl, 1995b, p. 13). Although Congress may see that it is important to examine the organizational structure of government, it also needs to reassess the broader rules of the game that drive existing performance and behavior. This would include rethinking congressional committee jurisdictions as well as the existing budget process in both the legislative and executive branches. For example, accountability for some agencies is so diffuse among congressional committees that congressional efforts in 1995 to eliminate the Department of Commerce took the concurrence of nearly all the committees in the House of Representatives. Likewise, the Environmental Protection Agency reports to over seventy congressional committees and subcommittees. Other agencies face similar situations. These factors drive each agency's structure as well as its culture. Unfortunately, past reorganization attempts have faltered because these issues were not part of the scope of the earlier studies. It's not clear that Congress is ready to address such issues (Kamensky, 1995, p. 8).

Conclusion

In spite of the initial skepticism about the Clinton-Gore reinvention initiative, a growing body of observers has concluded that the NPR is making measurable progress toward its vision of creating a government that works better and costs less. Several key reasons for this progress can be discerned from the reinvention implementation experience of the first four years of the NPR.

First is the importance of committed leaders at key levels in successful organizations—political as well as career leaders. Second, in the public sector it is essential to work simultaneously on several fronts in order to succeed in reform. It is important to act on specific recommendations to change organizations and their management from government-wide, agency-level, and individual perspectives. Third, it is important to have a clear and compelling goal, such as customer service, as the focal point for the rationale behind the changes under way. And finally, it is essential to engage the media and other public opinion makers in order to stimulate the political momentum for continued reform. These actions have been essential to the progress and credibility of the NPR effort to date.

Notes

1. Even with the initial bad publicity, by 1989 the OMB had concluded that progress had been made on nearly two-thirds of the recommendations. Some 1,607 recommendations had been implemented or were in the process of being implemented, but the dollar savings were unclear (Moe, 1992, p. 46).
2. Executive Order 12862, *Setting Customer Service Standards,* September 11, 1993.
3. Vice President Gore visited most large agencies not once, but twice, in the first two years of his reinvention initiative—the first time to learn from employees and the second time to teach them the principles of reinvention through his Hammer Awards.
4. The GAO independently assessed the NPR's claims of completed recommendations (U.S. General Accounting Office, 1996c). It concluded that it could verify 77 percent of the claims, 17 percent were claimed prematurely, and it could not verify the rest, largely because it had no authority to examine records in the intelligence community. The NPR disagreed with some of its assessments, saying that a number of recommendations that the GAO had determined not to be complete were open to interpretation.
5. "Large communities" are defined as the 183 cities with populations over 150,000, the largest city in each state, and counties with populations over 700,000.

6. This recommendation, creating a multiagency, boundary-spanning workforce development council, was criticized because it did not go far enough in reducing duplication and overlap in federal workforce training programs.
7. The National Academy of Public Administration received a Pew Charitable Trust grant in late 1996 to determine the relationship between public trust and the quality of government services.
8. Two independent studies suggest some limited improvement. A Roper Poll in late 1996 suggests that public satisfaction with services from federal agencies had improved by 9 percent since 1993 (Roper, 1996). Another limited study suggests that the public's perception of how well the federal government performs has improved since the 1980s, but the limited sample size and small shift in perception may not be indicative of a clear trend. However, the same study shows no increase in the public's trust of government (Yi and Hyde, 1995, p. 61).
9. Congressional involvement is seen as an important element in the success of performance measures and customer service standards. In mid-1996, congressional committees began holding hearings on measures in the science agencies and on whether the Department of Veterans Affairs was meeting its customer service standards.
10. This is equivalent to 125 cases of copier paper—for a single set of the rules abolished!

References

Australian Task Force on Management Improvement. *The Australian Public Service Reformed: An Evaluation of a Decade of Management Reform.* Canberra: Australian Government Publishing Service, 1992.

Barrett, K., and Greene, R. "How Well Run Is the Federal Government?" *Financial World,* Oct. 27, 1992, pp. 37–68.

Barrett, K., and Greene, R. "An Open Letter to the President." *Financial World,* Oct. 25, 1994, pp. 42–73.

Beard, D. P. "It Could Be You: Any Employee Can Change an Agency." *Public Manager,* 1995, *24*(3), 52–55.

Behn, R. D. "Regulators to Consultants: The Maine Top 200 Experimental Targeting Program, Occupational Safety and Health Administration." *Government Executive,* 1995, *27*(11), 19–20.

Clinton, W. J. "Remarks Announcing Federal Procurement Reforms and Spending Cut Proposals." *Public Papers of the Presidents: William J. Clinton,* Vol. 2. Washington, D.C.: U.S. Government Printing Office, 1993a.

Clinton, W. J. "Remarks Announcing the Initiative to Streamline Government." *Public Papers of the Presidents: William J. Clinton,* Vol. 1. Washington, D.C.: U.S. Government Printing Office, 1993b.

Clinton, W. J. "Remarks to General Services Administration Employees in Franconia, Virginia." *Public Papers of the Presidents: William J. Clinton,* Vol. 2. Washington, D.C.: U.S. Government Printing Office, 1993c.

Clinton, W. J. "Remarks Announcing the Report on Customer Service Standards." *Public Papers of the Presidents: William J. Clinton,* Vol. 2. Washington, D.C.: U.S. Government Printing Office, 1994a.

Clinton, W. J. "Remarks on the Middle-Class Bill of Rights and North Korea." *Public Papers of the Presidents: William J. Clinton,* Vol. 2. Washington, D.C.: U.S. Government Printing Office, 1994b.

Clinton, W. J. "Remarks on the National Performance Review and an Exchange with Reporters." *Public Papers of the Presidents: William J. Clinton,* Vol. 1. Washington, D.C.: U.S. Government Printing Office, 1994c.

Clinton, W. J. "Memorandum on Regulatory Reform." *Weekly Compilation of Presidential Documents,* Vol. 31, no. 9. Washington, D.C.: U.S. Government Printing Office, 1995a.

Clinton, W. J. "Remarks on Regulatory Reform." *Weekly Compilation of Presidential Documents,* Vol. 31, no. 8. Washington, D.C.: U.S. Government Printing Office, 1995b.

Clinton, W. J. "Remarks in Portland, Oregon." *Weekly Compilation of Presidential Documents,* Vol. 31. no. 20. Washington, D.C.: U.S. Government Printing Office, 1996.

Clinton, W. J., and Gore, A., Jr. *Putting Customers First: Standards for Serving the American People.* Washington, D.C.: U.S. Government Printing Office, 1994.

Clinton, W. J., and Gore, A., Jr. *Putting Customers First '95: Standards for Serving the American People.* Washington, D.C.: U.S. Government Printing Office, 1995.

Clinton, W. J., and Gore, A., Jr. *The Blair House Papers.* Washington, D.C.: U.S. Government Printing Office, 1997.

Corbin, L. "Going Leaner and Greener: Comprehensive Reinvention at the Bureau of Reclamation." *Government Executive,* Nov. 1995, pp. 35–36.

De Pree, M. *Leadership Is an Art.* New York: Bantam Doubleday Dell, 1990.

Drucker, P. F. "Really Reinventing Government." *Atlantic Monthly,* Feb. 1995, pp. 49–61.

Fosler, S. "The National Performance Review." Statement before the House Committee on Government Reform and Oversight, Subcommittee on Government Management, Information, and Technology, May 2, 1995.

Goodsell, C. "Did NPR Reinvent Government Reform?" *Public Manager,* Fall 1993, pp. 7–10.

Gore, A., Jr. *From Red Tape to Results: Creating a Government That Works Better and Costs Less.* Report of the National Performance Review. Washington, D.C.: U.S. Government Printing Office, 1993.

Gore, A., Jr. *Creating a Government That Works Better and Costs Less: September 1994 Status Report.* Report of the National Performance Review. Washington, D.C.: U.S. Government Printing Office, 1994a.

Gore, A., Jr. "The New Role of the Federal Executive." *Public Administration Review,* 1994b, *54,* 317–321.

Gore, A., Jr. *Common Sense Government: Works Better and Costs Less.* Washington, D.C.: U.S. Government Printing Office, 1995a.

Gore, A., Jr. "Reinventing Government Phase II Kickoff Meeting." Unpublished transcript, Jan. 12, 1995b.

Gore, A., Jr. "Remarks by the President and Vice President on the Second Anniversary of the National Performance Review." Unpublished transcript, Sept. 7, 1995c.

Gore, A., Jr. *The Best-Kept Secrets in Government.* Washington, D.C.: U.S. Government Printing Office, 1996a.

Gore, A., Jr. *Reinvention's Next Steps: Governing in a Balanced Budget World.* Washington, D.C.: U.S. Government Printing Office, 1996b.

"Highlights of '95 Hammer Award Winners." *Federal Times,* May 13, 1996, pp. S19–S22.

Hood, C. *Explaining Economic Policy Reversals.* Philadelphia: Open University Press, 1994.

Jasper, H., and Alpern, A. "National Performance Review: The Good, the Bad, the Indifferent." *Public Manager,* Spring 1994, pp. 27–34.

Johnson, P., and Stern, J. "From Good Enough to Best in Business: Benchmarking for Public Managers." *Public Manager,* Fall 1995, pp. 21–24.

Kamensky, J. M. "A Balanced Budget? Now What Do We Do?" *Public Manager,* Winter 1995, pp. 5–8.

Kamensky, J. M. "Role of the 'Reinventing Government' Movement in Federal Management Reform." *Public Administration Review,* 1996, *56*(3), 247–255.

Kettl, D. F. "Assessing the National Performance Review." Testimony before the House Committee on Government Reform and Oversight, Subcommittee on Government Management, Information, and Technology, May 2, 1995a.

Kettl, D. F. "Restructuring the Federal Government: Downsizing, Dumbsizing, or Smartsizing?" Statement before the Senate Governmental Affairs Committee, May 18, 1995b.

Kettl, D. F. "Building Lasting Reform: Enduring Questions, Missing Answers." In D. F. Kettl and J. J. Di Iulio, Jr. (eds.). *Inside the Reinvention Machine: Appraising Governmental Reform.* Washington D.C.: Brookings Institution, 1995c.

Koonce, R. "Reengineering the Travel Game." *Government Executive,* May 1995, pp. 28–34.

Koskinen, J. Statement of the Deputy Director for Management, Office of Management and Budget before the House Committee on Government Reform and Oversight, Feb. 12, 1997.

Moe, R. C. *Reorganizing the Executive Branch in the Twentieth Century: Landmark Commissions.* Report no. 92–293 GOV. Washington, D.C.: Congressional Research Service, 1992.

Moe, R. C. "The 'Reinventing Government' Exercise: Misinterpreting the Problem, Misjudging the Consequences." *Public Administration Review,* Mar.–Apr. 1994, pp. 111–122.

National Academy of Public Administration. *Revitalizing Federal Management: Managers and Their Overburdened Systems.* Washington, D.C.: National Academy of Public Administration, 1983.

National Partnership Council. *A Report to the President on Progress in Labor-Management Partnerships.* Washington, D.C.: Office of Personnel Management, 1996.

Organization for Economic Cooperation and Development. *Governance in Transition: Public Management Reform in OECD Countries.* Paris: Organization for Economic Cooperation and Development, 1995.

Osborne, D., and Gaebler, T. *Reinventing Government: How the Entrepreneurial Spirit Is Transforming the Public Sector.* Reading, Mass.: Addison Wesley Longman, 1992.

Osborne, D., and Plastrik, P. *Banishing Bureaucracy: The Five Strategies for Reinventing Government.* Reading, Mass.: Addison Wesley Longman, 1997.

"Reinvention Roundtable." [http://www.npr.gov]. Feb. 18, 1994.

Roper Polls. *Roper Report, 96–4.* Summary, Mar.–Apr. Survey, pp. 64–65, 1996.

Shoop, T. "True Believer." *Government Executive,* Sept. 1993, pp. 16–23.

Shoop, T. "Brave New Leadership." *Government Executive,* July 1994, pp. 23–30.

Singleton, A. L. "Customs Tailoring: The Remaking of a Bureaucracy." *Government Executive,* July 1995, pp. 30–35.

Szanton, P. *Federal Reorganization: What Have We Learned?* Chatham, N.J.: Chatham House, 1981.

Thompson, J. R. "Eureka?" *Government Executive,* June 1995a, pp. 31–34.

Thompson, J. R. "Joe vs. the Bureaucracy." *Government Executive,* Oct. 1995b, pp. 50–55.

Thompson, J. R. "The Reinvention Revolution." *Government Executive,* May 1996, pp. 39–41.

U.S. General Accounting Office. *Implementation: The Missing Link in Planning Reorganizations.* Publication no. GGD-81–57. Washington, D.C.: U.S. Government Printing Office, 1981.

U.S. General Accounting Office. *Government Management Issues: Transition Series.* Publication no. OCG-93–3TR. Washington, D.C.: U.S. Government Printing Office, 1992.

U.S. General Accounting Office. *Management Reform: GAO's Comments on the National Performance Review's Recommendations.* Publication no. GAO/OCG-94–1. Washington, D.C.: U.S. Government Printing Office, 1993.

U.S. General Accounting Office. *Management Reform: Implementation of the National Performance Review's Recommendations.* Publication no. GAO/OCG-95–1. Washington, D.C.: U.S. Government Printing Office, 1994a.

U.S. General Accounting Office. *Veterans' Benefits: Status of Claims Processing Initiative in VA's New York Regional Office.* Publication no. GAO/HEHS-94–183BR. Washington, D.C.: U.S. Government Printing Office, 1994b.

U.S. General Accounting Office. *Federal Downsizing: Better Workforce and Strategic Planning Could Have Made Buyouts More Effective.* Publication no. GAO/GGD-96–62. Washington, D.C.: U.S. Government Printing Office, 1996a.

U.S. General Accounting Office. *Management Reform: Completion Status of the National Performance Review's Action Items.* Publication no. GAO/GGD-96–94. Washington, D.C.: U.S. Government Printing Office, 1996b.

U.S. General Accounting Office. *Management Reform: Status of Agency Reinvention Lab Efforts.* Publication no. GAO/GGD-96–69. Washington, D.C.: U.S. Government Printing Office, 1996c.

U.S. General Accounting Office. *NPR Savings Estimates.* Publication no. GAO/GGD-96–149R. Washington, D.C.: U.S. Government Printing Office, 1996d.

U.S. House of Representatives, Committee on Government Operations. *Managing the Federal Government: A Decade of Decline.* Washington, D.C.: U.S. Government Printing Office, 1992.

U.S. House of Representatives, Committee on Government Reform and Oversight. *Making Government Work: Fulfilling the Mandate for Change.* House Report no. 104–435. Washington, D.C.: U.S. Government Printing Office, 1995.

U.S. House of Representatives, Committee on the Budget. *Management Reform: A Top Priority for the Federal Executive Branch.* Publication no. CP-4. Washington, D.C.: U.S. Government Printing Office, 1991.

U.S. National Performance Review. "Bureau of Taxation," Railroad Retirement Board [http://www.npr.gov/library/awards/hammer], 1997.

U.S. Office of Management and Budget. "Making Government Work." In *Budget of the United States, Fiscal Year 1997.* Supplement. Washington D.C.: Superintendent of Documents, 1996.

U.S. Office of Management and Budget. "Improving Performance in a Balanced Budget World." In *Budget of the United States, Fiscal Year 1998.* Supplement. Washington D.C.: Superintendent of Documents, 1997.

U.S. Senate. *Report of the Committee on Government Affairs to Accompany S.20, "Government Performance and Results Act of 1993."* Report no. 103–58. Washington, D.C.: U.S. Government Printing Office, 1992.

Yi, H., and Hyde, A. C. "Public Perspectives of the State of Management." *Public Manager,* Fall 1995, pp. 60–64.

Chapter Four

Reinventing Public Agencies

Bottom-Up Versus Top-Down Strategies

James R. Thompson
Ronald P. Sanders

Where does organizational change begin? Who decides and guides its nature and substance? These are central questions in effecting (and investigating) organizational change, and they both have to do with "vector"—the force, direction, and magnitude of the change process in any given organization. In its most basic form, vector has a vertical dimension, typically described in terms of either top-down or bottom-up approaches to organizational change; these approaches are often presented in the literature as a strategic, mutually exclusive choice for the change agent.

This chapter examines the top-down, bottom-up vector in the context of two case studies of complex organizational change, both part of the federal government's larger reinvention effort. The top-down, or "engineering," change model employed by the Internal Revenue Service (IRS) is compared and contrasted with the bottom-up, or "gardening," approach that has emerged in the Veterans Benefits Administration (VBA). The gardening and engineering metaphors are employed by Szanton (1981, p. 24), who states that "reorganization had best be viewed as a branch of gardening rather than of architecture or engineering. As in gardening, the possibilities are limited by soil and climate, and accomplishment is slow. And like gardening, reorganization is not an act but a process, a continuing job."

We begin by reviewing the multiple elements that comprise the top-down, bottom-up dichotomy, along with some of the arguments that have been offered concerning the relative merits of each approach; we also consider some of the hybrid models that have been developed to deal with the various deficiencies found in the two polar extremes. Within that theoretical context, we then examine in some detail the ongoing reinvention of the IRS and VBA, with particular attention to the impetus for their respective change efforts, the efficacy of their contrasting implementation strategies, and the operational impact of those strategies to date.

Top-Down Versus Bottom-Up Change Strategies

The strategy embodied in the National Performance Review (NPR) highlights the relevance of the top-down, bottom-up vector to an understanding of change processes. The NPR represents a distinct change in focus from previous efforts to reform the federal government. Whereas past reforms, such as those of the Brownlow and Hoover commissions, were directed toward macro-level changes such as strengthening the executive office of the president and consolidating many of the independent agencies of government within the executive branch, the NPR has placed its emphasis on more micro-level changes, improvements to the actual processes and procedures of government.

Consistent with their macro-level focus, past reform efforts have employed a predominantly top-down vector. The various presidential reform commissions, for example, were generally composed of individuals appointed by the president from outside government and implementation was generally accomplished through law and presidential decree. The NPR, in contrast, has applied a more mixed approach. Efforts at systemic reform have taken a conventional, top-down form with the passage of laws such as the 1992 Government Performance and Results Act and the Federal Acquisition Reform Act of 1994. Other elements, however, such as the several hundred "reinvention laboratories" that have been formed constitute a more bottom-up approach to change.

These reinvention laboratories, located mostly in agency subunits and field organizations, are intended to encourage managers to try new and innovative ways of delivering service by freeing them from internal constraints. The labs were described by Vice President Al Gore in a May 1, 1993, letter to department heads as places where "we can fully delegate authority and responsibility, replace regulations with incentives and measure our success by customer satisfaction." The labs were intended to allow a large number of innovations to be tested on a relatively small scale, with correspondingly less risk; those that proved successful were eventually to be adopted by other subunits and agencies. By encouraging those at lower organizational levels to initiate change, the reinvention lab model contrasts sharply with more traditional approaches in which both new ideas and the pressure for implementation were presumed to come from the top.

The top-down, bottom-up vector is also relevant to the actual procedures used in putting micro-level changes into effect. The type of behavioral change that process reform entails raises the issue of employee participation in the design and implementation of the changes. Much attention has been devoted by management theorists to the question of whether such participation is a prerequisite of successful micro-level change. Since the NPR has generally left such strategic decisions up to individual agencies, both top-down and bottom-up approaches are being employed.

The variegated nature of the change strategies being employed by different agencies under the general NPR rubric makes comparisons between them opportune. Consistent with our focus on the top-down, bottom-up vector, we have identified two change efforts, one at the IRS and the other at the VBA, that offer important contrasts in this regard. This comparison, in turn, offers insights on how the elements of that strategic dimension affect outcomes.

Theoretical Context: Change-Vector Models

Beer, Eisenstat, and Spector (1990, p. 68) highlight a key distinction between top-down and bottom-up strategies when they state that the most fundamental choice regarding the selection of a change strategy is "how unilaterally directive" management will be in its approach. Associated questions that they identify include: "To what extent will [management] rely on changes in systems, structure, and formal policies to transform the organization? How much employee participation will management invite in shaping the organization's response?" (p. 68). Finney, Bowen, Pearson, and Siehl (1988) present the issue as follows: "The two most popular change models involve either a top-down or a bottom-up change in control structure. In top-down change efforts, the top managers of the firm design the change strategy and then encourage or force middle managers to implement the strategy. In contrast, bottom-up change efforts encourage lower-level employees to act in a democratic fashion and attempt to force change up through the hierarchy" (p. 292).

Both of these characterizations of the difference between top-down and bottom-up change hint at multiple dimensions according to which the two approaches can be compared. Finney, Bowen, Pearson, and Siehl suggest that top-down and bottom-up approaches can be contrasted based on where the change was designed and how it is imposed on the organization, whether by coercion or choice. Beer, Eisenstat, and Spector also highlight the issue of coercion as a feature of top-down change, and they identify some of the levers ("systems, structure and formal policies") by which force is exerted. They also identify the issue of employee participation as relevant to distinctions between approaches to change.

Participation

Bottom-up approaches are often presumed to incorporate the participation of lower-level employees in the design of the changes. Leemans (1976, p. 52) describes the distinction in terms of "collaborative" and "noncollaborative" strategies as follows: "A noncollaborative strategy implies that reform decisions are taken by the top of the unit or organization in consultation only with close confederates. This strategy is usually coercive by nature. . . . A collaborative strategy, or in Mosher's terms a participative strategy, on the other hand, is one in which the subjects of the reform are consulted in some way or other and the lower strata of the organization are involved in the reform process."

Collaborative or participative change strategies have received the endorsement of a number of researchers and management theorists. They are thought to be "more enduring" (Kanter, Stein, and Jick, 1992), in that they allow differences to be exposed and resolved (Cummings, 1989) and elicit greater commitment by organizational personnel (Beer, 1980). Lawler (1988) asserts that "the involvement approach" is congruent with the "democratic values and education level of the current work force" (p. 53), and he argues that a shift away from a control orientation enhances "the quality of work life" for "lower-level participants" who "gain a greater degree of authority and responsibility" (p. 50). Others have argued that coercion is often insufficient to force an organization's members to change (Beer, Eisenstat, and Spector, 1990) and may breed opposition (Cohen, 1976); moreover, a top-down approach may cause participants to adopt coping strategies rather than to cooperate (Kanter, 1983).

Mosher (1967) hypothesized that "participation will enhance reorganization effectiveness . . . through two mechanisms: first, by reducing resistance to change among the participants, or, more positively, by increasing their motivation to make reorganization successful in accomplishing its intended goals; and second, by providing information and ideas to the planners and deciders, thus contributing to modifications (potential improvements) in the content of the reorganization proposals" (p. xvii). However, his review of multiple studies of government reorganization led him to conclude that the hypothesis was not supported by the evidence.

Gross, Giacquinta, and Bernstein (1971), challenging the seminal work of Coch and French (1948), reached a similar conclusion, stating that "it is assumed that a strategy of initiation involving a change agent and subordinate participation typically leads to the successful implementation of innovations; [however] there is a paucity of research evidence" to support that proposition (p. 29).

Empirical work has not resolved the dispute as to whether collaborative or noncollaborative approaches are more effective. Dunn and Swierczek (1977, p. 149) found "collaborative" change efforts and those in which the change agent had a "participative orientation" to be "more successful than change efforts undertaken with other modes of intervention." Nutt (1986), in contrast, has provided evidence that intermediate or hybrid strategies that incorporate both top-down and bottom-up elements may be more effective than "pure" versions of either. He identifies four primary implementation strategies—intervention, participation, persuasion, and edict. In this model, intervention and persuasion represent two intermediate or hybrid approaches. Nutt found that intervention had the highest rate of success, followed by participation, persuasion, and edict.

Elements of the Top-Down, Bottom-Up Vector

The research evidence regarding the relative merits of collaborative and noncollaborative approaches to organizational change remains somewhat inconclusive. However, other facets to the top-down, bottom-up dichotomy suggest that the difference between the two approaches is more complex than simply the extent of employee participation, upon which the focus is usually placed. In the discussion that follows, we identify five separate elements that comprise the top-down, bottom-up vector: (1) the locus of the recognition of the need for change, (2) the organizational levels that those involved in the design represent, (3) the stages in which lower-level participation occurred, (4) the change levers utilized, and (5) the nature of communication flows during the change process.

Recognition of the Need for Change and Levels Involved in the Design

Rogers and Shoemaker (1971) have developed a vector-like change typology that turns on the locus of (1) "the recognition of the need for change" and (2) "the origin of the new idea" (p. 17). Under their typology, a change may be characterized as top-down when both recognition and origin emanate from upper levels of management; when both impetus and ideas come from lower levels, a change may be described as bottom-up.

Stage

If organizational change can be viewed as having a distinct "life cycle"—that is, a discrete beginning, middle, and end—then the characterization of a particular change strategy as either top-down or bottom-up may be contingent on its stage of development. A model developed by Zaltman, Duncan, and Holbek (1973) suggests that there are at least two primary steps in any organizational change: initiation or design and implementation. A purely bottom-up approach presumes that participation occurs at both the design and implementation stages; a purely top-down approach, at neither. A hybrid approach may be characterized by participation and collaboration at the design stage but not at the implementation stage, or vice versa. For example, an organization's top management may conceive of and initiate a particular change, but then choose to devolve considerable discretion to individual units in its implementation.

Change Levers

Beer (1980, pp. 53–56) lists several techniques that are available to leadership for the implementation of top-down change: "decree," "technology," "replacement," and "structure." He argues that bottom-up change, by contrast, can be implemented by "training," "staff group" (such as an operations research or organization development group), or "experimental unit." Beer maintains that the premise of bottom-up techniques such as organization development is that "coercive," top-down strategies cannot get participants to change their "normative orientation" (beliefs about how things ought to be done). Rather, argues Beer, a "normative-reeducative strategy" such as organization development is required.

Leemans (1976, p. 48) describes the choice as between structural and behavioral change levers. He further associates structural approaches with the formal organization and behavioral approaches with the informal organization: "Emphasis on structure has usually been identified with the formal organization and its statics; emphasis on behavior with the informal organization and organization dynamics." He adds, "Traditionally, emphasis is given to the structural elements in reorganizations of the machinery of government. . . . Changes have to be enacted and . . . formalized" (p. 48).

Communication Flows

Both Burns and Stalker (1994) and Kanter (1983) investigate the structural characteristics that facilitate innovation. Burns and Stalker distinguish between "organic" and "mechanistic" organizations, analogous to Kanter's distinction between "integrative" and "segmentalist" organizations. Organic or integrative structures are presumed to facilitate innovation, whereas mechanistic or segmentalist structures, which are highly bureaucratic in nature, impede change and innovation. Burns and Stalker cite as a distinguishing element of organic organizations "a lateral rather than a vertical direction of communication through the organization, communication between people of different rank, also, resembling consultation rather than command" (p. 121). Kanter (1983) notes that the tall hierarchies and long chains of command that typify segmentalist companies inhibit communication and that organizational participants are measured by "rule obedience" (p. 78).

The conclusions reached by Burns and Stalker (1994) and Kanter (1983) with regard to innovativeness can also be applied to changes in the organization itself. Bottom-up approaches imply a two-way communication between top management and lower-level participants, whereas top-down approaches imply that communication emanates from top to bottom.

Table 4.1 summarizes these multiple elements of the top-down, bottom-up vector. In so doing, it makes it apparent that pure examples of either top-down or bottom-up strategies represent only a small fraction of the potential number of configurations, most of which would be categorized as hybrid forms, combining elements of both the top-down and bottom-up approaches. Further, the table omits reference to the middle layers of the organization, which, if they were added, would vastly increase the number of hybrid options available.

Hybrid Models

This discussion suggests that the top-down, bottom-up distinction is not a unidimensional one and that there are a variety of ways to configure hybrid approaches to change that include elements of both. A number of researchers have argued for not only the viability but the superiority of hybrid or contingent approaches. Greiner (1967, pp. 120–122), for example, emphasizes the differential use of coercion in designing and implementing change. He identifies a "power distribution continuum" of approaches that range from "unilateral" to "shared" and "delegated." The unilateral approach to implementation relies on hierarchical authority exercised through "decree," "replacement" of personnel, and ma-

Table 4.1. Dimensions of Change.

Dimensions of Change	Top-Down	Bottom-Up
Recognition of the need for change	Top	Bottom
Levels involved in design	Top	Bottom
Implementation—local autonomy	No	Yes
Change levers	Formal	Informal
Communication flows	One-way	Two-way

nipulation of structure; in contrast, a shared approach relies on "group decision making" and "group problem solving." Greiner concludes that success is most often associated with a hybrid, or "shared," approach to change: "The unilateral approach, although tempting because its procedures are readily accessible to top management, generally serves only to perpetuate the myths and disadvantages of omniscience and downward thinking. On the other hand, the delegated approach, while appealing because of its 'democratic' connotations, may remove the power structure from direct involvement in a process that calls for its strong guidance and active support" (p. 130).

Kanter (1983, p. 186) advocates a specific model intended to capture elements of both of the two polar approaches. She calls for a "parallel participative organization of cross-hierarchical task forces reporting to a steering committee." This approach is designed to avoid the tensions that may arise with an exclusively top-down approach because, "in the parallel organization, workers and managers are involved in more egalitarian teams[;] . . . status distinctions are leveled and all struggle together for a joint solution" (p. 203).

Beer, Eisenstat, and Spector (1990, p. 69) explicitly attempt to integrate what they call the "hard and soft approaches to change" in their "critical path" model. They comment that in the "top-down approach . . . employee commitment to the newly aligned organization may be low, and employee knowledge of how things get done in the organization may not be considered in the solution," whereas in the "bottom-up approach . . . change may be too slow and ill defined to respond effectively to short-term business demands" (p. 68). Thus, contingent or "recombinant" strategies may be most effective.

Alternative Change Models in the Federal Government

The federal government offers a rich source of empirical and experiential data concerning the effectiveness of alternative change strategies. Its ongoing reinvention efforts, spurred by pressures from Congress and the Clinton administration to restructure, downsize, reengineer, and deregulate, present numerous examples of top-down, bottom-up, and hybrid change models and provide an opportunity to examine empirical distinctions relating to the top-down, bottom-up change vector. Two alternative approaches are explored here, one at the IRS, a component of the Department of the Treasury, and the other at the VBA, part of the larger Department of Veterans Affairs. Information on the two change efforts was obtained from extensive interviews with key officials at each agency. The interviews at the IRS took place in three phases, beginning in the fall of 1993 and continuing in the fall of 1994 and the spring of 1996. Interviews with officials at the VBA took place during the spring and summer of 1995. Over thirty interviews were conducted with twenty-five different officials at the two agencies.

Despite apparent differences in size, mission, and clientele—the IRS employs 110,000 employees to collect taxes, while 16,000 VBA employees disburse benefit checks—the two agencies share some common characteristics that are relevant to our discussion. Both are involved in processing large volumes of data (tax and benefit claims forms) in an essentially assembly-line manner, and their respective outputs and outcomes are observable and measurable. According to the typology posited by Wilson (1989), the IRS and VBA would both be classified as "production" organizations. Significantly, the substantive changes being pursued by the two agencies are also similar, focusing on organization-wide work process reengineering.

However, while they may share common conceptual ends (that is, reengineered work processes), the IRS and VBA contrast fairly sharply in their choice of means—their respective change strategies. The IRS effort, conceived, planned, and directed by its senior leadership, reflects a top-down, "engineering" approach to change, while the VBA effort—comprised primarily of unleashing, monitoring, and eventually "harvesting" relatively independent subunit-level change efforts—is characteristic of the bottom-up, "gardening" strategy. A comparison of these two alternative strategies gives some insight into the advantages and liabilities of each; it also underscores the complexity of the top-down, bottom-up dichotomy.

The Internal Revenue Service

The IRS has committed to a major restructuring that will, when complete, result in dramatic changes in the way the agency does business. Most of those changes revolve around automation—a massive upgrade of the agency's computer systems called Tax Systems Modernization (TSM). Initially, the modernization program, directed by the IRS and managed by its chief information officer, concentrated on automating existing tasks and procedures. However, critical external reviews by the General Accounting Office (GAO) and the National Research Council (NRC) forced the IRS to undertake more radical change. The two outside agencies argued that by simply automating existing processes, the IRS would get only 10 percent of the potential benefits of systems modernization.

As a result of this external prodding, the IRS leadership, in the form of its executive committee, decided on a strategy that incorporated multiple, parallel tracks. The key track was the effort to modernize information systems; most of the resources requested of Congress for the overall effort were allocated to the Information Systems unit; that unit, in turn, decided what projects would be funded. As a result, the other tracks, most notably the attempt to reengineer business processes and the structural reconfiguration, were subsidiary to the modernization effort.

As part of the process orientation, a new organizational configuration was devised that was intended to represent a departure from the old functional divisions. The agency shifted from a hierarchy that included a senior deputy commissioner, two deputy commissioners, and ten assistant commissioners to a process-based organization headed by a deputy commissioner and six "business system owners." Functionally based units such as collection, examination, and taxpayer service and returns processing were reorganized into value tracking, informing and educating, managing accounts, ensuring compliance, resourcing, and developing and maintaining systems.

Agency leadership commissioned two key studies that served as a basis for the new organizational structure—the Service Center Organization Study and the District Organization Study—each corresponding to a key IRS subcomponent: its large service centers where tax returns are processed and the district offices that are responsible for compliance. The Service Center Organization Study, staffed by eight mid- and senior-level managers along with consultant representatives, can be characterized as a case of "reverse reengineering"; seeking to fully leverage TSM technologies, it called for new work processes that would allow taxpayers to make payments and conduct other transactions over the phone directly, without forms or direct contact with IRS employees. The District Organization Study, conducted by a team of similar size and composition, proposed to virtually eliminate functional specialization for activities involving face-to-face contact with the taxpaying public. It envisioned highly trained, multidisciplined professionals, supported by modern technology, serving customers in a substantially less hierarchical organization (U.S. Internal Revenue Service, 1993).

Both studies recommended major changes in the role of frontline personnel, and hence in the long and storied institutional culture of the IRS. For example, the tasks undertaken by customer service representatives were to be expanded so that 95 percent of all customer inquiries would be resolved in the first contact. A major emphasis was placed on electronic filing of tax returns and other forms; the Service Center Organization Study even asked Congress to pass legislation requiring electronic filing of all returns by preparers who file 100 or more returns per year. Paper tax returns would be scanned using imaging technology, tax refunds and payments would be made through the electronic transfer of funds, and processing of returns would take place at only five of the ten sites currently used. District offices—to be renamed customer service sites—would be reduced from forty-four to twenty-three.

These changes, now under way, will take at least until the year 2001 to fully implement. TSM will cost approximately $23 billion, $7.5 billion more than the cost of maintaining present IRS systems. The agency actively sought and received union cooperation for the changes, but the price it paid was high: a policy statement guaranteeing that no layoffs would result from the restructuring. In theory, the changes will engender dramatic improvements in productivity. Rather than downsizing, however, the IRS expects to retrain many of its employees and redeploy them to compliance activities, where, according to agency officials, there is a 5:1 payoff in revenue collected—in increased returns and penalties—for each dollar (and employee) invested (Thompson and Ingraham, 1996).

Based on interviews and other documents, it is clear that the IRS TSM program can be characterized as a top-down, organizational "engineering" approach to change.

- For example, many of the changes proposed by TSM were instigated at the top of the organization—indeed, by a staff component. The agency's Information Systems unit actively pursued systems modernization out of concern about the rising cost of maintaining existing systems and the reliability of those systems, and systems modernization drove the process reengineering effort (hence the notion of "reverse reengineering").
- Agency officials drew a clear demarcation between TSM and the largely bottom-up Total Quality Management (TQM) effort that had been under way in the IRS. TQM had a largely local orientation, implemented piecemeal at the discretion of the various district and service center directors. The former head of the Ogden (Utah) service center commented that he and his staff had used TQM to work on problems that were "unique to Ogden."
- Design of the new organizational structure was tightly controlled by the agency's top executive committee. The district and service center study groups were made up of a small group of carefully selected upper middle managers. No union representatives or front-line employees were included on either team. The recommendations made by the two study groups were submitted to the executive committee for ratification, and in the case of the District Organization Study, they made important revisions; they rejected perhaps the most radical change envisioned in the report, the creation of generalist "field service representative" positions that combined the duties of revenue agent, revenue officer, tax auditor, taxpayer service representative, and taxpayer service specialist (although a "blended group" concept is now being considered).
- Although an elaborate structure was devised for communicating downward to front-line employees, to convince them of the need to change, it is apparent that there was little or no substantive

upward communication between front-line employees and top career officials. Although a number of the top managers contended that front-line employees did not recognize the need for the agency to change its business methods, a representative of the communications division reported that, based on his experience in employee focus groups, 85 percent of the employees recognized the need for change. Moreover, one management official acknowledged that front-line employees recognized the need to change but conceded that they "don't see that the reorganization is going to resolve the concerns that they have—better equipment and simpler instructions."

- The lack of communication between the executive committee and the rest of the organization is revealed in the comments of several senior managers who acknowledged that even the "second tier" of the organization had not bought into the need to change. For example, the special assistant to the deputy commissioner commented in the fall of 1994 that of 250 to 300 senior executive service members in the IRS, "only forty or fifty understand the program now." One of these second-tier members confirmed the problem in the course of an interview. The deputy assistant commissioner for examination commented derisively that the entire reorganization effort consisted of "playing around with the damn boxes." He added poignantly that "nothing is going to change until we do something for the front-line workers."
- Perhaps most telling is the organizational architecture of the "new" IRS. The restructuring will result in a centralization of power within the agency. In addition to the reordering at the top of the agency's pyramid—and the replacement of the deputy commissioners and assistant commissioners by the business system owners—there will be a shift in power from the seven IRS regional offices to the national office. In the agency's last major reorganization in the late 1940s, regional offices were given considerable authority over policy issues. In the new structure, the number of regional offices will be reduced from seven to five, the size of each office will be cut from about 375 employees to about 100, and the major responsibilities of the regional commissioners will be transferred to the business system owners at the national office.

Ironically, the top-down approach to change itself was in sharp contrast to the way that members of the executive committee, the key management group, operated among themselves. One official emphasized the extent to which decision making by the executive committee was historically "consensus-based" and "low-risk." He stated, "We have traditionally taken a collegial approach to investment decision making and tried to divide our available investment funds into many pieces to ensure that all parts of the organization were perceived to win." The executive committee, consisting of the six business system owners, made the key decisions with regard to TSM based on this consensus approach, which, according to the director of the Office of Modernization, actually impeded implementation. He concluded that a more unilateral approach was in order and called for "rapid decision making by someone with 51 percent of the vote."

What about the results of this approach? As of this writing, TSM has run into severe problems. The chair of the House Appropriations Subcommittee that oversees the Department of the Treasury called the project a "fiasco" and threatened to withhold further appropriations, and an assistant secretary in the Department of the Treasury conceded that "TSM went off-track" (Hershey, 1996). Members of Congress have complained that there is relatively little to show for the $2.7 billion in funds expended. Some new systems have been installed and sites have been set up to test new work arrangements, but the processing of tax returns has not been changed in a fundamental way. Issues relating to the question of whether an alternative strategy would have produced better results are addressed in the concluding section of this chapter.

The Veterans Benefits Administration

The second case study we examine involves the VBA, which, along with the Veterans Health Administration and the National Cemetery System, comprises the Department of Veterans Affairs. In a strategy that literally inverts the organizational pyramid, the VBA's change efforts have been spearheaded by its New York regional office, one of fifty-eight regional offices in the agency and one of the NPR's reinvention laboratories. The primary function of the regional office is to process individual claims for veterans' benefits. The heart of each regional office is the Adjudication division, in which claims examiners review and decide each compensation and pension claim.

The adjudication process has traditionally resembled an assembly line; each claim passes through a series of review steps, accomplished by specialized employees with narrowly defined tasks. Regional offices are functionally organized: face-to-face contacts with veterans are handled by counselors in the Veterans Services division, while case and claim processing is done by claims examiners in the Adjudication division. When a veteran calls in with questions about a claim, the call goes to a counselor who must retrieve the case file from an examiner and call the claimant back; moreover, since counselors do not process cases, they are unable to respond immediately to additional questions. A single inquiry thus results in a series of telephone or personal contacts. To compound the matter, each time a claimant calls, he or she is likely to get a different counselor and have to explain the nature of the inquiry all over again. (See Figure 1.1, page 14.)

Applying the tenets of business process reengineering, the New York regional office devised a radically different approach to the processing of claims for benefits. Regional director Joe Thompson convened a working group of about a dozen employees, including front-line staff, and with the help of consultants whom the employees helped to select, members of the group redesigned the entire adjudication procedure from scratch. The solution that the group devised was to merge the Veterans Services and Adjudication divisions, combining the jobs of counselor and examiner into a single position of case manager. Assigned a set of customer-clients, each case manager was to be responsible for all aspects of their various claims, from start to finish. The proposed system would not only provide the claimants with a single point of contact, but would also allow direct contact with the workers who were actually making decisions on their claims. (See Figure 1.2, page 15.)

The newly reengineered claims process vastly simplifies the flow of work. Instead of a process with as many as thirty steps and multiple handoffs between employees and between divisions, there are now only four steps, with only one handoff between workers. This establishes clear accountability for each claim and reduces the chances for errors as cases are passed between case managers. As a companion initiative, case managers have been organized into work teams, further expanding the extent to which employees control their work environment. A total of sixteen teams have been created, each with twelve members. The teams are intended to be self-directing, although each is assigned a "coach," typically a former first-level supervisor.

To date, all the changes engendered by Thompson and his staff, including the reengineered and restructured claims-processing scheme, have been limited to the New York regional office and as with any bottom-up effort, the problem of export and replication remains. However, it appears that some of New York's ideas have begun to take seed across the agency. For example, under the old theory that "what gets measured gets done," Thompson has proposed a VBA-wide change in performance measures that he believes will lead to the adoption of his model (or something like it) in other regional offices. The New York office pioneered a set of performance measures that reflect the new emphasis on customer service and employee empowerment in addition to the traditional measures of quality, quantity, and timeliness.

These new measures are directly affected by the kinds of structure and process changes implemented in the New York region, and largely at Thompson's urging, it appears that they are going to be adopted across the entire VBA. In addition, the head of the agency, Veterans Affairs undersecretary for benefits Ray Vogel, issued a memorandum encouraging all regional offices to adopt one of four new alternative structures, each of which was a variation on the themes piloted in New York: consolidation of counseling and adjudication functions, generalist case workers, and teams.

The change effort at the VBA exhibits elements of both top-down and bottom-up approaches to change and can therefore best be described as a hybrid model. The change effort was initiated and designed at a subordinate organizational level—the New York regional office—and while it was driven by the head of that office, most of its substantive content came from teams of front-line employees and lower-level supervisors. Top VBA officials were aware of the changes but not directly involved in their design or implementation; however, deliberately or otherwise, they ceded considerable autonomy to the New York office that was consistent with its reinvention lab status, including a general waiver of standard agency operating procedures.

Both formal and informal levers were utilized to implement the changes in the New York office. For example, official job descriptions, reporting relationships, and reward structures were changed, largely as a result of employee input. This underscores what is perhaps the most important feature of this particular case, the extensive involvement and participation of employees in both design and implementation. However, the key "enabler" in this regard was the director, Joe Thompson. He and his immediate staff exerted control over the design effort to the extent that they reviewed and approved all of the changes devised by the employee working group; hence the hybrid label. Nevertheless, New York employees appear generally favorable toward the changes, and their local union has made no attempt to interfere; indeed, the union has entered into a partnership arrangement with office management. Most important, the wholesale nature of the changes and the participatory approach that was taken have contributed to what most participants perceive as a gradual change in the culture of the organization.

As a reinvention laboratory, the New York regional office may be characterized as an "experimental unit" (Beer, 1980) within the VBA, and as such, the overall change strategy employed by the agency is consistent with the critical-path model advocated by Beer, Eisenstat, and Spector (1990). They highlight the critical role of "unit level managers" in successful change efforts, rather than top leadership or lower-level participants, saying, "We found successful organizational innovations tended to occur disproportionately often in those plants and divisions managed by certain gifted managers" (p. 138) and "Revitalization in every company we studied began with unit leaders who were willing to risk being pioneers" (p. 224).

In the critical-path model, change begins at the subunit level and is then expanded throughout the organization. Unit managers are motivated to innovate because they are subject to performance pressures, and "they can find ways to start down the critical path by using those pressures to energize the organization" (Beer, Eisenstat, and Spector, 1990, p. 224). The role of top management in the critical-path model is threefold: to create a climate in which innovation is encouraged and rewarded, to communicate the need for change throughout the organization, and to provide opportunities for managers to learn about successful innovations.

Comparing the IRS and VBA models

Table 4.2 compares the IRS and VBA change strategies based on the elements listed in Table 4.1. It is apparent from Table 4.2 that neither approach could be described as purely top-down or bottom-up. However, the case has been made here, and is reflected in Table 4.2, that the IRS effort was predominantly top-down in orientation while the VBA strategy has been predominantly bottom-up.

Recognition of the need to change at the VBA came from the middle of the organization. Joe Thompson had gone through an awakening of sorts as a result of training he had received in quality management techniques. He became sensitized to the inability of his agency to respond to the needs and demands of its "customers," the veterans applying for different benefits, and to the effects of the assembly-line approach on the morale and job attitude of his employees. As soon as he was made director of the New York office, he began the search for new ways of organizing. In contrast, the initiative for the modernization project at the IRS came from three primary sources, all either at the top or external to the agency. The Information Systems unit, which was concerned about the functioning of the agency's antiquated computers, made a strong case for modernization; two outside organizations, the GAO and the NRC, urged a restructuring in conjunction with the modernization;

Table 4.2. Comparison of the IRS and VBA Models.

Dimensions of Change	Internal Revenue Service	Veterans Benefits Administration
Recognition of the need for change	Top	Middle
Levels involved in design	Top-middle	Middle-bottom
Implementation—local autonomy	No	Yes
Change levers	Technology	Culture
Communication flows	Middle-bottom	Middle-bottom

and a political appointee, former commissioner Fred Goldberg, endorsed reliance on electronic means of tax collection, which constituted the cornerstone of the new model.

At the VBA, front-line employees were allowed substantive input into the design of "their" new work processes, with extensive two-way dialogue between line employees and managers. In contrast, at the IRS, only the small number of employees appointed to the District Organization Study Committee and the Service Center Organization Study Committee were directly involved in design activities.

Little autonomy was granted to local IRS offices with regard to implementation of the new systems and processes. In each case, systems and processes were designed centrally and imposed on the field structure. In contrast, extensive autonomy was granted to the VBA regional offices by the undersecretary for benefits in deciding what structural configuration to adopt.

The change levers employed at the New York regional office were both formal and informal, but key to the successes achieved thus far appears to be a change in office culture. Bringing employees into the design process was a major departure from past practices and appears to have engendered widespread employee commitment to the new model. At the IRS, on the other hand, technology appears to be the predominant vehicle for generating behavioral change.

At the VBA, the entire design and implementation process was characterized by extensive dialogue between management and the workforce. While the IRS's top management encouraged communication between middle managers and line employees, it was principally one-way (downward) and focused on explanation and justification; moreover, the senior officials declined to enter into substantive dialogue with their workforce. Many top managers acknowledged that middle managers generally had not bought into the changes themselves.

It is no surprise, then, that employee commitment to—and even understanding of—TSM's grand vision was poor. To their credit, IRS leadership did enter into a precedent-setting partnership agreement with its employees' union, perhaps on the assumption that the union would serve as a communication conduit. (Indeed, the union has argued that it is the exclusive conduit in such matters!) However, while this partnership, and the expanded role it afforded the union in the change process itself, effectively precluded union opposition, it did little to engender a culture based on trust and commitment.

Ironically, although it has been described as top-down in nature, the IRS change strategy was impeded by a diffusion of authority at the top of the organization. The IRS's modernization executive (ME), who had overall responsibility for the TSM project, had to negotiate each project with his counterparts on the executive committee. A previous member of the ME's staff commented that the ME "was a matrix manager without line authority. He tried to cajole and persuade. Nobody was in charge"—at least until Congress insisted on a single point of accountability. In contrast, although the VBA effort was collaborative in nature, it was clearly a case of power sharing: the director retained ultimate authority over the direction of the project.

The VBA model also reveals another bottom-up advantage that may be unique to public sector (and especially federal) change management. Because it occurred at the subunit level, new systems and approaches could be tested without the intense scrutiny of external stakeholders such as the GAO, Congress, and the national media. In painful contrast, much of the IRS effort took place "in the sunshine" and was on such a large scale that it fell under the almost continuous scrutiny of multiple (and sometimes competing) units within GAO and Congress.

Top-down strategies are often characterized by a master plan, and the IRS effort fits that pattern, probably to its disadvantage. First, the conceptual basis for the TSM project's "design master plan" was flawed: it mandated the reengineering of work processes to fit anticipated technologies and systems, rather than the other way around. Second, the master plan suffered from a fatal inflexibility: it presumed a specific level of funding from Congress, and according to one IRS official, once that budget was cut, "the business master plan was out the window." Finally, the scope and magnitude of the master plan may have simply been too much for senior officials. Responsibility for its implementation was added to the already substantial operational portfolios of the business system owners, resulting in TSM "attention deficit disorder" and possibly contributing to unusually high executive committee turnover.

The VBA model also has liabilities. There, a lack of top-management commitment ultimately slowed the change process. Without the explicit sanction of top management for the innovations that emerged, their eventual adoption across the agency has become problematic. And while VBA headquarters did give its imprimatur to the generic concepts behind the New York model, it did so in a very ambivalent way, leaving its further implementation to the discretion of the remaining regional offices. Furthermore, what has been identified as the critical success factor in the bottom-up model, participation of employees in the design and implementation of the changes, itself mitigates simply exporting the changes to other offices. Extension of the participatory approach would presume that each office would devise its own model.

Conclusion

A theme that emerges from this discussion is the critical role of organizational leadership in engendering change. The leader is in a unique position to challenge and transform the culture of an organization by legitimizing, sanctioning, and condoning behaviors that contribute to substantive change. IRS interviewees characterized its senior leadership as conservative, hierarchical, and insular, before (and more important, during and after) the advent of TSM. Decision making has remained hierarchical in nature and the various business system owners are as insular as their functional predecessors—this in a project that demands effective integration at all levels! The uncertain future of TSM thus comes as no surprise.

On the other hand, VBA's New York leadership, and specifically Director Thompson, did challenge the traditional assembly-line culture of the regional office, first by triggering the change process from the top (at least the top of that particular subunit) and then by giving line employees a prominent role in the specifics of its design, more discretion over the disposition of the claims, and relief from the stifling specialization required by the pre-reengineered claims process. This is just the sort of hybrid change strategy—bottom-up from the standpoint of organizational origin, but with a top-down vector within that particular locus—that Beer, Eisenstat, and Spector (1990) advocate.

At least in theory, this hybrid strategy is consistent with the intent of the NPR's reinvention lab effort (as noted, the VBA's New York regional office is one such lab). In this regard, the NPR is unique in the long and frustrating history of attempts at management reform in the federal government. Like its predecessors, the NPR's most visible and public initiatives—its much publicized efforts to downsize and streamline the federal bureaucracy, restructure cabinet departments and programs, and reform certain management systems such as procurement and personnel—represent a classic top-down change strategy, and like its predecessors, it has met with mixed success. However, in contrast, the reinvention lab strategy "has been consciously structured to avoid hierarchy," according to Elaine Kamarck, Vice President Gore's senior NPR policy adviser. She says that the idea is "to get people to do things bottom-up."

But as we have seen, even a bottom-up strategy may require a top-down component. Thus, the strategic choice we posed at the outset of this chapter may have more to do with the timing and organizational origin of the change vector (that is, "corporate" versus subunit leadership) than with distinctions between employee and management or between collaboration and coercion. Implicit in this proposition, and in the hybrid critical-path model itself, is the notion that it is suitable for organization-wide application, employed as a deliberate (but decidedly subtle) strategy that comes from the top. Under this permutation, the role of top leadership shifts from that of an engineer who designs and imposes new work processes and structures on the entire organization to that of gardener who plants the seeds of innovation with subordinates, helps them grow, and then harvests the results and transplants them elsewhere. Under such a strategy, the key levers of change are informal in nature, with the leader primarily concerned with legitimizing innovative behavior and facilitating organizational learning.

This is a radically different change strategy for the federal government, one that may not even have a discernible endgame, and its prospects remain problematic as long as existing reward systems in government give agency leaders little incentive to make managerial issues a top priority and middle managers little incentive to attempt radical innovation in the interests of improved efficiency, service, and morale.

References

Beer, M. *Organization Change and Development: A Systems View.* Santa Monica, Calif.: Goodyear, 1980.

Beer, M., Eisenstat, R. A., and Spector, B. *The Critical Path to Corporate Renewal.* Boston: Harvard Business School Press, 1990.

Burns, T., and Stalker, G. M. *The Management of Innovation.* Oxford: Oxford University Press, 1994.

Coch, L., and French, J.R.P., Jr. "Overcoming Resistance to Change." *Human Relations,* 1948, p. 512.

Cohen, A. R. "Towards More Differentiated Strategies for Change." In A. F. Leemans (ed.), *The Management of Change in Government.* The Hague: Martinus Nijhoff, 1976.

Cummings, T. G. "The Actors in Large-Scale Organizational Change." In A. M. Mohrman Jr., S. A. Mohrman, G. E. Ledford Jr., T. G. Cummings, E. E. Lawler III, and Associates, *Large-Scale Organizational Change.* San Francisco: Jossey-Bass, 1989.

Dunn, W. N., and Swierczek, F. W. "Planned Organizational Change: Toward Grounded Theory." *Journal of Applied Behavioral Science,* 1977, *13*(2), 135.

Finney, M., Bowen, D., Pearson, C., and Siehl, C. "Designing Blueprints for Organizationwide Transformation." In R. H. Kilmann, T. J. Covin, and Associates, *Corporate Transformation: Revitalizing Organizations for a Competitive World.* San Francisco: Jossey-Bass, 1988.

Greiner, L. "Patterns of Organizational Change." *Harvard Business Review,* 1967, *45*(3), 119.

Gross, N., Giacquinta, J. B., and Bernstein, M. *Implementing Organizational Innovations: A Sociological Analysis of Planned Educational Change.* New York: Basic Books, 1971.

Hershey, R. D. "A Technological Overhaul of IRS Is Called a Fiasco." *New York Times,* Apr. 25, 1996.

Kanter, R. M. *The Change Masters: Innovation for Productivity in the American Corporation.* New York: Simon & Schuster, 1983.

Kanter, R. M., Stein, B. A., and Jick, T. D. *The Challenge of Organizational Change: How Companies Experience It and Leaders Guide It.* New York: Free Press, 1992.

Lawler, E. E., III. "Transformation: From Control to Involvement." In R. H. Kilmann, T. J. Covin, and Associates, *Corporate Transformation: Revitalizing Organizations for a Competitive World.* San Francisco: Jossey-Bass, 1988.

Leemans, A. F. (ed.). *The Management of Change in Government.* The Hague: Martinus Nijhoff, 1976.

Mosher, F. C. (ed.). *Governmental Reorganizations: Cases and Commentary.* New York: Bobbs-Merrill, 1967.

Nutt, P. C. "Tactics of Implementation." *Academy of Management Journal,* 1986, *29*(2), 230.

Rogers, E. M., and Shoemaker, F. F. *Communication of Innovations: A Cross-Cultural Approach.* (2nd ed.) New York: Free Press, 1971.

Szanton, P. *Federal Reorganization: What Have We Learned?* Chatham, N.J.: Chatham House, 1981.

Thompson, J. R., and Ingraham, P. W. "Organizational Redesign in the Public Sector." In D. F. Kettl and H. B. Milward (eds.), *The State of Public Management.* Baltimore: Johns Hopkins University Press, 1996.

U.S. Internal Revenue Service. *Final Recommendations of the District Organization Study.* Washington, D.C.: U.S. Internal Revenue Service, 1993.

Wilson, J. Q. *Bureaucracy: What Government Agencies Do and Why They Do It.* New York: Basic Books, 1989.

Zaltman, G., Duncan, R., and Holbek, J. *Innovations and Organizations.* New York: Wiley, 1973.

Part Two

The Tactics of Change in Public Organizations

By definition, planned change requires intervening in the functioning of an organization. These interventions, in turn, can have many, often unpredictable ramifications. Of paramount importance is understanding how employees of the organization will react. As David Frederickson and James Perry point out in Chapter Five, change agents need to address employee concerns at multiple levels. At the political level, tactics of resistance need to be anticipated and responded to; at the emotional level, employees' natural apprehensions concerning what change will mean for them must be addressed; and at a practical level, employees should be provided with the skills that will be required to perform any new tasks.

In Chapter Six, Hal Rainey identifies five key success factors that appear necessary in order for change to occur: a "widespread belief in the need for change," "clear, sustained leadership including support from top executives," "power sharing and broad participation in diagnosing problems and planning the change," "the development of a guiding vision for the change," and "flexible and incremental implementation, involving experimentation, feedback, adaptation, and building on successes to institutionalize changes." Rainey evaluates the National Performance Review on the basis of these factors and provides some suggestions on ways to enhance the prospects for the successful transformation of government agencies.

In Chapter Seven, Guy Peters adopts what could be described as a "contingency" theory of reform, arguing that the critical success factors may vary depending on circumstances. Peters analyzes three "models" of change, top-down, bottom-up, and "induced through external, imposed circumstances," and he identifies the circumstances in which each might be appropriate. Like Ronald Sanders and Hal Rainey, Peters highlights the need for competent leadership if change is to succeed. For Peters, a crucial element of that leadership is the ability to devise a change strategy suited to the organization and environment at hand.

Chapter Five

Overcoming Employee Resistance to Change

David G. Frederickson
James L. Perry

Harold Leavitt (1989a) reminds us that management has an emotional component. Attempts to influence human beings entirely through rational means are misguided. When managers endeavor to alter organizational structures, they must take into account how these actions will be perceived by all those affected by the organization. This chapter addresses the likely perceptions and reactions of internal stakeholders, primarily employees, when they are confronted with organizational change. Anticipating and confronting these perceptions and reactions is the cornerstone to enacting meaningful change. This chapter also provides strategies learned from successful and unsuccessful change efforts in public organizations.

Paradoxes of Public Sector Transformation

Despite the central importance of internal-stakeholder concerns, two conditions shift the focus of public sector organizational change away from these concerns. First, the genesis of government reform efforts (at least the most heavily publicized ones) is external rather than internal. Government reform has always played an important role in elections at every level of U.S. government. Such reform proposals blur the goal of administrative reform with that of political salience. Because little political gain results from attempts to assuage bureaucrats' apprehension about reform, such concerns have been largely absent in the drafting of these proposals. Due to their political nature, government reform efforts have traditionally been introduced with much fanfare and hyperbole. Without the impression of a current or impending crisis, there can be little political support for these efforts. Support for the work of the Hoover commissions, for example, came about through a substantial public relations effort. Many horror stories of waste and mismanagement were publicized to create the impression of a management crisis within the federal government. The creation of a perceived crisis was the initial step in garnering support for the commissions' endeavors (Moe, 1982). A crisis or emergency must be met with full force; mere modifications are inadequate against such a foe. A crisis justifies, even requires, that structures be "reformed," that organizations be "overhauled," and that institutions be "reinvented."

The hyperbole that precedes reform is accompanied by purported benefits of the reform effort that far exceed reality. These conditions lead to a pattern that Downs and Larkey (1986) refer to as "hubris to helplessness." Management problems are built up to seem daunting, and the reform effort is then sold as the panacea. This creates a paradox in which the prescription for curing government's ills conflicts with the lessons learned from previous government reform efforts. Despite calls for urgent, radical, and comprehensive reform crusades, evidence suggests that incremental changes are more realistic and healthy. When the reform effort fails to deliver as advertised, all that remains are the images of ineffective government created by the mismanagement anecdotes.

A second condition that shifts focus away from internal-stakeholder concerns is intimately tied to the external origins of change and accountability in public organizations. The external locus of proposals and accountability directs attention toward structural solutions and away from issues of individual compliance and adaptation. *Reinventing Government,* Osborne and Gaebler's 1992 book that is arguably responsible for the recent popular attention to government reform, and the National Performance Review (NPR), the federal government's reform effort based largely on reinvention precepts, frequently repeat the assertion that the problem with government is not incompetent public servants but the complex system of rules and regulations within which public servants must work. This line of reasoning creates the false impression that individuals will automatically adjust favorably to systemic and structural changes in public organizations.

Although being excused from responsibility for government's problems might somehow encourage dedicated public servants, who are often convenient scapegoats of both the left and the right, such structural and process-based reform efforts draw attention away from a critical element of any management reform effort. Management reforms that attempt change at the macro level, focusing mostly on structural issues, do so at the expense of micro-level (stakeholder) concerns. Change agents in the public sector must attend to both macro and micro considerations. Organization development (OD) theorists suggest that even if structures change, long-term transformational change occurs only when organizational actors alter their basic work-related behaviors. In other words, plans that merely change structures and processes are inadequate to effect meaningful reform.

A helpful distinction to remember when discussing organizational change is what Levy and Merry (1986) refer to as first-order and second-order change. First-order change refers to changes that alter systemic and structural characteristics alone. First-order change does not require alteration or even examination of the fundamental assumptions regarding cause-and-effect relationships (Porras and Robertson, 1992). The idea of first-order change is that structural changes will automatically lead to the desired work-related behaviors. Second-order change focuses on both the structure of the organization and the behaviors of the individuals working within the organization. In second-order change, "the original frames of reference are replaced by new ones, with the result that the new organizational condition is seen by members as conceptually quite distinct from the old" (Porras and Robertson, 1992, p. 721). If change of a second-order magnitude is intended, first-order structural changes are not sufficient. To effect reform, change agents in the public sector must alter work-related behaviors.

First-order changes generally emphasize the altering of organizing arrangements within an organization. Organizing arrangements—such as goals, strategies, formal structure, administrative policies, administrative systems, and reward systems—are the written rules and guidelines that instruct employees how they should carry out their work (Porras and Robertson, 1992). Attempts to change organizations are usually focused on these formal aspects. The OD contention is that the changes that result from alteration of organizing arrangements alone will be incomplete and unpredictable. "People do not respond consistently to what these organizing arrangements tell them to do"(Porras and Robertson, 1992, p. 730). To effect change that is more complete and predictable (second-order change), change agents should expand the scope of the change effort to include other aspects of an organization that greatly affect employee behavior. These other aspects include social factors such as culture and management style, technological factors such as technical equipment and technical procedures, and physical-setting aspects such as space configuration and interior design.

Previous reform efforts at all levels of government lend credence to the OD theorists' arguments. One example is the attempted reform of Florida's civil service system. Soon after the 1990 election, Governor Lawton Chiles and Lieutenant Governor Buddy MacKay put civil service reform at the top of their agenda. The general thrust of the reform effort was to grant managers greater authority for human resource issues. Deregulation and decentralization became the cry of reform. Through these techniques, reformers hoped to increase management capacity, employee involvement, commitment, and efficiency. Inattention to micro concerns, those dealing with individual employees, helped lead to the reform's failure. One of the reasons cited for this failure was demoralization of the state's employees (Wechsler, 1994). In the design and implementation phases of the reform process, little attention was paid to the concerns of individuals working within the system. This inattention was evident on three fronts: (1) employees were not sufficiently trained, (2) threats to managers were not mitigated, and (3) threats to workers were not mitigated.

The effects of poor training on Florida's civil service reform are nowhere more evident than in its Total Quality Management (TQM) initiative. Although TQM was to advance Florida's administrative capacity, "there was never enough understanding of this management approach or of what was involved in its adoption" (Wechsler, 1994, p. 74). Reorganization of the agency designated to carry out the bulk of the training heightened the implementation difficulties. Reductions in positions and budgets, a major concern of managers, were not addressed. One purported benefit of reform was savings. Managers were concerned that any savings would soon translate into smaller staffs and lower budgets. Workers' concerns included uncertainty about their new roles and potential job loss. It was not clear to workers that a decentralized system, in which managers would be granted greater authority in personnel matters, would be more fair than a centralized personnel system. In the previous system, personnel actions such as firings and demotions had to be approved by a central agency. After the reform, no prior central clearance was required.

Florida's experience raises a broader question for those seeking to transform government: what tactics must change agents employ to facilitate individual adaptation to and acceptance of change? In other words, what levers must change agents pull so that individuals within government agencies can adapt to and even thrive on organizational change? To answer these questions, we analyzed case studies of government agencies at the federal, state, and local levels, including federal "reinvention laboratories." Some of the cases involved recipients of awards for innovation conferred jointly by Harvard University's John F. Kennedy School of Government and the Ford Foundation. The findings in this chapter represent common threads that tie together these successful government transformation efforts.

Change Imperative 1: Change Agents Recognize and Manage Impediments to Change

For organizational change to take hold, change agents must first recognize that there are many impediments to change. The first step in the change process has been referred to as "unfreezing" (Lewin, 1951). The unfreezing process entails loosening the attitudes, outlook, and self-perception of organizational actors. Strategies for change that involve process and structural adjustments alone should be viewed with skepticism because they do not engage the deeply ingrained images and perceptions at the core of an organization's culture. To effect real change, change agents must recognize that the way organizational actors view themselves and their responsibilities, both consciously and subconsciously, will determine how they respond to proposed change. When the proposed change challenges these perceptions, it will be met with profound and unyielding resistance. As Lawrence Mohr suggests, the most efficacious route to initiating change "is through the undermining of those initial forces of resistance" (1995, p. 8). Some argue that acceptance of organizational change requires a secular equivalent of personal conversion. This conversion process is a radical one, involving the abandonment of one set of organizational assumptions and the adoption of another (Westley, 1990).

Tactic: Reduce Threat by Teaching Employees to Let Go

Change agents should recognize the natural human desire to hold on to existing attitudes, perspectives, and activities. Attempts to alter existing arrangements or to establish new ones will be met with anxiety. Some of the emotions associated with change are (1) the loss of something familiar and predictable, (2) feelings of uncertainty, and (3) the dissolution of meaning or loss of identity (Tannenbaum and Hanna, 1985). Change agents can facilitate a desire among employees to welcome and even embrace change. First, they must recognize that most employee fears are rational. Many employees fear that change might bring about increased scrutiny, an increase or decrease in their level of responsibility, or even unemployment. Also, certain fears are related to the change process rather than the specific change at hand. This aversion to change is often rooted in painful past events that taught that letting go can have negative consequences.

Does the natural fear of change preclude meaningful government transformation? Of course not. At the very least, it is the responsibility of change agents to allay fears about the negative consequences of change. Part of this responsibility is to help employees recognize and disaggregate the rational fears from generic ones. The rational fears should be met head-on, using some of the tactics discussed in the remainder of this chapter. The generic fears, on the other hand, accompany all changes regardless of the benefits change might bring. Change agents should teach employees to let go of these irrational fears. Ideally, change agents will uncover a vision of the organization's future, a transformed state that holds as many benefits for the front-line workers as it does for management. Each employee should understand the ways in which the proposed change will be an improvement from the status quo. Change agents must continually identify how the various attempts to restructure, reinvent, or transform government will affect individual organizational actors and how organizational actors will react. One question that should guide this inquiry is, does the proposed change contradict any element of the organization's culture? Every attempt should be made to align the wills of front-line employees and management.

Tactic: Cultivate Support from Career Civil Servants

Government transformation depends ultimately on the support of career civil servants. Change agents must recognize that earning their support is perhaps more critical than earning the support of elected officials, since the support of the latter tends to wane quickly (Berry, Chackerian, and Wechsler, 1995). Political support will often accompany the introduction of administrative change. Elected public officials run campaigns that exploit the actual and perceived shortcomings of government. They may support administrative reform efforts in an attempt to be seen as catalysts of government reform. Because reform is a slow process and the currency of electoral support is quick political gain, when the perceived political advantage of administrative reform diminishes, so does support from elected public officials (March and Olsen, 1983; Ingraham and Perry, 1994). Unfortunately, the support of career civil servants is partly dependent on elected officials' willingness to expend political capital (Savoie and Peters, 1996). When added managerial discretion and the pressure to be entrepreneurial lead to mistakes, the temptation for elected officials to exploit the situation for criticism will be substantial. If elected officials react with support, the fears of career civil servants will be partially allayed. An additional reason to enlist the support of career civil servants is that they bring a durability to the reform effort that elected or politically appointed public officials cannot provide (Rainey and Rainey, 1984).

The Occupational Safety and Health Administration

The Occupational Safety and Health Administration (OSHA) is one of two hundred reinvention laboratories charged with the first stages of implementing the NPR recommendations. One means OSHA has used to stimulate employees' support has been to appeal to their sense of mission. A strong sense of mission has the potential to foster change efforts. Employees can easily retreat into standard operating procedures to ensure that nothing goes awry. This attitude was prevalent in OSHA, which had placed heavy emphasis on the number of fines and citations it issued. Change agents within OSHA showed employees that the excessive focus on objective measures detracted from the overall goal of safer workplaces. The next step was to leverage the OSHA employees' sense of mission and convince them that the proposed changes would lead to safer workplaces (Sanders and Thompson, 1996).

Tactic: Defuse the Concerns of Resisters

Successful change agents defuse the most vocal resisters to change by accommodating their demands in a manner that does not violate the intent of the reform effort. Much of the organizational-change literature discusses methods of overcoming or bypassing resistance to change. Such managerial hubris is destructive to an organization, as it will likely lead to alienation of many organizational actors. Ignoring resistance can result in a failure to see valuable alternatives or revisions to the change proposal, deficient views of how change will affect individuals, and an incomplete understanding of the reality of the change proposal's probability of success (Nord and Jermier, 1994). Resistance to change should be taken seriously and met head-on. A genuine understanding of the resistance and its origins will inform the change process and increase its likelihood of adoption and success.

The Defense Personnel Support Center

The Defense Personnel Support Center (DPSC) of the Department of Defense is a model of how change agents met employees' resistance head-on, validated their concerns, and implemented change that was embraced rather than resisted. Instead of building up a coalition of support to gain the ability to overpower or ignore resisters, the DPSC sought an alignment of wills between management and the most vocal resisters.

The DPSC is a clearinghouse for supplies purchased from the private sector and provided to military mess halls, commissaries, and hospitals. In the 1980s and early 1990s, no one familiar with the DPSC, especially its customers, deemed it worthy of any award or distinction. By 1991, the Base Realignment and Closure Commission had targeted it for closure. DPSC warehouses were stocked with aging equipment and goods that none of the military services wanted.

Through various reform initiatives, the DPSC transformed itself from an outdated warehouse that took an average of over two months to deliver goods that most military outposts did not want to an innovative, electronically based organization providing military bases, commissaries, and hospitals with popular consumer goods, usually within three days. The changes initiated by the DPSC management posed a significant threat to some front-line DPSC employees. Many of these employees, quite justifiably, were afraid that the new system "would jeopardize their customer support and diminish their personal effectiveness" (Corbin, 1995b, p. 24).

How did management deal with this employee resistance? First, it gave the transformation's most vocal critics important roles in the transformation process, and second, it provided extensive training and supported employees through a comprehensive liaison effort.

Change Imperative 2: Change Agents Actively Manage Change

Efforts to change organizations are met with many defensive behaviors. These include overconforming, playing dumb, passing the buck, stalling, and adhering to organizational regulations to the letter while violating the spirit of reform (Ashforth and Lee, 1990). In addition to responding to the threat that reform efforts pose, these defensive strategies may be employed in an effort to avoid blame. Organizational actors' natural response is to behave in a way that reduces the effects of the actual or perceived threat that accompanies change. Added to the natural tendency to resist change are many organizational antecedents that lend themselves to defensive activities. Among these are bureaucratic rationality, specialization, formalization, and structures of accountability and reward (Ashforth and Lee, 1990). The breadth and depth of the barriers to change require that effective change agents be proactive. Managing change as a bureaucratic routine will not suffice.

Tactic: Involve Employees Appropriately

Our review of the award-winning government innovators suggests that some level of employee participation, at least in the method of implementation, allows for greater employee "ownership" of the change sought and a greater likelihood that its adoption will be successful. According to Wise (1996, p. 397), "When frontline employees consider themselves engaged in decision making and responsible for organizational outcomes, their commitment to achieving organizational goals is enhanced." When employees are organized and represented by unions, the award-winning government agencies have a good record of involving the union in establishing the objectives of change and in selecting a method of implementation. The opportunity for participation will not only help win over or defuse vocal resisters but also provide a greater understanding of the effects of change at all levels of the organization.

The Federal Quality Institute

The Federal Quality Institute's analysis of high-performing federal agencies lends its support to high levels of employee involvement in the change process. Its handbook states: "All of the organizations reviewed for this study made a concerted effort to increase the degree of employee involvement in various aspects of operations" (Federal Quality Institute, 1994, p. 92).

Tactic: Nurture Risk Taking by Reinforcing Appropriate Behaviors

Change agents must recognize that change poses threats to almost all actors within an organization. This is true even for the groups that seemingly stand to gain from the change process. This point is easily illustrated with a look at the trade-offs involved in current reinvention efforts. One of the main themes of reinvention is "empowerment" of individuals at the lower levels of government agencies by freeing them from onerous regulatory impediments. On the surface, it appears that the empowered front-line employees are the victors in this equation, and theoretically, because of their newly granted empowerment and added discretion, they should approve reinvention. From the perspective of those on the front line, however, such discretion can be very threatening.

In an era of governmental downsizing, where each government agency has to continually justify its existence, the call for innovation and risk taking is apt to go unheeded. The most likely response to change in such an environment is defensiveness. As Paul Light (1995) put it: "Who wants to go out on a limb when so many are sharpening saws?" Indeed, a study of Florida's extensive governmental reinvention efforts found that middle managers were reluctant to take the risks these efforts demanded (Berry, Chackerian, and Wechsler, 1995). This reluctance intensifies when the call to take risks is accompanied by a shift of organizational power away from management and toward front-line employees.

One tactic for getting employees to take risks is grounded in recognizing that risk taking is a learned behavior. Such learned behaviors must be nurtured by organizations over the long term. In their review of reform successes at the federal level, Ronald Sanders and James Thompson (1996) found that internal "champions," or upper-level managers supporting reform efforts by front-line change agents, smooth the change process considerably. These internal champions can provide protection for change agents willing to take risks.

Low-Risk Experimentation at the Bureau of Reclamation

The U.S. Department of the Interior's Bureau of Reclamation is one of the federal government's two hundred reinvention laboratories. For ninety years the Bureau has provided irrigation and electricity through the construction of dams, canals, and power plants. It has come to a crossroads, however, now that the irrigation and electricity potential of most western states' rivers has been almost entirely exploited. The bureau's former commissioner, Daniel Beard, explains the transformation: "We concluded that our original mission—to reclaim the arid West—was essentially complete and that we must change from an organization based on civil works projects to one based on water resource management" (Corbin, 1995a). In its transformation, the bureau encouraged employees to take reasonable risks through the use of "forgiveness coupons." The coupons were cashed in by employees who made mistakes associated with risk taking. Employees were instructed to cash in at least two coupons annually. Encouraging risk taking through forgiveness coupons was a simple method the bureau used to sustain morale during a period of considerable organizational flux.

Tactic: Hold Current Employees Harmless from Unintended Consequences

In every case we examined, reform was only a means to an end. Reforms are sold to the public as a way to reduce budgets and save taxpayers money. Employees understand that this often leads to personnel reductions. The purported savings from the NPR, for example, are to come primarily from reducing the number of federal employees. Change agents must recognize that employees' fear leads to attitudes and actions that run counter to the objectives of reform, which include the objective of delivering better public services at a reduced cost. Successful reform efforts start with the assumption that employees are an asset rather than a liability. Reform efforts that do not provide some form of job security for competent employees are destined to reduce employee morale, which will lead to decreased productivity.

Job Security Assurance in Indianapolis

During his campaign, Indianapolis mayor Stephen Goldsmith promised to privatize public services. Upon entering office, however, he decided that his goal was not to eliminate jobs in city government but to inject competition into the delivery of public services in order to provide the best value to the taxpayer. Instead of laying off hundreds of city employees, Goldsmith decided to open the provision of many city services to public bidding. City employees would merely be one of the several bidders competing to deliver each of these services. Despite the reprieve from immediate layoffs, the union representing city employees was not greatly relieved. It felt that city employees were at a significant disadvantage in these competitions. Mayor Goldsmith took a number of steps to level the playing field without compromising his objective of introducing competition.

The first public service put up for bidding was the city's pothole project. To get union support, the mayor had to assure employees that the playing field was level. The mayor "had to do more than offer public employees a chance to bid. He had to devise a way to help them structure a bid which could legitimately be compared to a private proposal" (Husock, 1995, p. B2). This required that the city employees provide dollar totals based on itemized expenditures. The city hired a consultant to give its employees the necessary accounting qualifications and promised them that the city would give them "the opportunity to make mistakes and . . . the benefit of the doubt on close calls" (p. B2).

Compared to the private bidders, it was evident that the city's bid on the pothole project was not sufficiently lean. Several middle-management positions would have to be eliminated. Even when it was necessary to fire city employees working on the project, the mayor did it in such a way as to decrease, rather than increase, the level of animosity between the union and the mayor's office. When the decision was made to eliminate twelve middle managers, the mayor's office, in consultation with the union, fired only city council political appointees from the mayor's own party who were serving as supervisors on the street repair crews. As a result of the reduced size of crews and other reforms, the city employees were able to reduce their cost of pouring asphalt by a remarkable 25 percent. Since private firms have been allowed to bid for these services, union workers have won about 80 percent of all bids for repairing potholes and resurfacing roads.

When a private firm won the right to operate Indianapolis's wastewater treatment facility, it agreed to hire as many city employees as possible. Soon after the firm took control of the facility, it decided to reduce its 340 employees by a third. The city adopted a no-layoff policy. It promised to move displaced workers into other, vacant public works positions or to provide training in preparation for work in the private sector. Within five months, more than 80 percent of the displaced workers had been placed in new jobs. The others were allowed to remain on the city payroll until they found work.

Tactic: Train Employees to Increase Capacity and Productivity

Because most reform efforts require employees to learn new skills, extensive training needs to be part of the reform process. The previously mentioned failure of Florida's civil service reform points to the importance of training. Florida's employees were expected to use TQM principles to make productivity gains, but the state failed to provide any formal TQM training. Training, if it is to have a positive impact on work-related behaviors and productivity, cannot be done in a single workshop or seminar. Permanent changes require follow-up mechanisms that reinforce the initial training

(Faerman and Ban, 1993). Training should be focused on the core competencies necessary for an agency to meet its primary objectives (Budd and Broad, 1996). The pressure to show savings generated by reform might lead some public managers to cut funds for training. Change agents must resist this temptation. The National Commission on the Public Service (1989) suggests that training be used in efforts to create a culture of performance.

Tactic: Recognize the Importance of Teams

Good managers have long recognized the advantages of work teams. Organizations that use teams in the right circumstances have demonstrated that they improve the quality of products and services, reduce the need for supervision, foster innovation, reduce absenteeism, enhance decision making, and decrease labor costs (Lawler, 1986). Leavitt (1989b) proposes that teams replace individuals as the building blocks of organizations. Team-based organizations, he contends, would cut operational levels and improve cohesiveness, motivation, and commitment.

In addition to the generic advantages of teams to organizations, teams can provide the specific advantage of facilitating organizational change. Teams facilitate change by creating a link between individuals and an organization, by amplifying small successes and providing support during setbacks, and by producing results that are greater than the sum of individual contributions (Marks and Shaw, 1994). Teams also encourage an attitude of inquiry and innovation as team members gain insights about themselves, the group, and organizations through the "observation, analysis, and diagnosis of interpersonal situations" (Schein, 1989, p. 435).

Chicago's Use of Teams

Chicago's Models of Excellence (MOE) program uses problem-solving teams to make the city's government more responsive, innovative, and efficient. The MOE program is an excellent example of the use of teams to encourage innovation, problem solving, and flexibility. Because one of the main obstacles to effective government is high turnover among senior-level, politically appointed managers, the MOE teams "decided to focus on the 'B' players, people who stick around as top management comes and goes" (Rategan and O'Hare, 1996, p. 95). Members of an MOE team in the Chicago Park District posed as ordinary citizens who were attempting to register for recreational activities to determine the average amount of time elapsed from first contact to enrollment in the activities. Enrollment times ranged from thirty minutes to 120 hours. The MOE team discovered over one hundred problems causing delays in enrollment and developed a system to ameliorate these problems. One simple solution was to create bilingual registration forms. At test sites, the average enrollment time was reduced to six minutes.

Prior to a pilot program developed by an MOE team, Cook County Hospital was plagued by dangerously low supplies in the critical care units: out-of-stock situations were reported an average of forty-four times a day. The MOE team's pilot program halved the procedures necessary to order supplies, added weekend deliveries, set up a supply catalogue, and designated certain elevators for supply delivery only. The program is now being extended throughout the hospital.

The ability of MOE teams to solve long-standing and deeply rooted management problems when individual managers could not is no fluke. Teams can provide the opportunity to gain quick wins, helping organizational members to see that change can make an organization not only different but also better for the individual (Marks and Shaw, 1994). The interaction between team players generates ideas and enthusiasm that are rarely generated by a group of unconnected individuals.

Using Teams in Hampton, Virginia

The city of Hampton, Virginia, used teams to transform itself into a high-performance organization. The city had been characterized by high tax rates, revenue shortfalls, and a declining economic base. But all that has changed. One example of the transformation is Hampton's Office of Human Resources. This office was originally organized along the lines of traditional segmented and specialized roles: recruitment, placement, employee relations, and training. The main component of the transformation was a push away from specialists who answered to supervisors in a conventional hierarchical structure and toward the creation of two self-directed teams of fully cross-trained generalists. The team approach was adopted by the entire Hampton city government, which soon reported declining tax rates and debt service (Perry and Mesch, 1997).

The benefit of teams is not found in the restructuring of work processes alone. Instead, teams allow organizational actors to change their basic work-related behaviors, as OD theorists suggest. Perry (1990) points out that the creation of teams provides not only the macro benefit of flattening organizational structures but also the micro benefits of increased employee commitment and a greater sense of ownership. Increased reliance on teams lets team members know that top management respects their abilities.

Change Imperative 3: Change Is Reinforced and So Endures

Once a successful innovation has been adopted, what conditions or actions allow the new practices, attitudes, and outlooks to take hold and gain permanence? Will success alone ensure that the innovations become routinized rather than merely being temporary changes in work habits? Research suggests that even change programs that have been successfully introduced in the public sector often have not been sustained over a long period of time (Mirvis and Berg, 1977; Walton, 1980; Goodman and Dean, 1982). After innovations have been introduced and implemented, what can change agents do to ensure that they continue?

An organization's culture is made up of observable activities, behaviors, processes, attitudes, and assumptions. It is elusive because it is only partially observable (Schein, 1992). Change must go beyond the surface realm of structures and processes to settle into the deep, unobservable elements of an organization's culture. Thus for change to gain permanence, change agents must build a strong organizational culture that legitimizes, promotes, and sustains the work habits, attitudes, outlook, and self-perception encouraged by the change. Simple communication of the values and behaviors that support innovation can help build a strong organizational culture. This can be communicated through physical symbols, the strategic use of language, narratives and myths, and repeated practices and events (Rainey, 1996).

Tactic: Align Human Resource Practices with New Cultures and Structures

Introducing new work practices is only part of the change equation. Equally important is eliminating the old practices (Yin, 1981). Every effort must be made to avoid contradictions between existing work practices and the values advanced by the change. One area that can be riddled with inconsistencies is the incentive structure. Changes to work structures and procedures must be accompanied by an incentive system that supports them. Nothing will dampen enthusiasm for change more quickly than an incentive structure built around the old way of doing things. What incentives can change agents offer to employees who embrace change and improve their work? Because altering monetary incentives can be difficult in the public sector, incentives might include choice office space, better work assignments, and various other forms of nonmonetary recognition (Cohen and Brand, 1993).

Tactic: Modify Reforms When They Prove Faulty or Unproductive

Even in successful change initiatives, some elements of the initiative may still run counter to organizational objectives. Similarly, it is not unusual for the behaviors and attitudes intended by a change initiative to differ from the actual behaviors and attitudes the initiative elicits. To protect an organization from change's negative results, change agents should institute auditing and recalibrating mechanisms (Goodman and Dean, 1982). Systematic auditing mechanisms allow change agents to detect when a change is producing unfavorable results due to flaws in its design or implementation. When unfavorable results are detected, the change agents must recalibrate or modify the change initiative. Instituting these mechanisms creates a self-correcting organization that can retain the positive results of change and modify or discard the negative results.

Fine-Tuning Change at the Indiana Department of Transportation

In 1992 the Indiana Department of Transportation (IDOT) underwent a significant transformation as it implemented a TQM program. Despite the substantial care and thought that went into the program's design, IDOT experienced some setbacks. The most difficult challenge was translating basic TQM concepts and principles into action. One problem was a diffuse implementation program. A TQM management team narrowed the focus of the TQM implementation program to four primary areas: project management, action groups, Opportunities for Improvement (an employee suggestion program), and training (Letts, 1993). Once the TQM program gained new focus, IDOT employees knew that the TQM efforts would be channeled into one of these four areas rather than into a difficult-to-understand, diffuse set of TQM instructions.

Tactic: Involve Career Employees to Ensure Continuity

In institutionalizing change, change agents must be wary of the possibility that turnover in elected or appointed leadership may bring the change effort to a sudden halt. Unless permanent staff are invested in change, an event such as the departure of a political appointee could have disastrous results, short-circuiting a reform's institutionalization. The best way to overcome the liability of discontinuities such as an executive's departure is to give career employees significant roles and responsibilities in institutionalizing change.

Conclusion

This chapter identified three strategic imperatives and associated tactics drawn from successful public sector transformation initiatives. The first strategic imperative is that change agents recognize and manage impediments to change. One step in managing impediments is to gain the support of career civil servants. Change agents must also communicate stakeholders' new roles and articulate the advantages and challenges that will accompany these roles. Another part of managing impediments is to defuse the arguments of resisters by accommodating their demands in a manner that does not violate the intent of the change effort.

The second strategic imperative is that change agents manage change actively. A key consideration in this phase of the process is to involve employees appropriately. Throughout the change process, risk taking must be nurtured by reinforcing appropriate behaviors, creating opportunities to succeed, and holding employees harmless from unintended consequences. Effective reformers make training an integral part of the change process. Training not only increases employees' capacity but also reduces the threat of change and its accompanying new roles. Change agents also use teams to communicate change and generate support for it. Teams allow groups of peers affected by the change to aid and encourage each other.

The third strategic imperative is to reinforce change so that it endures. This requires change agents to align human resource practices with new practices, structures, and cultures. Organizations must also be willing to adjust or change plans when they prove faulty or counterproductive. Involving career civil servants promotes continuity, just as it reduces resistance to change.

The strategic imperatives we discussed are based on Lewin's classic model of change (1951). Although Lewin's model is familiar, it would be a mistake to view it as merely commonsense or simple. The failure of thousands of change initiatives is testimony to the difficulty of "doing" change rather than just planning it. This is particularly true in the public sector, which is fraught with paradoxes that deflect the attention of change agents from the importance of many of the ideas reviewed here. Public sector change agents must recognize the paradox that although the design and planning of change are rational processes, change itself is inherently emotional. An equally important and no less perplexing paradox is that public sector change and accountability are externally initiated and focused, but their success is dependent on the acceptance, adaptation, and support of internal stakeholders.

References

Ashforth, B. E., and Lee, R. T. "Defensive Behavior in Organizations: A Preliminary Model." *Human Relations,* 1990, *43,* 621–648.

Berry, F. S., Chackerian, R., and Wechsler, B. "Reinventing Government: Lessons from a State Capitol." Paper presented at the Third National Public Management Research Conference, University of Kansas, Lawrence, Oct. 5–7, 1995.

Budd, M. L., and Broad, M. L. "Training and Development for Organizational Performance." In J. L. Perry (ed.), *Handbook of Public Administration.* (2nd ed.) San Francisco: Jossey-Bass, 1996.

Cohen, S., and Brand, R. *Total Quality Management in Government: A Practical Guide for the Real World.* San Francisco: Jossey-Bass, 1993.

Corbin, L. "Going Leaner and Greener." *Government Executive,* 1995a, *27*(11), 35–36.

Corbin, L. "Retooling the Supply Chain." *Government Executive,* 1995b, *27*(11), 23–24.

Downs, G. W., and Larkey, P. D. *The Search for Government Efficiency: From Hubris to Helplessness.* New York: Random House, 1986.

Faerman, S. R., and Ban, C. "Trainee Satisfaction and Training Impact: Issues in Training Evaluation." *Public Productivity and Management Review,* 1993, *16,* 299–314.

Federal Quality Institute. *Federal Quality Management Handbook: Lessons Learned from High-Performing Organizations in the Federal Government.* Washington, D.C.: U.S. Government Printing Office, 1994.

Goodman, P. S., and Dean, J. W. "Creating Long-Term Organizational Change." In P. S. Goodman and Associates, *Change in Organizations: New Perspectives on Theory, Research, and Practice.* San Francisco: Jossey-Bass, 1982.

Husock, H. *Organizing Competition in Indianapolis: Mayor Stephen Goldsmith and the Quest for Lower Costs.* Cambridge, Mass.: President and Fellows of Harvard College, 1995.

Ingraham, P. W., and Perry, J. L. "The Three Faces of Civil Service Reform." In H. D. Rosenbaum and A. Ugrinsky (eds.), *The Presidency and Domestic Policies of Jimmy Carter.* Westport, Conn.: Greenwood Press, 1994.

Lawler, E. E., III. *High-Involvement Management: Participative Strategies for Improving Organizational Performance.* San Francisco: Jossey-Bass, 1986.

Leavitt, H. J. "Pathfinding, Problem Solving, and Implementing: The Management Mix." In J. L. Leavitt, L. R. Pondy, and D. M. Boje (eds.), *Readings in Managerial Psychology.* (4th ed.) Chicago: University of Chicago Press, 1989a.

Leavitt, H. J. "Suppose We Took Groups Seriously." In H. J. Leavitt, L. R. Pondy, and D. M. Boje (eds.), *Readings in Managerial Psychology.* (4th ed.) Chicago: University of Chicago Press, 1989b.

Letts, C. W. *Introducing Total Quality Management to the Design Division of the Indiana Department of Transportation.* Cambridge, Mass.: President and Fellows of Harvard College, 1993.

Levy, A., and Merry, U. *Organizational Transformation: Approaches, Strategies, Theories.* New York: Praeger, 1986.

Lewin, K. *Field Theory in Social Science.* New York: HarperCollins, 1951.

Light, P. C. "Fear and Loathing Meet Reinvention." *Government Executive,* 1995, *27*(3), 56.

March, J. G., and Olsen, J. P. "Organizing Political Life: What Administrative Reorganization Tells Us About Government." *American Political Science Review,* 1983, *77,* 284.

Marks, M. L., and Shaw, R. B. "Sustaining Change: Creating the Resilient Organization." In D. A. Nadler, R. B. Shaw, A. E. Walton, and Associates, *Discontinuous Change: Leading Organizational Transformation.* San Francisco: Jossey-Bass, 1994.

Mirvis, P. H., and Berg, D. N. *Failures in Organization Development and Change.* Somerset, N.J.: Wiley-Interscience, 1977.

Moe, R. C. *The Hoover Commissions Revisited.* Boulder, Colo.: Westview Press, 1982.

Mohr, L. B. "One Hundred Theories of Organizational Change: The Good, the Bad, and the Ugly." Paper presented at the Third National Public Management Research Conference, University of Kansas, Lawrence, Oct. 5–7, 1995.

National Commission on the Public Service. *Leadership for America: Rebuilding the Public Service.* Washington, D.C.: National Commission on the Public Service, 1989.

Nord, W. R., and Jermier, J. M. "Overcoming Resistance to Resistance: Insights from a Study of the Shadows." *Public Administration Quarterly,* 1994, *18,* 396–409.

Osborne, D., and Gaebler, T. *Reinventing Government: How the Entrepreneurial Spirit Is Transforming the Public Sector.* Reading, Mass.: Addison Wesley Longman, 1992.

Perry, J. L. "Unleashing the Power of Teamwork." *Government Executive,* 1990, *22*(7), 40.

Perry, J. L., and Mesch, D. J. "Strategic Human Resource Management." In C. Ban and N. M. Riccucci (eds.), *Public Personnel Management: Current Concerns, Future Challenges.* (2nd ed.) Reading, Mass.: Addison Wesley Longman, 1997.

Peters, B. G., and Savoie, D. J. "Managing Incoherence: The Coordination and Empowerment Conundrum." *Public Administration Review,* 1996, *56,* 281–290.

Porras, J. I., and Robertson, P. J. "Organizational Development: Theory, Practice, and Research." In M. Dunnette and L. Hough (eds.), *Handbook of Individual and Organizational Psychology,* vol. 3. (2nd ed.) Palo Alto, Calif.: Psychological Press, 1992.

Rago, W. V. "Struggles in Transformation: A Study in TQM, Leadership, and Organizational Culture in a Government Agency." *Public Administration Review,* 1996, *56,* 227–234.

Rainey, G. W., and Rainey, H. G. "Breaching the Hierarchical Imperative: The Modularization of the Social Security Claims Process." In D. J. Calista (ed.), *Bureaucratic and Government Reform.* Greenwich, Conn.: JAI Press, 1984.

Rainey, H. G. "Building an Effective Organizational Culture." In J. L. Perry (ed.), *Handbook of Public Administration.* (2nd ed.) San Francisco: Jossey-Bass, 1996.

Rategan, C. A., and O'Hare, K. "The Debureaucratization of Chicago." *Training and Development,* 1996, *50*(5), 95–96.

Sanders, R. P., and Thompson, J. R. "Stalemates and Setbacks: From Headquarters Obstinacy to Outdated Systems, the Roadblocks to Reinvention Are All Too Real." *Government Executive,* 1996, *28*(3), 7A–9A.

Savoie, D. J., and Peters, B. G. "Managing Incoherence: The Coordination and Empowerment Conundrum." *Public Administration Review,* 1996, *53,* 281–290.

Schein, E. H. "Management Development as a Process of Influence." In H. J. Leavitt, L. R. Pondy, and D. M. Boje (eds.), *Readings in Managerial Psychology.* (4th ed.) Chicago: University of Chicago Press, 1989.

Schein, E. H. *Organizational Culture and Leadership.* (2nd ed.) San Francisco: Jossey-Bass, 1992.

Tannenbaum, R., and Hanna, R. W. "Holding On, Letting Go, and Moving On: Understanding a Neglected Perspective on Change." In R. Tannenbaum, N. Margulies, F. Massarik, and Associates, *Human Systems Development: New Perspectives on People and Organizations.* San Francisco: Jossey-Bass, 1985.

Walton, R. E. "Establishing and Maintaining High-Commitment Work Systems." In J. R. Kimberly, W. H. Miles, and Associates, *The Organizational Life Cycle: Issues in the Creation, Transformation, and Decline of Organizations.* San Francisco: Jossey-Bass, 1980.

Wechsler, B. "Reinventing Florida's Civil Service System: The Failure of Reform." *Public Administration Review,* 1994, *54*(2), 64–76.

Westley, F. R. "The Eye of the Needle: Cultural and Personal Transformation in a Traditional Organization." *Human Relations,* 1990, *43,* 273–293.

Wise, L. R. "Enhancing Employee Performance." In J. L. Perry (ed.), *Handbook of Public Administration.* (2nd ed.) San Francisco: Jossey-Bass, 1996.

Yin, R. K. "Life Histories of Innovations: How New Practices Become Routinized." *Public Administration Review,* 1981, *41*(1), 21–28.

Chapter Six

Ingredients for Success

Five Factors Necessary for Transforming Government

Hal G. Rainey

This chapter examines administrative reforms in government by drawing from the complex and sprawling literature on the management of organizational change. It looks at the National Performance Review (NPR) as an exercise in the leadership and management of large-scale organizational change. The chapter compares the leadership of the NPR from the top executive level to what experts on organizational change have concluded about successful change. The comparison leads to conclusions about good aspects of the NPR that make it relatively successful, as well as bad aspects that limit its success. More generally, the analysis leads to refinements of the propositions about leading and managing organizational change, especially in the public sector.

The National Performance Review as an Administrative Reform

Although the NPR is described and discussed in other chapters of this book, it is useful to review some of the main features of the reform effort. These aspects of the reform are important in its comparison with points about organizational change emphasized by experts on change. The NPR deserves attention as a major recent reform effort in public management that some experts regard as unprecedented in the attention and activity it has generated (Kettl, 1994).

Early in his administration, President Bill Clinton launched the NPR to operate under the leadership of Vice President Al Gore. A task force made up mostly of employees drawn from federal agencies would conduct an intensive review of federal operations and propose reforms. As part of the review, Vice President Gore conducted meetings with employees in federal agencies, ostensibly to gather ideas about problems and solutions, but with an obvious intention to have a symbolic impact.

The REGO Movement

David Osborne and Ted Gaebler's book *Reinventing Government* (1992) heavily influenced the reform effort. Osborne served as one of the primary consultants to the NPR. The book became a bestseller during the 1990s and has shaped many government reforms in the years since its publication. It provides provocative and challenging ideas about approaches to public management and the delivery of government services. The authors called for more "entrepreneurial" government through such strategies as the following:

- "Catalytic" approaches in which government induces private and nonprofit providers to deliver programs through privatization of public services and other means
- Decentralized and community-owned government, established through such means as encouraging control of programs at the community level and relaxing rules and red tape for government employees and citizens
- Customer-oriented government that increases the attention paid to the "customers" of government programs and responsiveness to their needs
- "Enterprising government," in which government finds ways to make money on its operations
- Competitive and market-oriented government, in which government uses more competition between government programs and between government and the private sector, as well as more market-type mechanisms such as vouchers, tax credits, and user fees
- A strong focus on mission and results, involving more use of performance measures and more emphasis on mission than on rules and procedures

Interestingly, the book's perspective on the state of performance in the public sector was mixed. The authors introduced the book with the claim that, in many ways, government is failing and breaking down. Yet they also argued that government plays an essential role in society and has to define and carry out that role effectively—hence the need for reinvention. In particular, the authors attacked the old-fashioned centralized, bureaucratic model that dominated many government agencies and programs. They called for more entrepreneurial governmental activities to supplant that approach. For proposals about the innovations that would support the entrepreneurial approach, however, they looked to effective practices they had observed around the country. They described many existing activities that illustrated their suggestions for decentralization of government, privatization, control of programs at the community level, attention to the customers of government programs and responsiveness to their needs, support of government's ability to make money on its operations, and creation of more competition between government programs and between government and the private sector. They did this with numerous examples from existing government programs. The purportedly failing government also served as the source of ideas for its own reinvention.

Their proposals had rapid, major impacts, including their influence on the NPR. REGO—for "reinventing government"—became a widely used term in the federal government and other governmental circles. The REGO movement sparked a broad array of developments, including such examples as a reinvention initiative in the state government of Florida and an entrepreneurial effort at getting a hotel built in downtown Visalia, California (Berry, Chackerian, and Wechsler, 1996; Wechsler, 1994; Gurwitt, 1994).

The Progress of the NPR

In many ways, the NPR had a tenor similar to that of *Reinventing Government*. The first report (Gore, 1993a) argued that the federal government needed a drastic overhaul to improve its operations, a reinvention similar to those of many corporations that had reformed themselves in the face of international competition in the 1980s. Yet the report, and Vice President Gore in his public statements and actions (such as his meetings with agency employees), took the position that federal employees were not to blame for the problems. The structures and systems were the problems, the report said, and it emphasized the effort that should be taken to listen to federal employees' ideas and observations.

The report spawned numerous initiatives to reform the structure and operations of the federal government, as well as many change efforts within federal agencies. Exhibit 6.1 summarizes some of the major priorities and initiatives announced in the first NPR report.

As the exhibit suggests, the NPR emphasizes reforms of many of the constraints on federal agencies and their management. The reforms would decentralize and relax personnel and procurement regulations, for example. In addition, many of the reforms reflect currently popular themes and ideas in management practice and writing, such as Total Quality Management, reengineering, and an emphasis on customers, decentralization, empowerment, and relaxing controls. The report thus provides an interesting example of the infusion into government reform of trends and ideas in management.

Predictably, the NPR has been controversial in public administration circles, because of questions about whether it was well conceived and whether it will have lasting and beneficial effects. Its ultimate effects remain to be seen, but without doubt it has caused a lot of activity in federal agencies, as described in Chapters One and Two and the Conclusion. Among other steps, the NPR announced a reduction of about 11 percent of the federal workforce, or over two hundred thousand employees. This gave rise to questions about whether such cuts were really the ulterior motive behind the glowing discourse about reforms, and whether the reform effort was simply part of a recent trend of presidents who have attacked the bureaucracy for political effect (Arnold, 1995). In addition, many of the NPR initiatives were implemented by presidential directives, such as one instructing federal agencies to reduce their internal regulations by 50 percent and one eliminating the elaborate federal personnel manual. Whether such directives will have substantial and lasting effects is also unclear at present.

Other NPR reports have announced additional developments that show the effects of the reform efforts. A presidential directive

Exhibit 6.1. The National Performance Review: Major Priorities and Initiatives.

Cut Red Tape

Streamline the Budget Process: Use biennial budgeting, relax Office of Management and Budget categories and ceilings, allow agencies to roll over 50 percent of funds not spent.

Decentralize Personnel Policy: Eliminate the Federal Personnel Manual; allow departments to conduct their own recruiting, examining, evaluation, and reward systems; simplify the classification system; reduce the time to terminate employees and managers for cause and to deal with poor performers.

Streamline Procurement: Simplify procurement regulations; decentralize General Services Administration authority for buying information technology; allow agencies to buy where they want; rely on the commercial marketplace.

Reorient the Inspectors General: Move from strict compliance auditing to evaluating management control systems.

Eliminate Regulatory Overkill: Eliminate 50 percent of internal agency regulations; improve interagency coordination of regulations; allow agencies to obtain waivers from regulations.

Empower State and Local Governments: Establish an Enterprise Board for new initiatives in community empowerment; limit the use of unfunded mandates; consolidate grant programs into more flexible categories; allow agency heads to grant states and localities selective waivers from regulations and mandates; give control of public housing to local housing authorities with good records.

Put Customers First

Give Customers "Voice" and "Choice."

Make Service Organizations Compete.

Create Market Dynamics and Use Market Mechanisms.

Empower Employees to Get Results

Decentralize Decision Making.

Hold Federal Employees Accountable for Results.

Give Federal Workers the Tools They Need.

Enhance the Quality of Work Life.

Exhibit 6.1. The National Performance Review: Major Priorities and Initiatives, cont'd.

Cut Back to Basics.

Eliminate What We Don't Need.

Collect More.

Invest in Productivity and Reengineer to Cut Costs.

Source: Adapted from Gore, 1993a. Reproduced from H. G. Rainey, 1997, p. 367.

ordered federal agencies to publish customer service standards, and a great many have (Clinton and Gore, 1995). Follow-up reports have announced indications of progress, such as reductions in regulations, cost savings of fifty-eight billion dollars, and a variety of steps in different agencies to improve operations and services (Gore, 1995). One of the efforts under the NPR involved a presidential directive ordering federal agencies to set up "reinvention laboratories" that would work on improving procedures within agencies. In some cases, these reinvention labs have reported success in finding improved and innovative ways of carrying out their agency's business, although they have also encountered many obstacles to change (Sanders and Thompson, 1996; see also Chapters One and Two).

Whether or not the NPR achieves significant long-term reforms depends in large part on political developments, such as whether the Clinton administration remains in office and continues to devote emphasis to the reforms. Controversy over the sincerity, design, and effects of the initiative will continue for years. The NPR nevertheless is one of the major developments in efforts to enhance excellence in public management. It illustrates many of the obstacles to such efforts, but it also illustrates some of the elements of effective public management and the leadership of reform and change. While critics may be right about many problems with the NPR, it has clearly exerted far more influence on the federal agencies than many other reform efforts, such as the Reagan administration's Grace Commission.

The Grace Commission (The President's Private Sector Survey on Cost Control) was an ad hoc independent commission staffed by employees loaned by the private sector to conduct an analysis of waste and cost-cutting opportunities in the federal agencies. It conducted such an analysis and proposed changes that purportedly would achieve four hundred billion dollars in savings across a number of years. The commission's activities, however, had virtually no impact on federal operations. The activities stimulated by the NPR, described in other chapters and above, provide a striking contrast to the ultimate impotence of the Grace Commission. What accounts for the moderate success of the NPR so far, at least relative to many other reform efforts? One way to look for answers is to compare the general leadership of the NPR to some of the prescriptions for leading organizational change from the literature on that topic. This comparison also leads to some suggestions about the limitations of the NPR, and to refinement of some of the prescriptions for leading change as they apply to government reforms.

Analyses of Large-Scale Organizational Change

The literature on large-scale organizational change is quite diverse and difficult to summarize succinctly (Facer and Rainey, 1996). However, two articles published some thirty years apart, whose authors summarize patterns of organizational change and transformation, provide valuable observations about analyzing and managing successful initiatives. Although they were published several decades apart, they show interesting similarities.

In 1967, Greiner reported an analysis of eighteen cases of major organizational-change attempts, in which he drew conclusions about the patterns of successful change. He found that some frequently used approaches to change usually fail. These unsuccessful approaches include unilateral actions, such as top-down decrees or commands for structural changes, and limited attempts at power sharing through group decision making. The successful change efforts that Greiner observed involved much more comprehensive approaches, as illustrated in Exhibit 6.2.

As the exhibit suggests, Greiner's observations about successful patterns of change emphasize the following conditions and steps:

Exhibit 6.2. Patterns of Successful Organizational Change.

Phase I: Pressure and Arousal

1. Significant External and Internal Pressure for Change.

   Widespread conviction of the need for change, perception of performance gaps.

   Pressure on top management.

Phase II: Intervention and Reorientation

2. A New Person Enters as Change Leader.

   The person has a record as a successful change agent.

   The person enters as a leader of the organization or a consultant working with the leader.

3. The New Person Leads a Reexamination of Past Practices and Current Problems.

   The newcomer uses an external, objective perspective to encourage examination of old views and rationalizations, attention to "real" problems.

4. Top Management Is Heavily Involved in Reexamination.

   The head of the organization and immediate subordinates assume a direct, heavily involved role in the reexamination.

Phase III: Diagnosis and Recognition

5. The Change Leader Engages Multiple Levels in Diagnosis.

   The change leader involves multiple levels and units in collaborative, fact-finding, problem-solving discussions to identify and diagnose current problems.

   The diagnosis involves significant power sharing.

Phase IV: Invention and Commitment

6. The Change Leader Stimulates Widespread Searches for Creative Solutions, Involving Many Levels.

Phase V: Experimentation and Search

7. Solutions Are Developed, Tested, and Proven on a Small Scale.

   Problems are worked out and solved. Experimentation is encouraged.

Phase VI: Reinforcement and Acceptance

8. Successes Are Reinforced and Disseminated and Breed Successes.

   People are rewarded. Successes become accepted and institutionalized.

Source: Adapted from Greiner, 1967. Reproduced from H. G. Rainey, 1997, p. 337.

1. A pressure for improvement is felt widely among people within the organization and among relevant actors outside.
2. A new person is brought in as head of the organization or as a consultant to lead the change effort.
3. Top executives involve themselves very heavily in beginning and sustaining the change process.
4. The change agent (new head or consultant), with the involvement of top executives, initiates a general diagnosis.
5. The change agent leads this diagnosis in a multilevel, collaborative, fact-finding and problem-solving process aimed at identifying and diagnosing the key problems. Representatives of many units and levels participate. The human resource or personnel unit is heavily involved.
6. Participants develop solutions.
7. The solutions are tested on a small scale, then implemented and tested on a wider scale.
8. Participants use successes to reinforce results, and the results become widely accepted.

As indicated in step 5 in Phase III of the exhibit and implied in other phases, Greiner concludes that power sharing serves as a crucial element in successful patterns: success requires it and it must occur through a developmental process. In many of the failed efforts at change, leaders sought to rely on unilateral pressures for change, with an illogical sequence of steps.

In 1995, John Kotter, a prominent author on leadership, organizational change, and other topics, published another article in the *Harvard Business Review* on organizational change. The article presented observations about failures in organizational "transformations" (a currently fashionable term for large-scale, comprehensive change efforts). Exhibit 6.3 summarizes the opposite of Kotter's observations—that is, the reasons for failure transposed into requirements for success. Kotter's observations differ from Greiner's in certain ways. Kotter places more emphasis on "vision." He also refers to a "guiding coalition," in contrast to Greiner's focus on a change leader who comes in from the outside (although Greiner did emphasize power sharing). Kotter's phrasing is consistent with other recent research on large-scale change in organizations. Very recent studies (Huber and Glick, 1993) emphasize the essential roles of "shared values," which can equate to "vision" in

Exhibit 6.3. Steps for Successful Organizational Transformations.

1. Establish a Sense of Urgency.
   Examine market and competitive realities.
   Identify crises and/or opportunities.

2. Form a Powerful Guiding Coalition.
   Assemble a group with enough power to lead the change effort.
   Encourage the group to work as a team.

3. Create a Vision.
   Create a vision to help direct the change effort.
   Develop strategies for achieving the vision.

4. Communicate the Vision.
   Use all available means to communicate the new vision and strategy.
   Teaches new behaviors by example.

5. Empower Others to Act on the Vision.
   Remove obstacles to change.
   Change systems or structures that present obstacles.

6. Create Short-Term Wins.
   Plan for visible performance improvements.
   Create those improvements.
   Recognize and reward employees involved in those improvements.

7. Consolidate Improvements and Produce Further Change.
   Use increased credibility to change systems, structures, and policies to pursue the vision.
   Hire and develop employees who can implement the vision.

8. Institutionalize the New Approaches.
   Articulate the connections between the new behaviors and cooperate for success.
   Ensure leadership development and succession.

Source: Adapted from Kotter, 1995. Reproduced from H. G. Rainey, 1997, p. 339.

important ways, and leadership teams, rather than individual, heroic leaders.

The similarities between these two views, thirty years apart, are striking and provide a simple but deceptively demanding framework and set of guidelines for large-scale organizational change:

1. A widespread belief in the need for change
2. Clear, sustained leadership including support from top executives
3. Power sharing and broad participation in diagnosing problems and planning the change
4. The development of a guiding vision for the change
5. Flexible and incremental implementation, including experimentation, feedback, adaptation, and building on successes to institutionalize changes

These elements appear luxurious for public sector organizations, since many of them face frequent turnover of top executives, interventions and constraints from external authorities, and other conditions that might block some of the steps. This raises the question of whether Greiner's and Kotter's analyses, concentrated as they are on private firms or other nongovernment organizations, can apply to the executive branch of government and its agencies. The next section describes an example of change in a federal agency that suggests that their conclusions certainly can be applied.

Change in a Federal Agency

In the 1960s, the Social Security Administration (SSA) became overloaded and backlogged in processing claims for Retirement and Survivors' Insurance (RSI)—that is, social security payments. Clients complained to the SSA and to members of Congress, who demanded that the agency solve the problem. At one point, the SSA struggled with a backlog of one million claims. Something had to be done. The agency ultimately solved the problem through a highly successful reorganization of its major claims-processing units. It reorganized the work process by forming work modules that contained all the specialists needed to process a claim from beginning to end. The change involved a major transformation, not just of structure and process, but also of culture. It also implemented a variant of team-based work design that, according to some accounts, received praise from prominent business executives as superior to their own attempts at such designs. The change included many elements of team-based work design and reengineering well before those concepts became hot topics in management.

The problem of backlogged cases had developed largely because Congress had added many new programs and new forms of coverage to the original social security program; for example, it extended coverage to dependents, farmers, the self-employed, and the disabled. Together with population growth, these additions continually expanded the number of claims to be processed.

The organizational system for handling the claims involved major functional bureaus for the RSI program, disability insurance, data processing and records, and supervision of the district offices. The district offices, located around the country, took in claims from clients applying for benefits. For the RSI program, the offices forwarded the claims to one of six program service centers (PSCs). These PSCs were located in six regions of the country. Each had around two thousand employees. When a claim arrived at a PSC from the district office, a clerical support unit would prepare a folder for the claimant and forward it to a claims unit. There, a claims authorizer would determine the type and degree of eligibility for social security payments. Then the folder would be forwarded to a payments unit, where a benefit authorizer would compute the amount of the benefit payment. Next, the folder would go to an accounts unit, which would assemble and code information about the case, then to another unit for entry into the computer, and finally to a records maintenance unit for storage. In some of these units, hundreds of people worked at desks in long rows, receiving deliveries of stacks of folders from shopping carts, with coffee and lunch breaks announced by the ringing of bells. Control clerks and supervisors, who heavily emphasized the technical issues and production rates of their unit, checked the work for accuracy.

Any incomplete information or disagreements among the technical specialists would delay a claim, because it would have to be sent back to an earlier point in the process for clarification or correction. The communication about the problem usually had to be in writing. There was no provision for getting it back to the same person who had done the earlier work. The increasing numbers of claims and the complications in many of them increasingly clogged the system.

Robert Ball, the long-term, highly respected SSA commissioner, appointed an experienced SSA official, Hugh McKenna, as director of the RSI bureau, with a mandate to correct the problems. McKenna initiated an open-ended process of change with four years of research, development, experimentation, and morale building. Several task forces with internal and external representation studied management processes, case handling, and labor relations. A consulting firm analyzed the case management process. Large team-building and morale-boosting meetings were held between the managers and staff of the PSCs, the district offices, and the RSI central office. The office staff worked with the PSCs to develop training courses on participatory management. Significantly, some of the participants reportedly commented that McKenna "*ordered* participatory management." He did, but obviously with crucial flexibility and sophistication in the way that the order was imposed.

Out of these developments emerged a concept for a modular claims-processing unit. The planning staff in the central office suggested setting up a smaller unit of fifty employees, containing all the technical specialists needed to process claims, and letting them handle a claim from beginning to end. Citing the ideas of Douglas McGregor, Frank Herzberg, Rensis Likert, and Abraham Maslow, the proponents of the module concept argued that it would provide job enrichment and participatory management. Employees would have more identity with the task and the clients as individuals, easier access to supervisors and managers, and more control over the flow of claims processing and their part in it.

One of the PSCs tried out such a unit on an experimental basis and then adopted a total of six modules. Problems arose. At one point, when productivity dropped in the modules, termination of the experiment was seriously considered. However, the staff decided that the problems could be corrected, and they ultimately did correct them. Relations with other agencies, such as the Civil Service Commission (now the Office of Personnel Management), required skillful handling in attempts to obtain new space and receive approval of new personnel structures. Ultimately, other PSCs adopted the modules.

The modular concept became widely accepted in the agency as a success. Processing time for new claims improved, and employee surveys showed increased job satisfaction in the modules. There were some bad results; for example, some long-term employees disliked the change and took early retirement, and later personnel cutbacks made it difficult to properly staff some of the modules. Nevertheless, many people in the agency regarded the modular concept as successful.

This success may simply reflect proper application of some of the principles of change noted earlier. The change involved widely shared recognition of the need for it; support from the top and sustained leadership; flexible implementation with adaptation, feedback, and experimentation; and a realistic strategy for achieving the objectives of the agency. The change did, in a sense, have a top-down character, but it appears to illustrate what the experts mean by support from the top: it must include process sponsors and process champions with sufficient authority and resources. In addition, the change did not involve leadership by an outside consultant or change agent, although McKenna could be regarded as having played such a role.

Some particulars about the SSA case may distinguish it from other cases involving federal agencies. The SSA had as its chief executive a long-term career civil servant who had enjoyed trust and support from key congressional figures and thus could gain a grant of authority to solve the agency's problems without interference. The SSA has strong support from a large clientele receiving a specific service, and the agency's tasks tend to be clear and mechanistic. The people in the agency were able to encapsulate their work processes and management and seal them off from political intervention.

While such factors, as well as the generic principles of successful change, may have provided the SSA with advantages, the case suggests additional considerations, summarized in Exhibit 6.4 (Rainey, 1990). The SSA had a durable, skillful power center, committed to successful change. Ironically, for all the stereotypes about career bureaucrats who resist change, in this case the long-term civil servants were the champions of change. They utilized their knowledge of the political and administrative system to sustain that change. Also, they were not leaving soon. They had a career commitment to the agency, so they wanted the changes to succeed, and they and others knew that they would be there for the duration.

Exhibit 6.4. Conditions of a Successful Change in a Federal Agency.

1. A Durable Power Center, Committed to Successful Change.

   Strong, stable leadership by career civil servants.

   An internal change agent (career agency executive) with authority and resources.

   Active, creative bureau staff.

2. Appropriate Timing for Collective Support.

   Political "window of opportunity."

   Political overseers (congressional committee heads) who were supportive but noninterventionist.

   Political sophistication of agency leaders and staff—effective management of relations with Congress and oversight agencies (Office of Personnel Management, General Services Administration).

   Strategies blending sincere employee involvement with decisive exercise of authority.

3. A Comprehensive, Clear, Realistic Alternative Process.

   A long-term change strategy, using group processes to develop new structures.

   A major structural reform, focused on measurable outputs, that decentralizes operational responsibility.

   Reasonable clarity about the nature and objectives of the new structure and process.

Source: Adapted from Rainey and Rainey, 1986a, 1986b. Reproduced from H. G. Rainey, 1997.

The SSA change took place at the appropriate time for collective support. No distracting crises or controversies weighed against it. The need for change was widely recognized inside and outside the SSA. In part, this reflects luck; in part, it reflects the skill of experienced public managers and staff members who knew when and how to work for better alternatives. Indeed, they did develop a better alternative, one that was comprehensive, clear, and realistic. Vague, prepackaged models, such as management by objective, will fail if they are not adapted to fit structural and cultural conditions within particular organizations. The sponsors and champions of the change in the SSA applied relatively firm, consistent pressure for a reasonably clear, realistic idea, while allowing a degree of experimentation and variation in its implementation.

In many ways, the conditions of successful change in this example coincide with the characteristics of successful change described by Greiner and Kotter. This point, however, does suggest an additional consideration. Greiner's analysis said little about the substantive characteristics of the change itself—about what would change, and into what. Kotter mentions a "vision" for the change, and thereby suggests that one has to develop a reasonable sense of the substance of the change—again, of what will change, and how—that people can buy into and implement. The SSA case suggests an additional item for our simple framework of successful organizational change:

6. The development of good ideas about what to do—of realistic, attractive alternative processes

We can now apply to the NPR our simple model, or outline, of change.

The NPR as a Large-Scale Organizational Change

The NPR represents an interesting example of how to manage, or at least try to manage, large-scale organizational change if we take our list of conditions as a model. We could debate the various characteristics of the NPR and its implementation endlessly, but we can give it relatively high marks on the factors in the list described below.

The Need for Change and Urgency of Change

Critics charge that the NPR focuses on incremental administrative repairs rather than on fundamental institutional issues such as the effects of pluralistic politics. It simply displaces public concern about excessive and ineffective government by essentially blaming it on the bureaucracy and not on the political forces surrounding it (Arnold, 1995). The emphasis on the poor performance of government agencies and programs and on the need for management techniques that mimic industry may well be another exercise in misdiagnosing the maladies of government that other reforms have represented (Peters and Savoie, 1994).

If we consider the problem of building support for change and the sense of urgency about change, however, the inflated and distorted references to bureaucratic malfunctions become more understandable. Faced with survey information and many other indications of widespread public disaffection with the federal government and the federal bureaucracy, it seems reasonable that a chief executive would attempt to harness those public sentiments, respond to them, and use them to fuel constructive changes. The president's ability to mobilize support from many external stakeholders, including Congress, has been complicated by the electoral success of the opposing party and consequent dramatic shifts in the leadership of Congress. Still, the NPR has received considerable public attention and press coverage, as well as generally favorable support from external stakeholders, for being a "good government" reform with limited potential for high political payoffs. The critics' concerns about the bureaucracy-blaming aspects of the NPR are well taken, but the criticisms implicitly acknowledge the energetic efforts of the administration to generate support for the initiative.

In addition, as noted earlier, in rhetoric launching the NPR and in its first report, the administration did absolve government employees of the blame for the problems and instead blamed the administrative "systems" that they worked in. The report announced the intention of involving federal employees in solving the problems because they are the ones who best know how to do so. (Those of us who lament the "bureaucrat bashing" in the United States and some other nations in recent decades need to remember that some of the most sustained criticisms of the administrative systems come from the bureaucrats themselves.) The vice president conducted meetings in agencies to further the symbolic emphasis on involving federal employees. The reinvention labs and many other features of the reform sought to encourage activities within the agencies, and they explicitly sought to stimulate bottom-up change processes. For these and other reasons, the NPR clearly has generated a great deal of activity in agencies, and many agencies obviously have taken the initiative very seriously. In spite of inevitable patterns of resistance, the initiative appears to have been effective in mobilizing considerable support from many internal stakeholders.

Leadership

The president has devoted considerable direct attention to the NPR. The vice president became the highest-ranking official to take direct charge of any of the major administrative reform efforts in recent history. As suggested above, he has devoted considerable time and attention to the initiatives. One might question the leadership role of the ad hoc task force that purportedly provides central guidance for the NPR, but executive leadership has been reasonably strong and sustained for an initiative of this type.

Participation and Power Sharing

The rhetoric of the reform and its various reports may make overblown claims about empowerment, but many features of the NPR do emphasize increases in participation and the authorization of actions within the agencies. Some of the efforts to involve federal employees and enlist their support have been described above. The reinvention labs are another such feature. The strategy behind their creation was to encourage bottom-up innovation and even, as Sanders describes in Chapter Two, a "guerrilla war." As described earlier, in spite of formidable obstacles, some of the labs are quite successful in generating innovative procedures (Sanders and Thompson, 1996; also see Chapters One and Two). Many of the NPR's proposals call for agencies to establish their own systems, such as performance management systems, recruitment and hiring systems, and incentive and bonus systems. The NPR also proposes authorizing or encouraging agencies to adopt such innovations as broadbanding systems, gain-sharing programs, and other programs for which demonstration projects and other evidence have provided promising results.

Good Ideas

As these examples of ideas for drawing on demonstration projects suggest, the NPR often seeks to draw on past experiences for relatively clear and feasible programs in human resource management.

In addition, many people in the agencies have evidently found the concept of the reinvention lab to be reasonably attractive and feasible, and the labs themselves have become a source of good ideas that can be disseminated.

Institutionalization of Successes and Small Wins

As this last point about the reinvention labs suggests, the NPR provides in various ways for the incremental, flexible, and experimental development of changes and their implementation. The NPR report on human resource management, for example, reads as if it had been developed under the influence of the analyses of organizational change depicted in Exhibits 6.1–6.3 and the simple model this discussion is following (Gore, 1993b). The report acknowledges the limited successes of earlier programs such as pay-for-performance plans, and especially the need to avoid imposing such plans rigidly across all agencies, as previous reform efforts have sometimes attempted to do. In proposing the adoption of ideas from demonstration projects, such as broadbanding, the report acknowledges the limits to the evidence provided by the demonstrations about how widely applicable the programs might be. The proposals then recommend authorizing and encouraging agencies to develop and shape the ideas in relation to their particular conditions. Obviously, this may be the point on which the reforms founder, in that gaining such authorization may be difficult. Nevertheless, the report and its proposals tend to follow the model one might draw from some of the research on the management of organizational change. That model discourages rigid, top-down, system-wide mandates and prescribes more participative, experimental, bottom-up development and dissemination of reforms. While there are myriad complications, the NPR follows that model in many ways; this appears to bode well for the success of at least some of its initiatives and to explain the successes thus far.

Limitations of the National Performance Review as an Organizational Change

To this point, this chapter has discussed the good aspects of the NPR as an exercise in the leadership and management of organizational change. Now we turn to the not-so-good features of the effort. The emphasis on the good things about the change so far in this chapter shows that the point here is not simply to criticize or deride the effort. The objective is to refine our thinking about successful change and to pinpoint needs and challenges.

Reinventing Government and Blurred Vision

Reinventing government, both as the subject of a book and as a reform movement, has been widely discussed and critiqued (see, for example, Kettl, 1994; Moe, 1994). Critics have complained that REGO tends to blame the administrative agencies for problems in government and to locate the solution there, when the problems often come from other sources, such as poorly conceived directives from the legislative branch. Hence, the diagnosis and the solutions should actually focus on other institutions in addition to the executive agencies. Critics also worry that applications of REGO often have a scattershot or patchwork quality. Berry, Chackerian, and Wechsler (1996) describe the reinvention effort in Florida as involving a diffuse array of directions and initiatives—reforming the civil service system, adopting strategic management, adopting Total Quality Management, using performance measures and new budgeting procedures, restructuring agencies, and reforming regulatory practices, as well as other efforts. Predictably, the results have been mixed.

Berry, Chackerian, and Wechsler see progress in some areas, such as strategic management, where the agencies themselves can control the process of change. Reforms involving larger systemic and institutional issues, such as civil service reform, have shown little success. Similarly, early in the process, Kettl (1994) expressed concern over the patchwork nature of the NPR, and his concern was prescient. The framework for successful change developed earlier in this chapter emphasized the importance of vision and of good ideas and alternatives. REGO offers little help with the full development of these matters and appears inclined toward shortcomings in these areas. REGO is both susceptible to and perhaps conducive to blurred vision, rather than strategic vision.

For all its virtues, Osborne and Gaebler's *Reinventing Government* essentially compiles a set of bright ideas about new—or at least underutilized—ways of doing business in government, with some glib and uncritical descriptions of examples of these ideas in practice, but with virtually no attention paid to the challenges of implementing them. REGO, in itself, devotes virtually no attention to the management and implementation of change. Its prescriptions raise many complex challenges for leading, motivating, designing, and strategizing for change, but it remains virtually silent on these matters. For example, privatization of public service, one of REGO's many prescriptions, is an issue as old as the Republic and replete with controversies and examples of failure. Ironically, privatization, often touted as necessary because of bad public management, requires excellent public management to be successful (Rainey, 1997, pp. 369–375).

Of course, one can defend REGO as a source of good ideas to be used strategically and selectively. The authors do not direct leaders in government to pursue all the ideas in scattershot fashion, and they have no authority to stop them from doing so. The book itself has energized government officials and employees. It supports a general vision of a government that will become more energetic, innovative, and responsive through harnessing the ingenuity and creativity of its employees. Yet the basic premise that government needs reinvention along many dimensions, using a diverse array of strategies that remain loosely described and articulated, tends to blur the vision of what is to be accomplished, and how, and to offer a series of often dubious alternatives, rather than attractive, persuasive ones.

As Berry, Chackerian, and Wechsler point out, political leaders often have a strong incentive to overpromise about reforms. We might also add that they feel the need for attractive ideas, for proposals that sound good and that they can tout to the public as bold, valuable steps they are taking. One lesson from the NPR and other REGO exercises is that leaders need to concentrate on developing a feasible, reasonable vision and set of alternatives that avoids the patchwork problem.

The Challenge of Sustained, Substantial Leadership

As indicated above, even if REGO is inclined to diffuse vision, leaders can work to refine and focus vision. Also, as suggested in the earlier discussion of the NPR, it has the general outline of effective executive leadership. The initiative has received considerable support and attention from the top executives—the president and vice president. The NPR includes encouragement of the agencies to select from a variety of possible reforms and to establish the reinvention labs. This approach conforms to the general outline of successful leadership of change described earlier. We can interpret the approach as involving executive encouragement and empowerment of the lower levels to experiment and innovate, under a broad vision of achieving a more responsive, more effective, more flexible, and less bureaucratic government. Then, presumably, the most effective alternatives may be recognized and disseminated.

Yet this perspective also raises some nuances about the leadership of organizational transformations. There must be some sustained support for innovations and innovators, which usually must involve higher-level executives. The political top executives must find ways to provide sustained, substantial support, and not merely symbolic support. Symbolic support can be very important. In Chapter Two, Ronald Sanders describes the valuable role of the vice president in providing general permission to innovators in agencies who are working in the reinvention labs. Sanders also describes the exciting developments that were seen as these innovators engaged in a guerrilla war after being incited to revolution by the vice president. The hope, of course, is that the new, effective practices will build upon themselves. Their success will stimulate others to adopt them, more guerrillas will join, and the revolution will spread. Symbolic "permission" has its limits, however. Sanders mentions disturbing instances in which the leaders who sought to be innovative and to press for change in the reinvention labs ultimately met with reprisals from their colleagues and superiors who had not joined the revolution. He also describes complaints from people working with the reinvention labs about political appointees from the administration who did not support the efforts of the labs.

Numerous examples are now coming in from industry and government that illustrate the problem that commonly is seen when a higher-level executive seeks to "empower" lower-level employees. Unless it is very skillfully managed, the empowerment effort can make managers at levels between those of the higher executive and the lower-level employees feel threatened. They tend to see the power that is going to the lower levels as coming at their expense. If the reinvention labs, as well as other innovations and changes, are to have sustained success, the top leadership of the administration has to find ways to provide sustained, substantive support for the reformers in the system and for dissemination of the reforms. The impediments to such support are well known in the public administration field. They include the rapid political turnover, or possible turnover, of politically elected executives and their appointees. Political rivals will seek to discredit and dismantle changes that the executives sponsor. There are well-known patterns of resistance in the agencies, including residual skepticism about changes because so many have failed in the past. The public and the press do not get particularly aroused over issues of administrative reform and good-government improvements.

Against such impediments, what might top executives do? The president and vice president can raise to a higher level on their own agenda the support and protection of innovators in the system. In some organizations, top executives have focused executives' and managers' attention on employee development by including this type of development as an element of the performance evaluations of all executives and managers. Political chief executives do not conduct formal performance evaluations in the way that executives in business firms and government agencies do, but they can certainly make it clear that encouragement and support for leaders and participants in reinvention labs is a very high priority for them, one that they will back up in a variety of ways. Executive attention to individual cases can have a supportive effect in itself, especially if it is handled skillfully and positively in a way that shows benefits, such as good publicity, for the superiors of the individual the vice president is attending to.

A stronger organizational base for the NPR can be considered, to translate executive leadership and support into organizational form. The obvious dilemma is to avoid the creation of still another bureaucracy as a purported means of reforming the bureaucracy, but to provide a more substantial base for NPR initiatives than the current ad hoc task force. The dilemma is aggravated further by the probable resistance in Congress to providing resources and authorization for another bureaucracy, especially one sponsored by the opposing party. An example from the state of Georgia suggests a possibility, however. The governor appointed a Commission on Economy and Effectiveness in Government to seek reforms and improvements. One task force of the commission concentrated on privatization. Rather than rushing to propose privatization of specific services, the privatization task force concentrated on developing an effective process for assessing privatization projects. Among other steps, the task force recommended establishment of a standing commission on privatization with a lean staff, headed by an experienced, reputable executive, to study, propose, and implement privatization initiatives. The commission has been appointed, headed by a well-respected executive with extensive experience in state government. Numerous privatization initiatives have gone forward successfully, with the commission receiving praise from the press for careful, deliberative handling of privatization initiatives.

Obviously, the example raises myriad complex political issues when it is applied to the NPR. It suggests, however, the value of considering a nonpartisan standing commission with an experienced executive leading it, a lean staff, sunset provisions, and a bipartisan board of directors or advisers. The commission could concentrate on identifying the most successful developments of the NPR and supporting them and their dissemination. The commission's activities could focus on a more clearly defined set of NPR initiatives, such as performance measurement, customer service standards, the reinvention labs, and carefully selected additions to this list.

Whether or not these proposals prove convincing to many people, they dramatize some of the challenges and nuances of leading organizational change in the public sector that we need to add to the frameworks and outlines of the sort illustrated earlier in this chapter. Practitioners and academics alike have to seek progress in understanding how to effectively define a vision and a feasible set of alternatives for reform efforts. We have to help leaders find ways to move effectively beyond rhetoric and ribbon cutting, as well as providing sustained, substantial support that will transform "guerrillas," who fight lonely battles at considerable odds, into a growing population of cohesive, mutually informative innovators in the public service.

References

Arnold, P. E. "Reform's Changing Role." *Public Administration Review,* 1995, *55,* 407–417.

Berry, F. S., Chackerian, R., and Wechsler, B. "Administrative Reform: Lessons from a State Capital." Paper presented at the American Society for Public Administration National Conference, Atlanta, July 2, 1996.

Clinton, W. J., and Gore, A., Jr. *Putting Customers First '95: Standards for Serving the American People.* Washington, D.C.: U.S. Government Printing Office, 1995.

Facer, R., and Rainey, H. G. "Organizational Change: Assessing the Public Sector Context and Learning from Studies of the Private Sector." *Society and Economy in Central and Eastern Europe,* 1996, *17,* 49–75.

Gore, A., Jr. *From Red Tape to Results: Creating a Government That Works Better and Costs Less.* Report of the National Performance Review. Washington, D.C.: U.S. Government Printing Office, 1993a.

Gore, A., Jr. *From Red Tape to Results: Creating a Government That Works Better and Costs Less. Reinventing Human Resource Management.* Accompanying Report of the National Performance Review. Washington, D.C.: U.S. Government Printing Office, 1993b.

Gore, A., Jr. *Common Sense Government: Works Better and Costs Less.* Report of the National Performance Review. Washington, D.C.: U.S. Government Printing Office, 1995.

Greiner, L. E. "Patterns of Organizational Change." *Harvard Business Review,* 1967, *45,* 119–128.

Gurwitt, R. "The Entrepreneurial Gamble." *Governing,* May 1994.

Horner, C. "Deregulating the Federal Service: Is the Time Right?" In J. J. Di Iulio Jr. (ed.), *Deregulating the Public Service.* Washington, D.C.: Brookings Institution, 1994.

Huber, G. P., and Glick, W. H. (eds.). *Organizational Change and Redesign.* New York: Oxford University Press, 1993.

Kettl, D. F. *Reinventing Government? Appraising the National Performance Review.* Washington, D.C.: Brookings Institution, 1994.

Kotter, J. P. "Leading Change: Why Transformation Efforts Fail." *Harvard Business Review,* Mar.–Apr. 1995, pp. 59–67.

Moe, R. C. "The 'Reinventing Government' Exercise: Misinterpreting the Problem, Misjudging the Consequences." *Public Administration Review,* 1994, *54,* 111.

Osborne, D., and Gaebler, T. *Reinventing Government.* Reading, Mass.: Addison Wesley Longman, 1992.

Peters, B. G., and Savoie, D. "Civil Service Reform: Misdiagnosing the Patient." *Public Administration Review,* 1994, *54,* 418–425.

Rainey, G. W. "Implementation and Managerial Creativity: A Study of the Development of Client-Centered Units in Human Service Programs." In D. J. Palumbo and D. J. Calista (eds.), *Implementation and the Policy Process.* Westport, Conn.: Greenwood Press, 1990.

Rainey, G. W., and Rainey, H. G. "Breaching the Hierarchical Imperative: The Modularization of the Social Security Claims Process." In D. J. Calista (ed.), *Bureaucratic and Governmental Reform.* Greenwich, Conn.: JAI Press, 1986a.

Rainey, G. W., and Rainey, H. G. "Structural Overhaul in a Government Agency." *Public Administration Quarterly,* 1986b, *10,* 206–223.

Rainey, H. G. *Understanding and Managing Public Organizations.* (2nd ed.) San Francisco: Jossey-Bass, 1997.

Sanders, R. P., and Thompson, J. R. "The Reinvention Revolution: A Special Report." *Government Executive* (Special Supplement), Mar. 1996, pp. 1–12.

Wechsler, B. "Reinventing Florida's Civil Service System: The Failure of Reform." *Public Administration Review,* 1994, *54*(2), 64–76.

Chapter Seven

Tailoring Change Strategies

Alternative Approaches to Reform

B. Guy Peters

The contemporary spate of organizational change, reform, and "reinvention" in the U.S. federal government, as well as in governments around the world, points to the need to understand better the processes through which change can be brought about successfully in the public sector (Aucoin, 1995). Scholars of public administration, and most especially practitioners of the arts of government, often assume that they can produce change when and where they perceive the need for that change. This presumed ease of producing desired changes within and among government organizations is manifestly not the case, and most histories of government reorganization provide instructive case studies of attempts at change that produced nothing, or sometimes worse than nothing (Szanton, 1981; Pollitt, 1984). The numerous exercises in planned organizational change now under way in the United States (at both federal and subnational levels) and almost everywhere else (Zifcak, 1994; Peters and Savoie, 1995; Kickert and van Vught, 1995) can serve as a useful laboratory for understanding the possibilities for planned organizational change.

One of the important, if generally unstated, features of this eruption of organizational change is that organizations, and the people who populate them, do matter in government. Much of the history of the 1980s in the public sector reflected the tendency to denigrate public employees and to attempt to discover some manner of eliminating as many employees as possible. The experience of the 1990s, on the other hand, has in some ways been more positive. The numerous attempts to "make government work better and cost less" and to achieve other, similar sets of goals have required political leaders to pay greater attention to the structure of government and the skills and motivations of their public employees. This (slightly) more positive conception of the public sector may be short-lived, given the negative political forces that are gathering in many countries, but for a short time the opportunity exists to produce positive change. This, then, is also a crucial time for public servants. They must demonstrate their willingness to change, while simultaneously finding some way to retain the values that have motivated them in the past and that continue to be important for managing a responsible public service (de Montricher, 1996).

This context helps us to understand contemporary efforts at change in American government. Efforts at administrative reform in American government appear to reflect three implicit models of the way to produce change, which can be compared and evaluated as they are being implemented. These three models are (1) change from the top down, (2) change from the bottom up, and (3) change induced through external, imposed circumstances. Although in practice it is not always clear how any particular reform should be classified, these categories are still analytically useful for understanding the sources of change and the unfolding pattern of its implementation. Also, all these change strategies must face the same barriers, as outlined by David Frederickson and James Perry in Chapter Five of this volume.

Comparison of these reforms is easier than is evaluation, however, given that they have rather different goals. Top-down reforms generally attempt to impose a uniform model of management across the public sector, while the other two models appear to provide greater freedom for individual organizations and their members to shape their own definitions of appropriate management. The budget-driven change strategy, in particular, tends not to notice differences between particular management strategies, as long as the overriding goal is to reduce public expenditure and/or public employment is achieved. In addition, as we will elaborate below, a reform strategy that is effective in one setting may not be in others.

Change from the Top Down

The first model for organizational change is a top-down imposition of change. This change strategy has been the most common historically, but it is probably the least commonly observed strategy in the contemporary reforms in the United States. Still, there is some tendency for current reforms to demand that organizations invent their own changes, even if they are content with the way they already function. The National Performance Review, for example, provided some principles by which organizations were to restructure themselves and assumed that those principles would be followed by organizations' "reinventing themselves." It is not clear how the supportive, fostering attitude that emanates from many of the contemporary change advocates would react to an organization that wanted to retain a more hierarchical structure, or even to increase its internal hierarchy, when it was given the opportunity to design its own future. It may be that, ironically, the old top-down model may be reasserted if organizations do not want to change in an appropriate manner. (This is perhaps unfair, given that organizations that have been reinvented have tended to follow the assumed lines of reform.)

In general, any reforms imposed from the top tend to enjoy limited success. Most organizations have a culture of their own and tend to resist imposition of external ideas (Schein, 1985). In the public sector this resistance appears to be manifested whether the ideas come from the administrative head of the organization itself or from a political leader operating totally outside the organization. The one major exception to this general rule appears to emerge when a political leader is able to develop an ideological or value-based statement to justify the changes and then get the employees to "buy in" to that thought pattern. For example, the success of a number of Republican state governments in reforming social programs over the past several years can be seen as a form of change imposed from above. This change was successful in part because the governors were able to convince employees that the changes were better for the state and perhaps even for the clients. In some settings these ideas have been adopted almost as if they were the ideas of the workers themselves (Thompson, 1993).

There are other instances in which changes emanating from above have produced effective change (Kotter, 1995). Perhaps the principal types of organizations in which imposed reforms can be reliably successful are those that are themselves hierarchical, such as the military, paramilitary organizations, criminal justice services, and some traditional corporate settings. This assumption of hierarchy now appears somewhat suspect; even military management is now adopting the more participative style associated with the most effective change. In addition, imposed change would have been easier historically because society itself was more hierarchical, and it may still be easier in societies within the United States that remain more hierarchical, for example, some of the southern states.

In general, attempting to generate effective organizational change from above is unlikely to produce the types of outcomes intended by the designer (Hage and Finsterbusch, 1989). This may be a result of malice and designed resistance to change, but it is more likely merely the result of inertia and the resilience of organizational cultures. Even if an externally imposed change can generate compliance in the short run, it may well fail in the longer run as organizations revert to type. For example, administrative reforms over the years in the United States and elsewhere appear to have been swallowed up as the inertia of government agencies drives them toward persistence rather than change. (One of the interesting exceptions to this generalization has been the success of the British government under Margaret Thatcher in institutionalizing a series of very radical changes; Hood, 1996.)

Even within the top-down approach, however, there can be different approaches to generating change. One of the more common approaches to contemporary reform has been to shop around for reform packages that can be "bought" off the shelf. Most of these are ideas that have been imported from the private sector and then made to more or less fit the demands of the public sector, such as Total Quality Management, business process reengineering, and performance pay. There may be a few cases in which reform programs developed specifically for the public sector have been spread around among the leadership of government organizations. For example, Ronald Reagan appointed a group of businessmen to the so-called Grace Commission with the mandate to identify potential savings in government programs. The idea of such executive cost-control commissions was tried in almost all the states prior to being brought to Washington.

The obvious alternative strategy is for the leaders of public organizations to devise their own approach to reform and then implement it, even if it must be from the top down. While Margaret Thatcher may not have devised the reform plans in Great Britain herself, the experience of the Thatcher government in implementing reforms would appear to fit this model (Greer, 1994). These reforms included major changes in financial management within government (the Financial Management Initiative), structural changes (the creation of the "Next Steps" agencies), and the opening of top management positions to competition from outside government. The reform schemes were very much top-down in origin and certainly were implemented in that manner. Furthermore, although some ideas were borrowed from other public sectors (for example, "Next Steps" from the Scandinavian countries), most of the ideas were home-grown and designed to fit a particular diagnosis of the problems in British government, rather than being a generic solution to management problems wherever they might arise. Critics are quick to argue that the diagnosis of the problems was incorrect, and that therefore the medicine applied was also incorrect, or at least excessive. Still, this was an attempt to create a custom-built solution to problems rather than merely pulling something off a guru's shelf, and it does appear to have been able to persist.

If we accept the proposition that there is only so much "space" for change and reform in any one organization at any one time, then choosing generic solutions rather than custom solutions may fill that space in a less effective manner. Everything else being equal, using purposely built solutions should meet the particular needs of an organization better than any generic solution. Further, purposely built reforms are more likely to be "owned" by the members of the organization, even if they are proposed from the top down. The leaders of an organization that is attempting to impose reforms from above may still find it impossible to formulate appropriate home-grown reforms on their own. One virtue of rejecting the generic strategy may be, therefore, to indirectly mandate the involvement of other segments of an organization in change even when the major impetus comes from the top.

Finally, a planned organizational change coming from the top, regardless of its indigenous or foreign roots, may appear to be a simple matter to the reformers. The experience of most practitioners and students of organizational change is that simple remedies produce complex results (Brunsson and Olsen, 1993). Relatively few reformers have the capacity to adjust to changes as they occur. This is especially true when the reformers are buying the reform from outside with the assurance that it will perform as expected and produce certain predictable results. It may well be that a more adaptable solution from within will surpass a presumably clear solution from the outside.

Change from the Bottom Up

The second model of reform in the public sector is a bottom-up, or organization development, approach to generating change (Golembiewski, 1990). Rather than relying on directions from political masters or organizational superiors, this approach to change relies on the employees within the organization to design their own directions for change. In a pure case this might mean that the lower echelons of the organization initiate the process of change and then implement the new ideas. The assumption is that workers in an organization know best what the structure needs and the ways in which the goals can best be achieved. If the leaders in the organization would simply get out of the way, so the argument goes, the rank and file would be able to make the organization perform better.

In the public sector, the idea of the "street-level bureaucrat" as a source of guidance for policy has substantial support, academically and practically (Lipsky, 1980; Adler and Asquith, 1981). This is especially true as the goal of "serving the whole client" becomes more important. Often, the best way to integrate potentially conflicting social service and economic development programs is through the lower echelons of the organizations, which must deliver them. The deals that must be struck to provide services then can become the basis for policy changes at the top of the organization. It is not that the lower echelons are able to make the changes they want directly, but that they are able to make these changes inevitable.

Although there is some sense that the lower echelons have ideas about how best to change their own organization, when we consider the public sector as a whole, implementing empowerment can produce an even more chaotic system of government than the one that existed prior to reform. The upper echelons of the political system may merely empower the lower tiers to produce changes, or they may encourage them to do what the lower tiers would have liked to do for some years but were prevented from doing. If the changes are all in the same direction, the system as a whole may function better; if they are not, the endemic problems of coordination and coherence in the public sector may be exacerbated (Peters, 1996; Davis, 1995).

In the other version of reform from the bottom up, organizational leaders or leaders of government establish guidelines and then allow individual organizations to respond to these stimuli. While this may appear to be a top-down change in disguise, in effect it is a bottom-up perspective on change. The statements from the leaders may be seen as a means of empowering the lower echelons to develop change strategies that might have been impossible without this affirmation. The real question that emerges from this strategy of change is just how much latitude the lower echelons of an organization will be granted to make change. Are certain types of change "good" and others "bad," based on an ideology in the center? If that is so, will the center permit the organization to engage in experiments that its members choose but that run counter to that ideology?

The approach to organizational change that enables the workers to make changes within their organization is reflected very clearly in the creation of the numerous reinvention laboratories resulting from the National Performance Review. One of the principal strategies for promoting change in the current environment has been to empower organizations, or components of organizations, to design their own plans for change. Osborne and Gaebler's ideas about reinvention (1992), for example, are extremely vague and would permit individual organizations to have substantial latitude in the types of reform that might be implemented. On the other hand, the Gore report (1993) and the ideas of the leaders of that movement within the federal bureaucracy are somewhat clearer. Their vision of the future is one of government organizations that are more decentralized and participatory than traditional organizations, public or private.

Almost all of the examples of reinvention, as manifested through the reinvention laboratories, are clearly in conformity with the more participatory approach to managing organizations expressed in the Gore report. This is true even for laboratories developed in military or quasi-military organizations, such as the Army Chemical and Biological Defense Command. These experiments all depend upon forming teams within the organization that manage their own work and participate heavily in forming the goals of their organization. What is less clear is whether these changes reflect the true wishes of these workers or merely the preferences expressed by the leadership of the reinvention movement. Also, it is not clear what would have happened if one of the reinvention labs had decided that the best way to improve its performance was to reinforce traditional Weberian bureaucracy within the organization.

Everything else being equal, this reform strategy appears most compatible with the more highly professionalized public organizations. In these organizations, the members often have clear ideas about what they would like their organization to do and how they would like to do it. They also are in touch with other similarly situated professionals who serve as sources of ideas (Bjorkman, 1982). The success of the reinvention labs, for example, appears clearer either when they have a highly professionalized public service ethos or when a number of members are from the conventional "liberal professions" or the sciences. For change from the bottom up to be successful, the organization must have a lower echelon with innovative ideas and the ability to effectively advocate them.

Exogenous Change

The final, and less clearly articulated, model for contemporary organizational change can be called an exogenous approach. The concept here is that if essential factors in the environment of a government organization can be changed, the organization will be required to adapt its structure and behavior to that new environment. This approach to change is related to the broad strand of organization theory that believes that environmental dependency is the crucial factor in explaining differences in organizations. The assumption is that if the organization is not able to adapt itself to the available niches in the environment, it must go out of business (Peters and Hogwood, 1992).

The most extreme version of this source of change in current government has been the administrative adjustments to democratization in Central Europe and Latin America (Peters, 1995; Geddes, 1991). In the most important contemporary example of this model in the developed democracies, the budgetary environment of a public organization is changed and the organization is then required to adjust its own internal functioning to cope with this change. This strategy contains many features of the bottom-up approach, although it lacks even the loose framework of principles associated with reform projects like the National Performance Review. In some countries, such as Sweden (Ericksson, 1983) and Ireland, this is a well-institutionalized strategy for producing change, with the "cheese slicer" taking a small percentage from the operating budget each year. Each agency is expected to make up the difference through gains in efficiency. In most countries, however, this strategy is merely a reaction to increasing fiscal scarcity. The strategy appears to be most applicable to organizations with "machine" functions—bureaucracies that perform simple, repetitive tasks—that may be amenable to substantial gains in efficiency. (There are interesting parallels here to the "cheese slicer" budgeting plans used in Sweden.)

Another exceedingly important exogenous factor motivating change in contemporary public organizations is technology (Perry and Kraemer, 1993). The development of information technology has presented new opportunities, and new imperatives, to most public organizations. Some organizations are naturally more affected by these changes than are others because of the nature of their workforce and of the tasks they are performing. In addition to dealing with more fundamental aspects of the information revolution, organizations with a technically competent workforce will also be forced to develop means of coping with electronic mail. Although largely a positive feature that speeds up internal communications, e-mail also presents problems in documentation and record keeping, and potentially in confidentiality. Roles are changed within the organization and therefore the internal power distribution becomes altered. The changes imposed by technology are more than technical; they may go to the heart of the functioning of the organization.

The Objects of Organizational Change

As well as differentiating among the various sources and strategies for producing change, we should also differentiate among the objects of change. What factors do the advocates of organizational reform visualize as the principal sources of problems and failures in government? Likewise, what components of organizations do the reformers argue to be the easiest and/or the most effective targets for change. Unfortunately, the factors within organizations that are the easiest to manipulate may also be the least effective, at least in the long run. Easily manipulable variables may not change the cultural and attitudinal characteristics that undergird other aspects of behavior within organizations.

Probably the simplest aspect of an organization to change is its structure. In most instances the existing structures of organizations reflect little intrinsic logic. Rather, they are the products either of following traditional patterns of government organizations (for example, making cabinet departments responsible for policies from formulation through implementation) or of making decisions for political reasons rather than according to the logic of organization theory. There is little evidence that organizational structures reflect the environment within which they function or the tasks with which they are charged. In part because of the absence of such a clear empirical connection, manipulating the structure of public organizations is easy, but it is also unlikely to generate predictable benefits of any real consequence.

A second level of change targets the formal regulations and rules within organizations for change or termination. For some critics of the functioning of government, these rules constitute a major part of the problem (Di Iulio, 1994; Barzelay, 1992). Indeed, the Gore report (1993) pointed out that much of the apparent inefficiency in the federal government was a function of the excessive regulations imposed on the government, and it recommended internal deregulation of the public sector. The solution proposed was to change radically the manner in which formal rules governed the conduct of government, especially the role of central agencies in imposing direction and coordination on the system of government as an entity.

Probably the most difficult component of an organization to change is its internal culture. This set of values and understandings is integral to the manner in which an organization functions, even if the attributes are sometimes difficult to identify in any unambiguous way. It appears clear that if reformers are able to change the values and culture of an organization, they are likely to have the most enduring impact on its performance (Peters and Waterman, 1982). However, these values tend to persist in the face of numerous challenges, and organizations often capture the changes and even use them to reinforce the dominant culture (March and Olsen, 1989, pp. 88–94). Further, there is no clear methodology for making the changes as there is for making structural or procedural changes.

The Contingencies of Organizational Change

Contingency theories have not enjoyed great success in the study of public sector organizations (but see Hal Rainey's discussion in Chapter Six). It is plausible to assume that guidance in structuring organizations should be based upon the tasks they have to perform or the nature of the constituencies they are intended to serve. To date, however, the empirical evidence is, at best, not strongly supportive of contingency approaches (Pitt and Smith, 1981). Nevertheless, there has been a good deal of useful sectoral analysis of public policies, and the hypothesis that policy areas are more similar across countries than within the same country has received substantial support (Freeman, 1985; Burstein, 1991). The evidence for linkages between those sectoral policy variables and the organizational structures for delivering the policies is not nearly as supportive.

If the evidence supporting contingency theories for organizational structures is limited, there is perhaps even less support for this theoretical approach as a guide for planned organizational change. If, however, the above analysis of the possible roots of change is useful, we should attempt to provide substantial guidance about when one style of change is more suitable than another. These contingencies may be based upon a number of factors, including the formal structure of the organization prior to reform, the nature of the policy area being administered, or the goals of the reform being undertaken. No one factor appears to be determinate; instead, multiple interaction effects exist that require analysis and interpretation.

One of the most important contingencies to be considered in the development of organizational-change strategies is the nature of the workforce within an organization. As a result of downsizing and the reduction of the large clerical workforces that have been a dominant feature of government, a government employee is now more likely to be a professional or paraprofessional. Organizations dominated by this type of worker are especially suitable for the bottom-up strategy of change and are likely also to demand this style of change. The increasingly participative nature of society in the 1990s makes participation a common demand, but it is especially common among professional employees. In addition, these workers have the skills and knowledge that can make participation in change more than the mere window dressing that it sometimes becomes. "Machine" bureaucracies, on the other hand, may respond very readily to change being implemented from the top down, although again that acceptance may be diminishing.

Externally imposed, budget-driven change obviously works better when budget constraints are real, rather than having been created for political purposes. They also appear to work best when the reductions imposed are differential and are related to some transparent criterion. Employees tend to react negatively to across-the-board cuts, despite their apparent equality. For example, part of the relative success of the Programme Review in the Chrétien government in Canada—a systematic analysis of all public expenditures conducted with an eye toward reducing the public deficit—has been that different ministries had differential cuts and differential targets (Savoie and Peters, 1997). This gave the appearance, and indeed reflected the reality, of giving careful thought to the ability to save money in different programs and the relative priority the government was willing to attach to each program. Employees did not always like what happened to their organization, but they were more willing to engage in change when it appeared that there was some reason for it.

A question that must be asked when attempting to promote organizational change is, What is the diagnosis and target of the change? As already pointed out, organizational change may have the rather meager goals of changing formal structures or internal processes, or it may be directed at altering more fundamentally the culture and behavior of an organization. Changing the culture of the organization is probably the most effective mode of change in the long run: if values are changed there is less need for monitoring and enforcement within the organization. The problem is that changing values is also the most problematic component of a change strategy, given the capacity of cultures to resist change and of role occupants to engage in rote compliance with the goals of a change without the underlying value change.

In contingency terms, we would argue that producing cultural change almost has to be done through a top-down process. It is difficult to expect members of an organization who are the carriers of the organization's culture to be particularly interested in modifying that culture. They may be able to do so, but only after the need for the change and its basic direction have been established externally. Even then, if the cultural change being proposed is in sharp contrast to the culture that has existed previously, then continuing, forceful involvement from the top of the organization may be needed. For example, institutionalizing effective change in the Internal Revenue Service required some movement away from a highly consensual culture to a more top-down culture. Some critics have charged that an impediment to effective implementation of the Tax Systems Modernization project (see Chapter Four) was a "culture of consensus" at the executive committee level that precluded the type of assertive action needed for the project to move forward. A similar pattern of change was observed in the case of the transformation of components of the Social Security Administration (Rainey and Rainey, 1986).

Finally, from an institutional perspective, the stability of the organizational processes being addressed appears to be a crucial determinant of success for any reform process. Organizations vary markedly in their degree of institutionalization, or the extent to which processes and values are internalized and accepted as stable components of their operations (Scott, 1995). Would-be reformers appear capable of exploiting incomplete processes to produce change, whereas more institutionalized processes will inhibit successful change.

Conclusion

The above discussion should point to the simple fact that different strategies of reform may be appropriate for different organizations and for different types of policies. This "horses for courses" approach to change has by no means produced reliable laws for organizational performance; in addition, clear cases of successful change have occurred outside the parameters arising from the conventional wisdom about change. Everything else being equal, bottom-up changes will be more enduring, simply because they can be expected to match the needs of a particular organization better than any imposed change, whether that change was imposed by the hierarchy or by external factors. The paradox is that bottom-up change has to be fostered from the top down, and perhaps with more than a nod and a wink saying that it is permissible. The leadership of the organization may have to become genuinely involved if the change is to be accepted and enduring.

As well as being a contingent phenomenon, organizational change is also a continuing phenomenon, contingent on the fads and fashions of the time. The administrative reforms being imposed and adopted in the late 1990s may appear well suited for the age in which they are being implemented, but they will soon manifest their own difficulties and will cry out to a new generation of reformers for other types of change. The decentralizing and entrepreneurial nature of contemporary changes will almost certainly generate problems of accountability and control that will engender a set of more hierarchical reforms. This is good news for those of us who are interested in reform and change, but probably not for the individuals who must live through the changes and attempt to manage them.

Finally, we have not yet addressed the question of how to evaluate administrative reform and change. Most reformers enter into the process rather blithely, in the expectation of being able to produce positive results and create a new era of productivity and excellence within their organization. Even when the reformers are successful in producing the expected changes, unintended consequences and interactions with other changes that are occurring simultaneously often escape adequate planning or prediction. Change in any organization is complex, but change in public sector organizations is even more difficult to assess because of the numerous values involved and the large number of constituencies being served.

Effective planned change is not impossible, but neither is it easy, and therefore allowing those involved to participate in the process may be the best means, on average, to produce enduring changes. The experience of the National Performance Review, to date, appears to substantiate that point. Of course, there is also good evidence for the contrary position: organizational change requires strong leadership from the top and persistent efforts by the leadership of the organization. If nothing else, this demonstrates that we have a great deal more research to do to be able to understand organizational change.

References

Adler, M., and Asquith, S. *Discretion and Power.* London: Heinemann, 1981.

Aucoin, P. *The New Public Management: Canada in Comparative Perspective.* Montreal: Institute for Research on Public Policy, 1995.

Barzelay, M. *Breaking Through Bureaucracy.* Berkeley: University of California Press, 1992.

Bjorkman, J. W. "Professionalism in the Welfare State: Sociological Savior or Political Pariah?" *European Journal for Political Research,* 1982, *10,* 407–428.

Brunsson, N., and Olsen, J. P. *The Reforming Organization.* London: Routledge, 1993.

Burstein, P. "Policy Domains: Organization, Culture and Policy Outcomes." *Annual Review of Sociology,* 1991, *17,* 327–350.

Davis, G. *A Government of Routines.* Melbourne, Australia: Macmillan, 1995.

de Montricher, N. "Public Sector Values in the Face of Administrative Reforms." Paper presented at the Conference on Taking Stock of Administrative Reform, Canadian Centre for Management Development, Ottawa, May 9–12, 1996.

Di Iulio, J. J., Jr. *Deregulating Government.* Washington, D.C.: Brookings Institution, 1994.

Ericksson, B. "Sweden's Budget System in a Changing World." *Public Budgeting and Finance,* 1983, *3,* 64–80.

Freeman, G. "National Styles and Policy Sectors: Explaining Structural Variations." *Journal of Public Policy,* 1985, *5,* 467–496.

Geddes, B. "A Game-Theoretic Model of Reform in Latin America." *American Political Science Review,* 1991, *85,* 371–392.

Golembiewski, R. *The Ironies of Organizational Development.* New Brunswick, N.J.: Transaction, 1990.

Gore, A., Jr. *From Red Tape to Results: Creating a Government That Works Better and Costs Less.* Report of the National Performance Review. Washington, D.C.: U.S. Government Printing Office, 1993.

Greer, P. *Transforming Central Government: The Next Steps Initiative.* Buckingham, England: Open University Press, 1994.

Hage, J., and Finsterbusch, K. "Three Strategies of Organizational Change." *International Review of Administrative Sciences,* 1989, *55,* 29–57.

Hood, C. "The United Kingdom: From Second Change to Near-Miss Learning." In J. P. Olsen and B. G. Peters (eds.), *Lessons from Experience: Experiential Learning in Administrative Reforms in Eight Democracies.* Oslo, Norway: Scandinavian University Press, 1996.

Kickert, W.J.M., and van Vught, F. A. *Public Policy and Administration Science in the Netherlands.* Brighton, England: Wheatsheaf, 1995.

Kotter, J. P. "Leading Change: Why Transformation Efforts Fail." *Harvard Business Review,* 1995, *37,* 59–67.

Lipsky, M. *Street-Level Bureaucracy.* New York: Russell Sage Foundation, 1980.

March, J. G., and Olsen, J. P. *Rediscovering Institutions.* New York: Free Press, 1989.

Osborne, D., and Gaebler, T. *Reinventing Government: How the Entrepreneurial Spirit Is Transforming the Public Sector from Schoolhouse to State House, City Hall to Pentagon.* Reading, Mass.: Addison Wesley Longman, 1992.

Perry, J. L., and Kraemer, K. L. "The Implications of Changing Technology." In F. J. Thompson (ed.), *Revitalizing State and Local Public Service: Strengthening Performance, Accountability, and Citizen Confidence.* San Francisco: Jossey-Bass, 1993.

Peters, B. G. *Managing Horizontal Government.* Ottawa: Canadian Centre for Management Development, 1996.

Peters, B. G., and Hogwood, B. W. "Applying Population Ecology Models to the Public Sector." In J. L. Perry (ed.), *Research in Public Administration.* Westport, Conn.: JAI Press, 1992.

Peters, B. G., and Savoie, D. J. *Governing in a Changing Environment.* Montreal: McGill/Queens University Press, 1995.

Peters, T., and Waterman, R. *In Search of Excellence.* New York: Harper-Collins, 1982.

Pitt, D. C., and Smith, B. C. *Government Departments: An Organisational Perspective.* London: Routledge, 1981.

Pollitt, C. *Manipulating the Machine: Changing the Pattern of Ministerial Departments.* London: Allen & Unwin, 1984.

Rainey, G. W., and Rainey, H. G. "Structural Overhaul in a Government Agency." *Public Administration Quarterly,* 1986, *15,* 206–223.

Savoie, D. J., and Peters, B. G. *Reviewing the Reviewers.* Ottawa: Canadian Centre for Management Development, 1997.

Schein, E. H. *Organizational Culture and Leadership.* San Francisco: Jossey-Bass, 1985.

Scott, W. R. *Institutions and Organizations.* London: Sage, 1995.

Szanton, P. *Federal Reorganization: What Have We Learned?* Chatham, N.J.: Chatham House, 1981.

Thompson, F. J. *Revitalizing State and Local Public Service: Strengthening Performance, Accountability, and Citizen Confidence.* San Francisco: Jossey-Bass, 1993.

Zifcak, S. *New Managerialism: Administrative Reform in Whitehall and Canberra.* Buckingham, England: Open University Press, 1994.

Part Three

Lessons for Continuing Transformation

The previous selections dealt with issues of change at strategic and tactical levels. Barbara Romzek, in Chapter Eight, and Donald Savoie, in Chapter Nine, take a more thematic approach. For Romzek, the critical issue is accountability. The bureaucratic model, for all its flaws, has at least one very important strength: it provides a clear and straightforward means of accountability. That accountability is enforced primarily through hierarchy and rules. Osborne and Gaebler (1992) and Gore (1993) complain, however, that these same elements deter effective management and the delivery of quality service.

What, then, are to be the new mechanisms of accountability? Romzek sees a shift to accountability based on assessment of outputs and outcomes, in which "the emphasis is on deferring to the discretion of managers as they work within broad parameters, rather than on close scrutiny to ensure compliance with detailed rules and organizational directives." She acknowledges, however, that a reliance on output and outcome modes of accountability requires that effective performance measures be devised. The technology for devising such measures, however, remains imperfect.

Savoie investigates the political context of reform, questioning whether and to what extent significant transformation of the organs of government can occur in the absence of changes to the political system. He identifies the critical role played by central staff agencies such as the Office of Management and Budget in the United States; here the rhetoric of reform often defers to the reality of politics and institutional dynamics that require centralized control. Savoie notes that all too often, the facilitation of broad-scale change conflicts with the dynamics of the political system. He hypothesizes that in future years, this period will be looked upon not as a time of dramatic transformation of government institutions but as a time of much ferment, highlighted by individual leaders seeking sufficient autonomy in the bureaucratic monolith to proceed with their own version of reinvention. A key question, to which only time can provide the answer, is whether the cumulative effect of all the activity at the individual and unit levels, in conjunction with pressures for improved service and fewer resources, will be sufficient to force the institutional changes that, as Savoie observes, have yet to occur.

In the concluding chapter, Patricia Ingraham reviews the lessons that can be drawn from the reinvention lab experience, one of the most important of which is that leadership counts, that lower-ranking individuals can provoke change and can make a difference even in an environment seemingly as hostile to innovation as the federal government.

References

Gore, A., Jr. *From Red Tape to Results: Creating a Government That Works Better and Costs Less.* Report of the National Performance Review. Washington, D.C.: U.S. Government Printing Office, 1993.

Osborne, D., and Gaebler, T. *Reinventing Government: How the Entrepreneurial Spirit Is Transforming the Public Sector.* Reading, Mass.: Addison Wesley Longman, 1992.

Chapter Eight

Where the Buck Stops

Accountability in Reformed Public Organizations

Barbara S. Romzek

Efforts to reform operations within federal, state, and local governments are widespread these days (Di Iulio and Kettl, 1995; Osborne and Gaebler, 1992; Gore, 1995; Ingraham and Romzek, 1994; Walters, 1996), as are changes in intergovernmental relationships (Radin and others, 1996). Calls for administrative reform have been widespread and urgent (Gore, 1993, 1994, 1995; Volcker Commission, 1989; Winter Commission, 1993). Most of these reforms, some under way and others under consideration, aspire to change the culture of American government and the context within which public managers do their jobs.

Reinvention reforms represent efforts to change the culture of government away from being a rule-bound, risk-averse culture to being one that emphasizes entrepreneurial and innovative approaches to implementing government programs. Reinvention initiatives under the National Performance Review were "consciously structured to avoid hierarchy" (Thompson and Ingraham, 1996, p. 293). Greater flexibility and innovation necessitate a loosening of rules and constraints, as Peters and Savoie (1996, p. 283) have noted: "By its very nature, entrepreneurial behavior is less constrained by conventional norms of hierarchy and public law." Regarding the management of human resources, a General Accounting Office–sponsored symposium summed up this orientation under one of its principles for managing people: "*Hold managers responsible for achieving results instead of imposing rigid, process-oriented rules and standards.* Give managers the authority to manage their people flexibly and innovatively so they can focus on achieving results rather than doing things 'by the book.' Hold them accountable for outcomes and for furthering the mission and vision of the organization rather than for adhering to a set of minutely defined procedures" (U.S. General Accounting Office, 1995, p. 5; emphasis in original).

Reforms emphasize increasing responsiveness and effectiveness by removing layers of regulations and constraints on how governments operate and by increasing the discretion, autonomy, and responsiveness of public employees. For example, of the forty-eight different federal reinvention laboratory innovations identified by Thompson and Ingraham (1996, pp. 294–295), only four could conceivably be unrelated to the loosening of accountability relationships. Most were categorized as seeking a waiver of regulations or review rights or directly requesting autonomy. Calls for eliminating red tape, streamlining procedures, reducing middle management, adopting a customer service orientation, and engaging in entrepreneurial management are examples of this trend.

Most of these initiatives reflect a recognition that government operations are cumbersome and unwieldy and a perception that government simply is not as effective as the American public would like. These various reform trends reflect a widespread sentiment that the pendulum in the United States has swung too far in the direction of control and rigidity and needs to swing toward greater discretion and flexibility for government. The expectation is that the reforms under consideration will increase government's effectiveness and accountability. The presumption is that removing layers of constraints and empowering public employees will change how they do their jobs—and increase the chances that government employees will do what is expected of them.

As in most efforts to change organizational cultures, the challenges presented by these governmental reforms are substantial. Reinvention reforms have implications for the accountability relationships of government agencies and public managers. Successful implementation of these reforms requires consideration of the accountability dynamics and a change in the culture of accountability. Yet most of these reinvention reforms have been proposed and undertaken with the presumption that accountability will somehow take care of itself once the reforms are successfully implemented (Garvey, 1995; Moe, 1994).

This chapter explores the accountability implications of the reinvention reforms currently under consideration at various levels of government. To begin, a brief review of the dynamics of accountability as a governance issue in the American political system is in order.

Accountability

Accountability is a relationship in which an individual or agency is held to answer for performance that involves some delegation of authority to act. Accountability in the public sector is a fundamental concern of the American political system, in part because the cultural norm of distrust of government is deep-seated in the United States. Such sentiment preceded the writing of the Articles of Confederation and is currently embodied in the principle of separation of powers that underlies our government structures. As early as the time of the country's founding, James Madison articulated a sentiment that is one of the cornerstones of American interest in government accountability, namely, that an important challenge of democratic government is to "oblige it to control itself" ([1788] 1961, p. 322).

Criticism of government and public employees' performance is frequently couched in terms of a need for greater accountability. Often calls for "more accountability" are really somewhat imprecise calls for different accountability relationships—ones that utilize the kinds of incentives, represent the degree of control, and promote the underlying behavioral expectations that the critic prefers. The fact is that the American public sector has a great deal of accountability at all levels. Public employees typically work enmeshed within several different accountability relationships simultaneously (Romzek, 1996). Among the kinds of accountability relationships utilized in the public sector in this country, some are better suited to the current managerial reforms than others (Romzek and Dubnick, 1994). Critics who deplore the lack of accountability of public employees would be more accurate if they deplored the lack of a "preferred" accountability relationship—the one they would prefer to see used to hold public employees answerable for their performance.

In Search of Accountability: Weaving a Web

While everyone agrees that governments and their employees should be accountable, there is little consensus regarding which kinds of accountability relationships are preferred. The debate was engaged in earnest in the mid-twentieth century (Friedrich, 1940; Finer, 1941) and has yet to be definitively resolved. One perspective emphasizes extensive oversight by democratic institutions (Finer, 1941; Gruber, 1987); another emphasizes self-control by professionals (Friedrich, 1940; Burke, 1986). This lack of consensus can be seen in the general dynamic that the American political system has followed regarding accountability relationships for public employees.

The pattern has been to design accountability relationships in reaction to undesirable situations that have arisen. For example, in the personnel arena, the infamous spoils system used during the mid-nineteenth century (Mosher, 1982) was a reaction to a sense that government had not been sufficiently responsive to changes in the electoral will. The spoils system relies on accountability relationships based on the responsiveness of employees to external actors (the elected officials who made the appointment). The merit system, instituted in the late nineteenth century, was a reaction to the excesses of responsiveness under the spoils system and a sense that insufficient attention had been given to the knowledge, skills, and abilities of job holders. The merit system relies on accountability relationships that emphasize obedience to internal organizational and supervisory directives, not responsiveness to external actors. Although the federal merit system was instituted with the Pendleton Act of 1883, a political appointee system was retained for the highest-level positions of government. So while the merit system established new accountability relationships (which emphasized obedience to rules), the political appointee system and its accountability relationships (which emphasized responsiveness to elected officials) were not discarded entirely.

This early pattern of layering accountability relationships has been repeated time and again. As a management problem or scandal arises, new accountability relationships are instituted to prevent such a circumstance from arising in the future. These new accountability relationships are not substituted for those that were in place at the time of the problem and are now perceived to be inadequate; they simply are added to the accountability relationships already in place. The result is the weaving of a thick web of multiple, overlapping accountability relationships within which public employees must work. For example, most observers agree that the paperwork and permissions necessary for government purchasing and travel are excessive at all levels of government. This pattern of requiring excessive documentation represents an accumulation of rules and regulations designed to eliminate the potential for any reoccurrence of accountability problems that have arisen in the past.

The presence of these webs of accountability relationships reflects the American pragmatic approach to governance. While the use of several accountability relationships simultaneously does not reflect any elegance of design, the multiplicity of relationships provides numerous opportunities for holding public managers answerable for their performance. Any trade-offs in efficiency that may result generally are deemed an acceptable price to pay for accountability.

The metaphor of a web of accountability relationships captures the situation for government agencies and managers fairly well. The different strands of the web of accountability represent the different relationships that government agencies and managers have with the various actors or institutions with legitimate performance expectations of public agencies and managers. These relationships vary in how they hold public employees accountable and what performance standards are used.

Types of Accountability Relationships

The web of accountability relationships reflects both internal and external sources of expectations and/or control and differing degrees of autonomy in administrative actions. There are four different types of accountability relationships: hierarchical, legal, political, and professional (Romzek and Dubnick, 1987). The first two, hierarchical and legal, emphasize low degrees of autonomy and close, detailed scrutiny of employees' performance. Hierarchical relationships rely on supervisory and organizational directives, including rules and standard operating procedures, for the standards to which employees are answerable for their performance. Obedience is the behavioral expectation. This type emphasizes directives that tell employees what to do, through rules, standard operating procedures, supervision, and organizational directives.

Legal accountability relationships emphasize compliance with some externally derived expectations or standards of performance and close scrutiny and oversight as the means by which employees are held to answer for their performance. This type focuses on external oversight to check on whether the appropriate behaviors and desired events have occurred. Audits, oversight hearings, inspectors general, and the courts are commonly used in legal accountability relationships.

Political and professional accountability relationships rely on much higher levels of autonomy. Here, behavior is scrutinized at less detailed levels and greater discretion is granted to employees to pursue their assigned tasks. Political accountability relationships emphasize responsiveness to the expectations of key external stakeholders, such as elected officials, clientele, and other agencies. These types emphasize accountability based upon whether the administrators have been sufficiently responsive to the expectations of the agency clientele, or "customers." Professional accountability relationships emphasize responsibility and deference to expertise. Performance standards are established by professional norms and the prevailing practices of one's peer or work group. The behavioral expectation is that discretion will be exercised responsibly. This type of accountability emphasizes deference to the administrative experts; it is based on trusting administrators to exercise their discretion responsibly, in a manner consistent with accepted administrative and professional norms of responsible practice. See Figure 8.1 for an illustration.

Accountability Under Government Reform

Numerous governance problems are related to accountability issues, including those of establishing expectations, verifying performance, maintaining responsiveness of agents, assessing blame,

Figure 8.1. Types of Accountability Relationships.

		Source of Expectations and/or Control: *Internal*	Source of Expectations and/or Control: *External*
Degree of Autonomy	*Low*	**Hierarchical** Relationship: Superior/Subordinate	**Legal** Relationship: Principal/Agent
Degree of Autonomy	*High*	**Professional** Relationship: Layperson/Expert	**Political** Relationship: Constituent/Representative

sorting out responsibility, determining who the masters are, and managing under conditions of multiple accountability systems (Romzek and Dubnick, 1997). While all of these problems are interrelated parts of the accountability challenge facing governments, the current era of reform has important implications for the challenges of establishing expectations and managing under conditions of multiple accountability relationships.

Changing Expectations and Culture

Holding public employees answerable for their performance implies some prior expectations regarding that performance. Situations involving public managers and agencies typically involve multiple expectations that are numerous, diverse, changing, and often contradictory. This circumstance is in part due to the various stakeholders public managers face, but it is also a result of the range of management reforms that are currently popular. These reform efforts that have been proposed and are under way typically embody conflicting expectations (Kettl, 1995, p. 47). For example, the reinvention movement advocates downsizing and lowering expenditures. Reengineering efforts seek efficiency through discontinuous breakthrough strategies. Total Quality Management reforms, which emphasize continuous improvement of processes, support responsiveness to customers through cooperation. Public managers face the challenge of trying to accommodate these conflicting expectations, each of which is being pursued under the rubric of reform.

The biggest change in expectations reflected in the current wave of government reform relates to the way managers and public agencies should approach their responsibilities. The hope is that public managers and government agencies will shift from a risk-averse approach to doing their jobs (Light, 1994) toward more entrepreneurial and innovative strategies (Osborne and Gaebler, 1992; Gore, 1995). A recent report by the U.S. General Accounting Office (U.S. General Accounting Office, 1995, p. 5) characterized recent civil service reforms as focused on emphasizing "mission, vision, and organizational culture," holding managers "accountable for outcomes . . . rather than for adhering to a set of minutely defined procedures," and choosing "an organizational structure appropriate to the organization rather than trying to make 'one size fit all.'"

The basic direction of these changes is to deemphasize performance expectations that are focused on rules and directives from central authorities, including the widely publicized example of eliminating the federal personnel manual. Other changes relate to decentralizing personnel functions and deemphasizing the monitoring and compliance roles of centralized personnel offices, such as the U.S. Office of Personnel Management. Another direction of change encourages decentralized decision making and, where possible, collaborative decision making across agency boundaries. Collaboration has been fruitfully pursued in some intergovernmental arenas such as agriculture and economic development, as seen in the National Rural Development Partnership. Participants in the partnership have seen a shift in the expectations they face, away from "stovepipe" management toward localized collaboration in problem solving among actors in the public and private sectors (Radin and others, 1996).

Accountability Alignments

In designing agencies and structuring reporting relationships, three factors influence the choice of the accountability relationship under which an agency or manager will operate: the agency's institutional environment, the managerial strategy employed, and the agency's or individual's tasks. Exploring the accountability implications of the various reforms requires some systematic thinking about how the various kinds of accountability relationships fit with the current environment, managerial strategies, and tasks.

The cultural norm of distrust of American government, as was noted earlier, gives rise to the institutional environment of fragmented government, and American government's current institutional environment has been highly critical of its administrative capacity and effectiveness. American public service has been subjected to a steady stream of severe criticism from elected officials, popularly known as "bureaucrat bashing" (Garvey, 1995). Clearly the current political environment favors reform.

Managerial strategies vary in their emphases, with most reforms in the direction of flexibility, discretion, and responsiveness. Some focus on inputs and processes; others emphasize outcomes and others outputs. Still other reforms seek improved responsiveness, a customer orientation, entrepreneurial behavior, or employee empowerment. Agency tasks are also shifting under these reforms as governments attempt to downsize, deregulate, shift responsibilities, and contract out many of their former functions (Milward, 1994). The nature of an agency's mission or individual job tasks will determine whether such changes warrant adjustments in accountability relationships as well. Current reforms suggest the need for a shift from those that emphasize rules and oversight toward those that emphasize discretion and responsiveness.

Among the various kinds of accountability relationships utilized in the U.S. government, some are better suited to the current managerial reforms than others (Romzek and Dubnick, 1994; Romzek, 1997). In order to change the operations of agencies and managers, it is essential to have a corresponding shift in accountability relationships. While the conditions of public administration are rarely ideal, it is possible to discuss "ideal" accountability configurations in the same way that Max Weber (Gerth and Mills,

1973) afforded us a profile of "ideal" bureaucracy. Figure 8.2 presents a baseline framework that illustrates how current managerial reform strategies and core tasks can be aligned in terms of accountability relationships.

A traditional *input* orientation focuses on the resources an agency or manager has available to carry out the program or activity, such as the budget levels, number of employees, or number of doses of vaccine available for distribution. This input orientation is reflected in the U.S. Occupational Safety and Health Administration's performance goal of "focusing resources on achieving workplace hazard abatement through strong enforcement and incentive programs" (Bowsher, 1996, p. 9). Public service tasks that are relatively routine and emphasize inputs lend themselves to hierarchical accountability relationships. Executive orders as agency directives, traditional performance evaluations by supervisors, administrative program checklists, and management within personnel ceilings and position classifications typically fall into this category of accountability.

A *process* orientation emphasizes proper paper flow and consultation with relevant, appropriate actors. In a social service agency, where transactions are the main mission, a process measure might focus on whether proper procedures and formulas were being applied and whether individuals who were denied benefits were being accorded appeal opportunities. In an agency with a record-keeping task, such as a tax assessor's office, process measures might focus on whether tax notices were being mailed to all property owners in a timely fashion. When an agency's managerial focus is on processes and its tasks are still relatively routine, legal accountability relationships are typically an effective alignment. Investigations by the Merit Systems Protection Board, inspectors general, and congressional committees, as well as external audits of various kinds, are examples of this type of oversight and monitoring function.

Outputs are the quantity and quality of the services delivered or products made. An output standard might focus on the number of payment vouchers processed during a certain fiscal year or the number of workers' compensation claims paid. In law enforcement, outputs are often measured in the number of arrests made and traffic citations issued. Circumstances where agency tasks are less routine

Figure 8.2. "Ideal" Accountability Alignments: Type of Accountability, Basis of Relationship, and Examples.

Core Agency Tasks

Routine → Nonroutine

Strategic Management Focus

	Routine			Nonroutine
Inputs	**Hierarchical Accountability** Supervision, Rules, Procedures Merit systems, SF-171, Federal Personnel Manual, executive orders, agency reorganizations			
Process		**Legal Accountability** Oversight, Monitoring, Auditing U.S. Office of Personnel Management, U.S. Merit Systems Protection Board inspectors general, the courts		
Outputs			**Political Accountability** Responsiveness to Stakeholders Political appointee, customer service orientation, community-based policing	
Outcomes				**Professional Accountability** Deference to Expertise Broadbanding of pay systems, employee empowerment, "Manage to Payroll," agency-based personnel authority

and managerial strategies focus on outputs lend themselves to political accountability relationships, where the emphasis is on responsiveness to some external stakeholder. Labor-management partnerships that are part of the National Performance Review and customer service orientations fall into this category.

Outcomes reflect the quantity and quality of the results achieved by the outputs in satisfying the client, taxpayer, or customer. An outcome might measure a change in the level of environmental pollution or the occurrence rates of a targeted disease, crime, teen pregnancy, or poverty in a given area. Professional accountability relationships represent the best alignment when the task is very specialized and the managerial strategy is focused on outcomes. This allows for the exercise of discretion and the application of expertise. Self-directed teams; experiments in the broadbanding of personnel classifications, such as the China Lake federal demonstration project (U.S. Office of Personnel Management, 1992); and the relaxation of purchasing restrictions are examples of efforts to allow public managers to exercise discretion responsibly, in accordance with accepted professional practices. In such accountability relationships, scrutiny over administrative decisions continues, but the emphasis is on deferring to the discretion of managers as they work within broad parameters, rather than on close scrutiny to ensure compliance with detailed rules and organizational directives.

Agencies often pursue multiple tracks simultaneously. For example, the Texas Commission for the Blind used a combination of output and outcome measures to assess the extent to which it was meeting its strategic goals. The commission established as an output measure the number of adults receiving skills training (U.S. General Accounting Office, 1994). The performance target outcome was the percentage of blind or visually impaired people who avoided a dependent living environment. Similarly, the city of Hampton, Virginia, reports the use of multiple measures of accountability, tapping inputs, outputs, and outcomes: "For people in self-directed teams, we have a model for pay based on results [*outcomes*], demonstrated skills [*inputs*], and what the group accomplishes [*outputs*], customer satisfaction ratings [*outputs*], and budget performance [*inputs*]." (italics not in original) (U.S. General Accounting Office, 1995, pp. 21–22).

In summary, the accountability landscape for public administrators in the United States is in a great deal of flux these days as efforts are made to reform administrative processes, redefine agency missions and values, and adjust reporting relationships. Reforms under reinvention represent a shift in emphasis in accountability relationships rather than an attempt to discard one or another type of accountability relationship altogether. Most of the managerial reforms currently under way and under consideration are intended to break up an overemphasis on inputs and processes. They emphasize deregulation, increased discretion and flexibility, and greater emphasis on outputs and outcomes. Hence the accountability relationships that are best suited to these reforms are professional and political types that rely on deference to expertise, increased discretion, and responsiveness. Failure to align accountability relationships with government reforms will seriously undermine the likelihood that the changes will be successfully implemented.

The Hard Reality of Accountability Patterns Under Reform

The public management accountability arena is best characterized as a work in progress. Some reforms have been implemented; some rules have been relaxed and some constraints have been eased. Efforts have been made toward redefining accountability for outcomes and outputs. Changing anything as fundamental as accountability relationships takes time. And in a system such as that of the United States, where the change amounts to a shift in emphasis rather than a substitution of one accountability relationship for another, clear transitions or demarcations are often absent. At present there is still more talk than action, more heat than light, in this area.

Because government reforms and accountability alignments are still in flux, patterns have not yet emerged and synthesis or analysis of broad trends is not possible. As a first step toward mapping the changes, the following discussion reviews selected areas of reform and examines the accountability alignments evident in these examples. Recent accountability reforms have taken two different but interrelated approaches. One is to broaden the scope of the input used in judging whether the performance of individuals and agencies has met expectations for accountability purposes. The other approach is to shift the standards that are emphasized when individuals and agencies are scrutinized to determine whether they have met the various expectations they face. Each approach represents an effort to update accountability relationships and better align them with contemporary management practices.

Broadening the Scope of the Evaluation

For starters, consider the relationship that comes to mind first when most people hear the word *accountability,* the individual performance appraisal. Performance appraisals are the primary instrument by which individuals are held accountable for their performance. In government these appraisals typically involve detailed (usually annual) scrutiny of an individual by his or her immediate supervisor according to predetermined expectations and criteria. Supervisory review of an individual's performance is a good example of hierarchical accountability: an internal actor (the employee's boss) scrutinizes the employee's behavior in some detail for whether or not performance expectations are being met. The behavioral expectations are that the employee will obey organizational directives, follow standard operating procedures, and fulfill supervisory expectations. In such instances performance is judged by how the individual deploys the organizational inputs at his or her disposal: time, effort, the workforce, or funds.

Depending on the nature of the job tasks, public employees typically must meet important legal obligations in performing their jobs, including evaluating the performance of any subordinates. If questions about compliance with legal obligations emerge in the course of an individual's job performance, legal accountability may be invoked. This would manifest itself as detailed external scrutiny to determine compliance with external expectations, through processes such as an audit, grievance, or lawsuit. In American public management, legal accountability relationships are closely, perhaps inextricably, intertwined with hierarchical accountability relationships. When legal accountability is invoked, hierarchical accountability is often quick to follow; for example, an employee is often placed on administrative leave or suspended during an investigation of serious misconduct. The legal accountability of a supervisor conducting a performance appraisal can be triggered through an appeal for external scrutiny of the appraisal on matters of substance or process. At the federal level, the scrutiny might be by the Merit Systems Protection Board, the Equal Employment Opportunity Commission, or a congressional oversight committee. At the state or municipal level, the scrutiny would be by equivalent bodies—a civil service commission, civil rights commission, or legislative oversight committee.

Experimentation with broadening the scope of the input used for performance appraisals beyond the judgment of immediate supervisors takes the form of feedback from coworkers and clientele or "customers." In this kind of reform, known as a "360-degree" performance evaluation, the range of inputs for determining accountability is broadened considerably. These evaluations continue to encompass supervisory judgment, and hence to retain some traditional hierarchical accountability. They also incorporate peer judgments about the individual's performance, including whether the performance was consistent with work-group norms of accepted practice. They incorporate a form of professional accountability to the extent that workers exercise discretion in offering their judgment of their coworkers' performance. Measures of clientele or "customer" satisfaction with service represent a form of political accountability, reflecting the extent to which individuals or programs were responsive to the clientele's expectations. Of course the possibility of external audits or oversight (legal accountability) is ever present, although it may be infrequently used. The full range of expanded inputs is visually presented in Figure 8.3. The individual is represented by the circle at the center of the figure; the fact that the circle straddles all the boxes indicates that each of the different evaluation standards and accountability relationships is relevant. While this technique represents all four kinds of sources of accountability expectations, wider sources of input on evaluations do not necessarily guarantee more accurate evaluations.

The next logical step in performance appraisal reform is to bring performance appraisals in line with the team orientation embedded in many of the broader reforms, especially those pursued under the rubric of Total Quality Management or continuous process improvement. This issue has received a great deal of rhetorical attention, especially for its emphasis on shifting from individual to group or team assignments. The accountability challenge in

Figure 8.3. Types of Accountability Relationships Under 360-Degree Performance Appraisals.

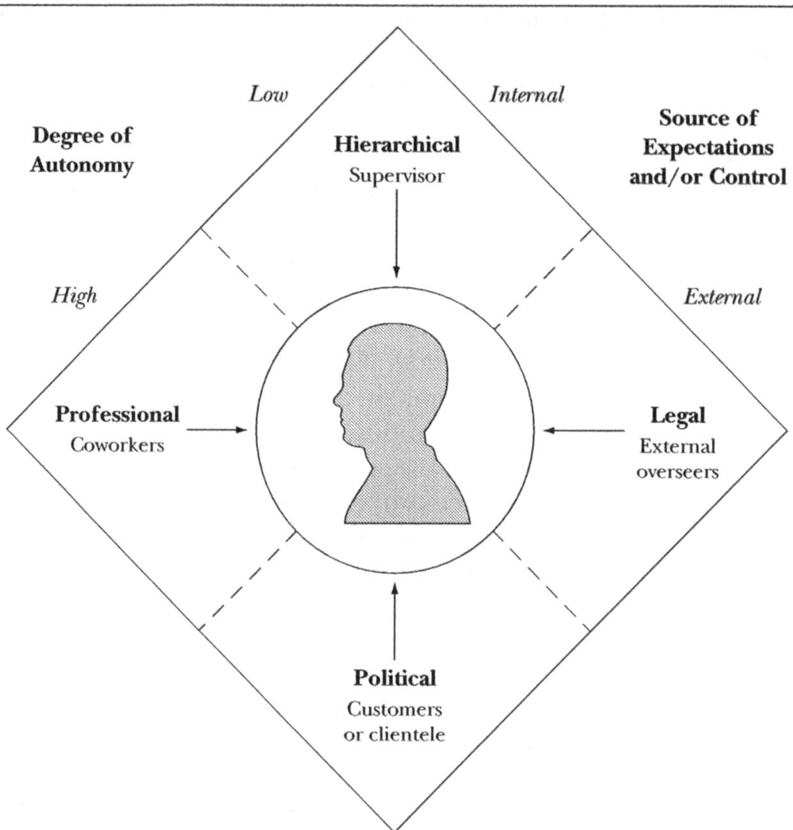

shifting to a team approach to work assignments is to develop a team-based performance evaluation system to accompany the team assignments.

Public agencies in general have been slow to adjust to evaluating and rewarding team behavior. The individualistic nature of our public service rules and regulations makes group-based evaluations very difficult. Most agencies that utilize teams evaluate the performance of *individuals* for their contributions to team projects, rather than the team as a whole. Some reinvention labs report experimenting with group-based bonus awards, but they are quick to note that they keep two sets of records—one that is consistent with the individual performance appraisals that headquarters or central agencies want to see and one with the group performance levels that the reform effort values and seeks to reward.

Some limited team-based activity is under way at state levels as well. The National Association of State Personnel Executives (1995) reports that six states have instituted or are developing team-based pay-setting approaches and bonus systems: Alaska, Colorado, Georgia, Idaho, Maryland, and Montana. A 1996 survey by the International Personnel Management Association found that 3 percent of the 270 federal, state, and local governments responding to the survey use some team-based evaluation (International Personnel Management Association, 1996). For example, Hampton, Virginia, reports that it has eliminated its personnel classification system and shifted to cross-functional and self-directed teams; the city bases pay in part on what the group accomplishes collectively (U.S. General Accounting Office, 1995, pp. 21–22).

The team approach to government reform has been evident at the agency level as well. It is most visible in intergovernmental contexts, where several agencies and levels of government work together to accomplish policy goals. The National Rural Development Partnership (NRDP) is one example. The NRDP involves interagency cooperation among some twenty-three different federal agencies and another thirteen national associations with rural development responsibilities and interests, as well as with the various governmental and nongovernmental interests in the states. The NRDP represents an effort to reform the way government agencies administer rural development policy away from federal funding and top-down directives. Instead, it places federal agencies in the role of facilitators for state rural development councils (SRDCs). The SRDCs emphasize inclusive, collaborative, localized responsibility and problem solving by agents representing federal, state, local, and tribal governments as well as private and not-for-profit organizations interested in rural development (Radin and others, 1996).

Needless to say, such a complex intergovernmental operation presents substantial challenges for traditional accountability relationships because of the difficulty in assigning relative contributions or responsibilities to individual agencies or actors (Southern Growth Policies Board, n.d.). NRDP participants report feeling as if they are working in two different worlds: one where they are judged by traditional performance appraisal processes for their agency-based roles and a second that encourages entrepreneurial, facilitative behaviors and team-oriented problem solving that crosses agency and intergovernmental boundaries (Radin and Romzek, 1996). State-based participants report similar double duty. They are accountable in two administrative worlds: their traditional, home-based organizational duties by which they are formally evaluated and the world of interorganizational collaboration that is supported rhetorically but that in reality is considered an "add on" duty. This same dynamic exists at the agency level as well: agencies face tension between their "regular" missions and their desire to deploy energies into and get credit for collaborative NRDP projects.

These various efforts represent experiments with changes in the scope of performance evaluation. Some changes have expanded the scope of input; others have expanded the unit of analysis to teams and interagency collaborations. While most of these experiments are still fairly limited, they nonetheless are important because they reflect the spirit of experimentation and enthusiasm for administrative reform that is necessary for long-term success. We next turn our attention to another way to adapt accountability reform, by changing the standards for performance used for evaluation.

Change Standards for Evaluation

As noted earlier in this chapter, most contemporary government reforms advocate shifting from the traditional emphasis on inputs and process to an emphasis on outputs and outcomes. The Government Performance and Results Act (GPRA), which is currently in the pilot phase of implementation, is an example of government's aspiration to move toward outcomes and outputs, this time with congressional support. With the GPRA, "Congress recognized that, in exchange for shifting the focus of accountability to outcomes, managers must be given the authority and flexibility to achieve those outcomes" (Bowsher, 1996, p. 11). The GPRA requires agencies to develop five-year strategic plans and identify program performance goals and quantifiable measures (Committee on Government Reform and Oversight, 1995, p. 36). Thus far the

GPRA has seventy first-stage "pilot projects" in which agencies are developing strategic goals that include output and outcome measures for which they will subsequently be held accountable.

Output measures include standards for *services* that the clientele can expect when they contact the agency. Outcome measures are the quantity and quality of the *results* achieved by the outputs. A great deal of activity has been concentrated on setting up output measures; outcome measures have proved much more difficult. When relying on outputs, there is a tendency to emphasize measures that are easily obtained, for example, number of arrests made, patients examined, checks issued, or citizens satisfied. Agencies have control over their outputs; they have much less control over outcomes.

Examples of output measures include the time callers have to wait to get through by telephone to the Social Security Administration, the time visitors have to wait for service at the National Archives and Records Administration, or the time veterans have to wait to see a benefits counselor. The U.S. Postal Service developed a consumer affairs tracking system that records and reports every customer contact. The medical centers of the Department of Veterans Affairs have an ongoing complaint-tracking system and conduct annual surveys of patients. Reliance on outputs and outcomes includes the use of executive-performance contracts for outputs in goods and services. New Zealand used this concept for its chief executive officers (U.S. General Accounting Office, 1995, p. 20), and by the end of 1995 the Clinton administration had signed similar performance agreements with eight agency heads (Gore, 1995).

The Defense Mapping Agency directly connects employees with customers through customer support teams to help customers plan, prioritize, and produce products, services, and information for the operational armed forces (National Performance Review, 1995, p. 12). An output of the NRDP was the development of a one-page form for a loan application through the Small Business Administration that takes about three days from start to finish. It replaces an earlier seventy-eight-page application that typically took ninety days for processing (Radin and others, 1996).

This discussion about shifting emphasis away from inputs and processes and toward outcomes and outputs reflects the rhetoric of government reforms. The language of reform is enticing. It is a fairly simple task to repeat the various reform mantras: "Cut red tape; empower employees; emphasize results, not rules; delight your customers." On the surface, these phrases appear to be obvious and straightforward prescriptions for action: simply tell public managers what outputs and outcomes they are expected to achieve and then give them the flexibility and discretion to do so. The fact of the matter is that following these prescriptions involves difficult work and some important shifts in decision-making authority. Political, managerial, and methodological challenges are associated with using outcome measures for accountability.

Political problems lie in the difficulty in getting agreement on qualitative and subjective measure of outcomes. Government programs are often infused with highly charged political issues; consequently, it is often extremely difficult to get agreement on definitions of good outcomes. This is evident in the education field's current pressures and difficulties associated with developing outcomes for assessment purposes. Or consider the different definitions of good outcomes for prisons. Is a good outcome for prisons the successful warehousing of inmates or successful parole and rehabilitation? What is meant by successful parole?

The difficulties experienced by an agency whose mission is research into outcomes illustrate some of the political challenges that can emerge. The health services area enjoys greater consensus regarding definitions of good outcomes than is characteristic of most government programs. Mortality and morbidity, physical functioning, mental well-being, and immunization rates are widely accepted measures of good outcomes in health care (Guadagnoli and McNeil, 1994). The experience of the Agency for Health Care Policy and Research (AHCPR), a unit of the Public Health Service in the U.S. Department of Health and Human Services, with group reactions to its findings on patient-oriented outcomes is illustrative. The agency's statutory authority includes the funding of research on patient outcomes from various medical practices. Its research focuses on "the relative effectiveness and cost effectiveness of different treatment modalities" and determines "not only what is working in health care, but what is *not* working" (emphasis in original) (Gaus and Simpson, 1995, p. 133). The research team examining patient outcomes for lower back pain found that treatment by general practitioners and chiropractors was efficacious but surgery for lower back pain was not indicated.

In response to these findings, the AHCPR found itself the target of intense opposition by back surgeons who vehemently disagreed with the research conclusions. The surgeons found political support among House Republicans; the result was that the agency was almost completely defunded for fiscal year 1996. The agency's final budget for fiscal 1996, $125.3 million, was one-third lower than it had been in fiscal 1995 (AHCPR, 1996, p. 18). And House Republicans remain committed to eliminating the agency completely over the next few years.

Managerial problems arise from using outcomes for accountability purposes because of the time lag between the administrative action and the desired outcomes, which may be measured in years. Results frequently are not immediately evident and can be determined only through formal program evaluation (Southern Growth Policies Board, n.d.). Achievement of goals often lags behind administrative action by several years or more. (This is similar to the problem that elected officials have in balancing short-term and long-term interests in policy making.)

One way to deal with this time lag is to develop intermediate outcome measures to supplement the final outcome measures. For example, the Minnesota Trade Office used intermediate outcome measures to identify outcomes because two to three years might elapse from the time the Trade Office assisted a business until the desired outcome was achieved, for example, "making a foreign market contact" or making a "decision to export" (U.S. General Accounting Office, 1994, p. 11). Similarly, the NRDP, with its emphasis on outputs and outcomes, has not had an easy time producing quantifiable indicators of improvement in rural access to jobs, health care, and education. However, it has had success with intermediate outcomes, such as the development of new projects, players, relationships, and ways of problem solving in the rural development arena, as well as increased participation, activity, and legitimacy (Radin and Romzek, 1996).

Program evaluation research has alerted us to the tendency of evaluations based on output measures to displace behavior. People perform in ways that maximize the outputs by which they will be measured. This has been known to happen when job training and placement services spend their energies on the job service candidates who can most easily be trained for jobs, rather than taking on the candidates who will be most difficult to place.

Another problem with using outcome measures for accountability is that managers are not always in total control of outcomes, which often depend on other factors besides the programs themselves. So a change in crime statistics might be due to shifting demographics among the population in the jurisdiction rather than to any change in the performance of law enforcement officials.

Methodological problems with outcomes emerge from the difficulty and expense of developing sound measures of outcomes, which tend to be qualitative and subjective (Committee on Government Reform and Oversight, 1995, p. 37). Another challenge is to overcome the limits of our knowledge of cause-and-effect relationships in areas of government policy (Walters, 1994). For example, it is not clear that we understand the cause-and-effect relationships in the area of economic policy, let alone the more complex social problems that government undertakes such as education, crime, youth gangs, and poverty.

Conclusion

Reforms of public management are being vigorously pursued at federal, state, and local levels of government. The pendulum is swinging toward flexibility and discretion and away from control and rigidity. These reforms, which seek to change the management culture, necessitate a change in the culture of accountability that has developed in this country over the years. The accountability culture calls for multiple, overlapping, and redundant relationships to ensure that proper behavior is the norm and that public employees are held to answer for inappropriate behavior.

The general reform pattern is a shift in emphasis in the approach to accountability, from inputs and processes to outputs and outcomes. This shift to outcomes and outputs presents substantial political, managerial, and methodological challenges. The reality of government reform is that it is very hard to make these changes, especially given the American political culture's disinclination to discard existing accountability relationships. The American political culture is unlikely to discontinue completely the use of hierarchical and legal accountability relationships, and the necessary changes in organizational culture that these reforms entail will require substantial adjustment on the part of public managers. Changes in organizational culture are rarely quick or easy (Schein, 1992).

It is unclear whether the American populace, its political institutions, and its managerial culture are ready to afford public agencies and their employees the discretion and flexibility that such reforms entail. The challenge of contemporary government reform is to change the underlying culture of accountability in this country, which has a distrustful, punitive orientation. It will be difficult to foster entrepreneurial behaviors in a culture that has a "gotcha" mentality toward accountability.

The institutional context within which public management operates in the United States has never been very trusting of government and its administrators, and there is no sign that trust is on the upswing; rather, it is declining (Ruscio, 1996). Currently public managers in the United States have strong disincentives for taking bureaucratic risks. And the American political culture has demonstrated an increasing intolerance with any missteps in government; a single error can be fatal to one's standing or career. Until the political culture can forgive "honest mistakes committed in an effort to improve the way things are done," the incentive system for entrepreneurial management will be inadequate (National Academy of Public Administration, 1994, p. 23).

These reforms may be deemphasizing old, familiar accountability relationships *before* the American polity is comfortable with a heavy reliance on accountability relationships that are appropriate for the new reforms. If history is a good predictor of the future, then at the first sign of problem or scandal under these reformed management systems, a reactivation of hierarchical and legal accountability mechanisms is likely. The pattern is all too common: an early search for someone to blame, identification of individuals at fault or scapegoats, and generation of new rules and regulations to ensure that such mistakes do not reoccur.

In summary, the accountability dynamics in American public service are complex. Deemphasizing inputs and processes and emphasizing outcomes and outputs does not necessarily mean more or less accountability from government administrators. Rather, it means that different kinds of accountability relationships should be emphasized, ones that encourage entrepreneurial management, increased discretion and worker empowerment in daily operations, and greater responsiveness to key stakeholders and customers. According to Kettl (1995, p. 71), "The key is not to avoid all risk . . . but to develop bureaucrats' judgments about which risks are prudent and to improve the system's ability to reduce the level of risk in general." The reality is that the American political system has traditionally been willing to trade efficiency and effectiveness for reassurances about accountability and control of administrative activity. It is not clear whether this resurgent interest in efficiency and effectiveness is stronger than the longstanding distrust of government.

This is an exciting and tumultuous time in government management, and it is not for the fainthearted. There are risks for managers and agencies and for the political system in granting more discretion to managers and encouraging more responsiveness to customers, not the least of which is the substitution of the judgment of individual managers and customers for that of supervisory and organizational directors. Paying some attention to accountability relationships can ensure that accountability patterns are in reasonable alignment with the nature of the reforms that are under way. Without changes in alignment, the reforms are unlikely to take firm hold in the administrative culture. Instead, we will witness yet one more wave of reform that breaks on the shores of administrative culture.

References

AHCPR [Agency for Health Care Policy and Research]. "AHCPR Receives $125.3 Million in FY 1996 Funding." *Research Activities,* Apr. 1996, p. 18.

Bowsher, C. A. "Managing for Results: Achieving GPRA's Objectives Requires Strong Congressional Role." Testimony of the comptroller general of the U.S. General Accounting Office before the Committee on Governmental Affairs, U.S. Senate. GAO/T-GGD-96–79. Washington, D.C., Mar. 6, 1996.

Burke, J. *Bureaucratic Responsibility.* Baltimore: Johns Hopkins University Press, 1986.

Committee on Government Reform and Oversight. *Making Government Work: Fulfilling the Mandate for Change.* Third report. U.S. House of

Representatives, Dec. 21, 1995. Washington, D.C.: U.S. Government Printing Office, 1995.

Di Iulio, J. J., Jr., and Kettl, D. *Fine Print: The Contract with America, Devolution, and the Administrative Realities of American Federalism.* Washington, D.C.: Center for Public Management, Brookings Institution, 1995.

Finer, H. "Administrative Responsibility and Democratic Government." *Public Administration Review,* 1941, *1,* 335–350.

Friedrich, C. J. "Public Policy and the Nature of Administrative Responsibility." In C. J. Friedrich and E. S. Mason (eds.), *Public Policy.* Cambridge, Mass.: Harvard University Press, 1940.

Garvey, G. "False Promises: The NPR in Historical Perspective." In D. F. Kettl and J. J. Di Iulio Jr. (eds.), *Inside the Reinvention Machine: Appraising Governmental Reform.* Washington, D.C.: Brookings Institution, 1995.

Gaus, C. R., and Simpson, L. "Reinventing Health Service Research." *Inquiry,* 1995, *32,* 130–134.

Gerth, H. H., and Mills, C. W. (eds.). *From Max Weber: Essays in Sociology.* New York: Oxford University Press, 1973.

Gore, A., Jr. *From Red Tape to Results: Creating a Government That Works Better and Costs Less.* Report of the National Performance Review. Washington, D.C.: U.S. Government Printing Office, 1993.

Gore, A., Jr. *Putting Customers First: Standards for Serving the American People.* Report of the National Performance Review. Washington, D.C.: U.S. Government Printing Office, 1994.

Gore, A., Jr. *Common Sense Government: Works Better and Costs Less.* Report of the National Performance Review. Washington, D.C.: U.S. Government Printing Office, 1995.

Gruber, J. *Controlling Bureaucracies.* Berkeley: University of California Press, 1987.

Guadagnoli, E., and McNeil, B. J. "Outcomes Research: Hope for the Future or the Latest Rage?" *Inquiry,* 1994, *31,* 14–24.

Ingraham, P. W., and Romzek, B. S. (eds.). *New Paradigms for Government: Issues for the Changing Public Service.* San Francisco: Jossey-Bass, 1994.

International Personnel Management Association. *Personnel Program Inventory.* Alexandria, Va.: Center for Personnel Research, International Personnel Management Association, 1996.

Kettl, D. "Building Lasting Reform: Enduring Questions, Missing Answers." In D. Kettl and J. J. Di Iulio Jr. (eds.), *Inside the Reinvention Machine: Appraising Governmental Reform.* Washington, D.C.: Brookings Institution, 1995.

Light, P. "Creating Government That Encourages Innovation." In P. W. Ingraham and B. S. Romzek (eds.), *New Paradigms for Government: Issues for the Changing Public Service.* San Francisco: Jossey-Bass, 1994.

Madison, J. "Federalist Paper No. 51." In A. Hamilton, J. Madison, and J. Jay, *The Federalist Papers.* New York: New American Library, 1961. (Originally published 1788.)

Milward, H. B. "Implications of Contracting Out: New Roles for the Hollow State." In P. W. Ingraham and B. S. Romzek (eds.), *New Paradigms for Government: Issues for the Changing Public Service.* San Francisco: Jossey-Bass, 1994.

Moe, R. C. "The 'Reinventing Government' Exercise: Misinterpreting the Problem, Misjudging the Consequences." *Public Administration Review,* 1994, *54,* 111–122.

Mosher, F. *Democracy and the Public Service.* (2nd ed.) New York: Oxford University Press, 1982.

National Academy of Public Administration. *Helping Government Change: An Appraisal of the National Performance Review.* Washington, D.C.: National Academy of Public Administration, 1994.

National Association of State Personnel Executives. *NASPE Survey Summary.* Lexington, Ky.: National Association of State Personnel Executives, 1995.

National Performance Review. *Reinvention Roundtable,* Winter 1995, p. 12.

Osborne, D., and Gaebler, T. *Reinventing Government: How the Entrepreneurial Spirit Is Transforming the Public Sector.* Reading, Mass.: Addison Wesley Longman, 1992.

Peters, B. G., and Savoie, D. J. "Managing Incoherence: The Coordination and Empowerment Conundrum." *Public Administration Review,* 1996, *53,* 281–289.

Radin, B., and Romzek, B. S. "Accountability Expectations in an Intergovernmental Arena: The National Rural Development Partnership." *Publius,* 1996, *26,* 59–81.

Radin, B., and others. *New Governance for Rural America: Intergovernmental Partnerships and Rural Development.* Lawrence: University Press of Kansas, 1996.

Romzek, B. S. "Enhancing Accountability." In J. L. Perry (ed.), *Handbook of Public Administration.* (2nd ed.) San Francisco: Jossey-Bass, 1996.

Romzek, B. S. "Accountability Challenges of Deregulation." In C. Ban and N. M. Riccucci (eds.), *Public Personnel Management: Current Concerns, Future Challenges.* (2nd ed.) Reading, Mass.: Addison Wesley Longman, 1997.

Romzek, B. S., and Dubnick, M. J. "Accountability and the Public Service: Lessons from the Challenger Tragedy." *Public Administration Review,* 1987, *47,* 227–238.

Romzek, B. S., and Dubnick, M. J. "Issues of Accountability in Flexible Personnel Systems." In P. W. Ingraham and B. S. Romzek (eds.), *New Paradigms for Government: Issues for the Changing Public Service.* San Francisco: Jossey-Bass, 1994.

Romzek, B. S., and Dubnick, M. J. "Accountability." In J. M. Shafritz (ed.), *International Encyclopedia of Public Policy and Administration.* New York: Henry Holt, 1997.

Ruscio, K. P. "Trust, Democracy, and Public Management: A Theoretical Argument." *Journal of Public Administration Research and Theory,* 1996, *6,* 461–478.

Schein, E. H. *Organizational Culture and Leadership.* (2nd ed.) San Francisco: Jossey-Bass, 1992.

Southern Growth Policies Board. *Alliance for Redesigning Government: Primer on Performance Measurement.* Washington, D.C.: National Academy of Public Administration, n.d.

Thompson, J. R., and Ingraham, P. W. "The Reinvention Game." *Public Administration Review,* 1996, *56,* 291–298.

U.S. General Accounting Office. *Managing for Results: State Experiences Provide Insights for Federal Management Reforms.* Publication no. GAO/GGD-95–22. Washington, D.C.: U.S. Government Printing Office, 1994.

U.S. General Accounting Office. *Transforming the Civil Service: Building the Workforce of the Future.* Report to the U.S. Committee on Governmental Affairs, U.S. Senate. Publication no. GAO/GGD-96–35. Washington, D.C.: U.S. Government Printing Office, 1995.

U.S. Office of Personnel Management. *Broad Banding in the Federal Government: A Technical Report.* Washington, D.C.: U.S. Office of Personnel Management, 1992.

Volcker Commission. *Leadership for America: Rebuilding the Public Service.* Task Force Reports to the National Commission on the Public Service. Washington, D.C.: National Commission on the Public Service, 1989.

Walters, J. "The Benchmarking Craze." *Governing,* Apr. 1994, pp. 33–37.

Walters, J. "Flattening Bureaucracy." *Governing,* Mar. 1996, pp. 21–24.

Winter Commission. *Hard Truths/Tough Choices: An Agenda for State and Local Reform.* First Report of the National Commission on the State and Local Public Service. Albany, N.Y.: Rockefeller Institute, 1993.

Chapter Nine

Making Government Reform Stick

Lessons Learned

Donald J. Savoie

Every government in Anglo-American democracies has in recent years launched ambitious measures to reform its operations (Savoie, 1994). Indeed, a good number of them have done so repeatedly in the hope that this time they were on to a winner. Unfortunately, success stories have been rare. Thus, over the past fifteen years or so, high-profile government reforms have been unveiled, strongly endorsed and publicly applauded, only to die on the vine within a few years. We are told that career public servants have developed a well-honed capacity to give the appearance of instituting change while, in fact, moving very slowly or even doing nothing (Savoie, 1994, p. ix). One well-known student of government observes: "Reading evaluations of major government reform efforts from a number of national settings appears to indicate that a finding of no significant results is often the indicator of a reform success, while a failure often is characterized by serious negative side effects" (Peters, 1991, p. 1).

Yet not everyone has stood still: some reform measures have had or are having an impact. For example, in all Anglo-American democracies, more administrative power is being given to line departments and agencies. In addition, financial management has changed a great deal during the past fifteen years. Governments are busy restructuring their operations, shedding jobs, and attacking red tape and administrative overhead. Some government units and line departments have reengineered their own operations and way of doing things, and parts of government departments and agencies "have changed dramatically" in recent years (Wilson, 1994, p. 671).

A number of questions jump to mind: What are the key conditions for success in planning and implementing government reform measures? What works and what does not? What can politicians do to increase the chances of success in reforming government? The purpose of this chapter is to answer these questions by mapping out key circumstances, conditions, and initiatives likely to result in real change.

Managing Expectations

One can easily appreciate why politicians on the outside looking in or on the day they assume office tend to offer dramatic, action-oriented phrases to describe their proposals to reform government. The rhetoric sells very well with the electorate; it plays on the negative stereotype of an inept public bureaucracy sorely in need of an overhaul. Nor does the rhetoric stop when politicians assume office. For example, in the United States, Vice President Al Gore forwarded his National Performance Review report to President Bill Clinton standing on the south lawn of the White House before forklifts of personnel, budget, and procurement manuals. Gore explained that his report was "about change. It will get us moving from red tape to results" (Gore, 1994, p. 7). The problem, of course, is that the actual reforms are assessed against the backdrop of these dramatic assurances and they invariably fall short of expectations. While politicians do not hesitate to promise "big answers," they are, in fact, rarely willing or able to take the first step: reforming their own political institutions. Big answers to get at the root cause of the woes of the civil service can only be contemplated—if indeed they should be contemplated at all—in tandem with equally ambitious reforms of political institutions.

Thus the role of politicians in government reform is far more important than is generally assumed. Good government has a lot more to do with good politics than with good public administration. After all, public administration begins and ends with political institutions—with the presidency, Congress, the Cabinet, or Parliament. If there are any big answers, they can only be found by fixing these institutions. Accordingly, senior career officials have every right to remind politicians in search of the big answer of St. Luke's famous caution to the physician: "heal thyself."

Unless politicians are prepared first to overhaul their own institutions and their way of doing things, they should keep their rhetoric in check. "Management by event" may offer short-term political benefits, but it can have only limited lasting impact unless politicians are also prepared to reinvent what they themselves do, how they do it, and how their own institutions operate.

Tailoring Change to the Circumstances

Henry Mintzberg has observed that one can "no more prescribe the best way to run all organizations than prescribe one pair of glasses for all people" (1989, p. 93). Empowerment and delayering, for example, may make sense in one government agency but not in another. Unthinkingly assuming that the latest fashion or fad will automatically fit the requirements of your department is no solution. Paul Thomas explains: "The beginning of practical wisdom for public managers is not to ask: What are the so-called best organizations doing? Rather, they should begin by asking: What does this particular organization need, given its purpose, history and current circumstances?" (Thomas, 1997).

The "one change fits all" mindset is not realistic. Many observers are now suggesting that government managers should look to the outside rather than inside the organization to plan change (Morgan, 1988, p. 2). However, the outside holds both threats and opportunities for the organization, and change agents need to understand both to successfully plan new reform initiatives.

Some observers are also suggesting that public sector managers should rank proposed changes according to their scope and complexity. Paul Thomas (1997) explains: "Writers make the distinction between *first order, second order* and even *third order* changes, referring respectively to relatively minor changes within the framework of existing organizational realities, more fundamental changes which involve modifications to the existing paradigm of the organization, and finally . . . the substitution of completely new definitions of reality" (p. 102; see also Levy, 1987). Understanding the scope and complexity of the proposed changes will enable managers to plan the resources necessary to make them stick, map out a proper strategy, and establish appropriate benchmarks to see if the reform measures are successful.

Managers must also assess the overall political climate to determine what change it can accommodate. Is the political environment stable or turbulent? Is it open to change? Change in government invariably entails a political risk. A popular administration riding high in public opinion polls will be more open to risks than one that is losing public support. In addition, opportune moments for introducing change should be taken advantage of. For example, in the United States the environment was particularly propitious in the immediate aftermath of Vice President Gore's National Performance Review report but less so after the midterm election when the Republicans won control of both houses of Congress.

Political Will Works

Announcements of reform measures, however modest, invariably are accompanied by expectations of action; nevertheless, any actual improvement in performance takes time. This, in turn, can lead to frustration, discouragement, and resistance (Thomas, 1997). Dealing with the gap between expectation and results requires a strong political will if the reform measures are not to be completely discarded. Political will is also necessary when tough decisions are needed to challenge long-established ways of doing things and to maintain the momentum of change.

Past experience reveals that politicians will often want to be front and center when measures with jazzy names are announced, but that they then go on to other, more pressing, issues immediately after the announcement. It may well be that government reforms can never hold the kind of political appeal that sustains a long-term interest in their implementation, or perhaps some politicians believe that their responsibility ends with painting the broad picture: someone else will handle the details. Whatever the reason, few political leaders are prepared to keep government reform at the top of their political agenda. This is what former U.S. defense secretary William J. Perry was getting at when he observed: "Many people have vowed to reform the government, but after they start that undertaking they mysteriously disappear, never to be heard from again. It's as if they had decided to take a vacation to Jurassic Park" (Perry, 1994, p. 5).

President Clinton insists that he is well aware of the need to provide long-term political commitment to government reform. When Vice President Gore submitted his report, Clinton explained: "Here's the most important reason why this report is different from earlier ones on government reform. When Herbert Hoover finished the Hoover Commission, he went back to Stanford. When Peter Grace finished the Grace Commission, he went back to New York City. But when the vice-president finished his report, he had to go back to his office—20 feet from mine—and go back to working to turn the recommendations into reality" (Clinton, 1994, p. 365).

Former prime minister Margaret Thatcher had more success in reforming government operations in the United Kingdom than her contemporaries elsewhere, not only because she stayed the course, but also because she took a strong personal interest in implementation of the reforms. She insisted on regular briefings and in many instances sought to master administrative details. From time to time, she even transferred administrative decisions to her own office. She did this, for example, in the case of the scrutinies process (Savoie, 1994). If nothing else, this sent a strong signal to permanent officials that she meant business.

In Florida, Governor Lawton Chiles and Lieutenant Governor Buddy MacKay launched an ambitious comprehensive reform effort after making administrative reform the centerpiece of the 1990 gubernatorial campaign. They took dead aim at rigid bureaucratic structures and outmoded management systems and established a reform commission that laid down a number of principles to guide the reform measures. Government agencies were reorganized, a performance-based budgeting process was introduced, decentralization of government activities was strongly encouraged, and new management techniques such as Total Quality Management were promoted.

Observers (Berry, Chackerian, and Wechsler, 1996, p. 16) now report that "there have been real successes" in Florida. The state government is "clearly more results focused" and a new strategic planning process has been implemented. In addition, the state is now "modestly more community-oriented and relies on more citizen input." If anything, Chiles and MacKay may have "over-promised" in the heat of the election campaign; in the end, the expectations were such that they could never have been fully met. The promise of big savings may be necessary to gain the necessary political support to launch reform measures, so politicians have to walk a thin line between promise, expectations, and reality. What they cannot do, however, is introduce ambitious reform measures and then go on to something else as if the job has been done. This is precisely what happened in Canada during the Mulroney years.

Canadian prime minister Brian Mulroney very rarely took any interest in the implementation of government reform measures. However, this never prevented him from introducing one initiative after another (Savoie, 1994). Within months of coming to office, he declared that front-line managers would be granted more power to make decisions. His government unveiled, with considerable fanfare, a bold new initiative to empower line managers called "Increased Ministerial Authority and Accountability" (IMAA). However, within months the initiative had lost credibility, largely because managers discovered that the paperwork required to make IMAA work was not worth the effort. The Mulroney government did not try to fix this problem. It simply came back with another high-profile plan, "Public Service 2000." Still more reforms followed, including the introduction of "special operating agencies" and a fundamental overhaul of the cabinet committee and budget-making systems. These initiatives were also largely discredited, again because they lacked the political commitment required to make them stick (Savoie, 1994).

Yet British and Canadian prime ministers work with political institutions that are much more amenable to making government reform measures stick than is the case for American presidents. Prime ministers with a majority mandate have a relatively free hand in shaping their political agenda. In addition, parliaments are much less likely to involve themselves in administrative details and government operations than are the U.S. Congress and its committees. Clinton and Gore may well have been strongly committed to the implementation of the National Performance Review report, but Congress could easily trip them up. Newt Gingrich's Contract with America, for example, does not easily square with Clinton and Gore's "reinventing government" initiative. Clinton and Gore want to reinvent government in order to save it, to ensure that it continues to have a strong role "to play on a wide spectrum of challenges—helping to spur economic growth, provide wider success to affordable health care, devise a long-term solution to crime, and so on" (Gore, 1994, p. 9). Gingrich's objective is vastly different. He would like to cut the federal government down to size and see its role in society attenuated on most policy fronts. The Contract with America was in many ways nothing short of a broadside directed at the reinventing government initiative. One practitioner involved with this initiative observed that "the environment is one of turbulence, flux that makes cultural change more problematic; what you change to now might not be relevant in the future."[1]

The above, perhaps more than any other factor, explains why many government reform efforts never live up to their initial billing. Mixed messages from political leaders lead to confusion, if not cynicism, among government managers. Mixed messages or a lack of firm political direction and commitment can derail the most well-thought-out plan. In turn, the inability to make a government reform measure stick serves to fuel the "disbelief culture" found among many civil servants.

Career officials have seen political leaders take turns at pledging reform only to lose interest once the announcement was made. Thus, public servants have learned to batten down the hatches at such times and wait out the passing storm. Experience has taught them that politicians will quickly lose interest in such matters and turn to the next pressing political crisis, of which there is never a shortage. According to Les Metcalfe and Sue Richards, this disbelief culture has also come to act as a psychological defense mechanism against any proposals that threaten the status quo of the public service (Metcalfe and Richards, 1987, pp. 18–19).

In the absence of strong and sustained political support, government managers will very often adopt a "steady as she goes" management style. They know that there will always be a market for their skills in acting as a kind of fire brigade to help extinguish political fires and the inevitable political crises. Thus, unless politicians are prepared to spend political capital on government reforms and to provide lasting commitment to this goal, the chances that the reforms will succeed are not high.

Communication Is Key

A participant at the Maxwell Symposium reported that it was impossible for government managers to overcommunicate when planning and implementing change.[2] He pointed out that managers have outside stakeholders as well as employees who are always interested in the nature of the changes being proposed or the progress being realized during the various implementation phases. Outside stakeholders, he explained, do not only include clients but also elected politicians and other government officials. These include members of key congressional committees and congressional staffers, as well as officials in the Department of the Treasury and the Office of Management and Budget (OMB).

Why is communication key? Unless one is satisfied to play at the margins, any important reform attempt must seek to change the organization's culture in some way. At the risk of overgeneralization, the organizational culture found in most government departments and agencies has the following characteristics: a consensus-based decision-making process, a strong emphasis on low-risk conservative approaches, and planning geared to the short term or at best the medium term. Again, at the risk of overgeneralizing, the reinventing government initiative promotes a more entrepreneurial approach to decision making, encourages risk taking, promotes rapid decisions, and attaches a strong importance to serving "client needs." President Clinton summed up the difference in this fashion: "Our goal . . . is to change the culture of our national bureaucracy away from complacency and entitlement toward initiative and empowerment" (Gore, 1994, p. 7).

Changing an organization's culture is no small task. Government departments and agencies have developed their culture over many years, and some employees no doubt have become comfortable with their departmental culture. They know what is expected of them and intuitively know how to survive in the organization. It is wrong to assume that change, even well-thought-out change, will always be welcomed within or even outside the organization. Hence, if the objective is to change the culture, it is impossible to overcommunicate. People can have a stake either in the old culture or in any plan for change. To win over employees will be the first priority, of course, but there will be others. Many outside groups will need to be informed of the proposed changes and what the impact will be on them. These include client groups and potential client groups. But there are also several oversight bodies or, as one participant at the Maxwell Symposium put it, the "external stakeholders" in the Treasury, the Office of Management and Budget, the General Accounting Office, and key congressional committees. He added, "You need to communicate until you are sick and tired of communicating, and then you do it some more."[3]

How to communicate? Participants at the Maxwell Symposium talked about the need for bottom-up communication, top-down communication, and team communication, as well as the need for champions to communicate the proposed changes. Several stressed the importance of identifying ways to make it as easy as possible for employees everywhere in the organization to voice their ideas and suggestions for change. Some reported that they had installed a "reinvention hotline" that enabled all employees to phone in their suggestions. Others said that suggestion boxes had been installed in strategic locations to enable employees to submit suggestions or comments anonymously. Yet others reported that new mailboxes had been established in the electronic-mail system where employees could register their suggestions or observations. Still others reported that special newsletters had been prepared to keep employees fully informed of the changes being introduced. Managers and supervisors were also strongly encouraged to maintain an open-door policy so that employees could discuss their suggestions in person. The means of communication that are used are important, and the participants identified the ones above. No doubt there are more, and some are probably better suited to some organizations than to others.

The central purpose in promoting a strong communications strategy is to develop a feeling of team spirit and a sense that all employees can contribute directly to a new way of doing things. Most government agencies have various field offices, and communication between offices, let alone between employees, is not always easy or evident. Indeed, different organizational cultures can take root in the head office and the field offices. When important changes are contemplated, unless strong communication mechanisms are put in place, rumors or stories in newspapers may be where employees get their information.

To be successful, top management has to commit a great deal of time to explaining the proposed changes and how all employees can contribute. Senior managers must also show the way through leadership and concrete examples. The surest way to kill change is for senior managers to send out uncertain signals. They can hardly talk about breaking down internal fiefdoms or cutting back on administrative overhead unless they take the lead on these fronts in their own offices. In short, imposing a new framework on the organization while senior management continues to do things the way it always has is a formula for failure.

Those at the bottom of the organization are no less important than top management in successfully implementing change. Top management often comes and goes while the rank-and-file employees, much more often than not, stay with the organization for the long term. Some previous initiatives that denigrated rank-and-file government employees, such as those attempted by the Grace Commission in the United States, had very limited lasting impact. In contrast, reforms such as the Rayner scrutinies in the United Kingdom, which had some lasting success, sought to directly involve public servants in the process (Savoie, 1994).

Changing an organizational culture may well require the development of a "better carrot." But developing a better carrot in times of government cutbacks is no easy task. How do you keep your most competent people when you cannot offer to give them more money? In government, as elsewhere, promotion has traditionally been the reward of success. Organizations wishing to introduce lasting management changes now have to become creative and identify incentives other than promotion to motivate rank-and-file employees. The new carrot will invariably consist of mostly nonfinancial incentives. Here it is wise to look at what many effective private sector firms have done. They have discovered that letting people carry out their pet projects can be a significant reward. Once these projects are successfully completed, employees are further rewarded by being encouraged to carry out more or bigger projects. As in pinball, the payoff comes from doing well enough to win a free game (Kanter, 1983, p. 143). This is a careerist-oriented strategy that doesn't involve promotion. People are moved sideways, not up. Its essence is empowerment: employees are gratified when they feel that the organization trusts them. Things like money, prizes, and bonuses are less important in the long run than emotional and intellectual satisfaction. Rosabeth Moss Kanter argues, for example, that "the incentives for initiative derive from situations in which job charters are broad; assignments are ambiguous, nonroutine and change-directed; job territories intersect, so that others are both affected by action and required for it; and local autonomy is strong enough that actors can go ahead with large chunks of action without waiting for higher-level approval" (Kanter, 1983, p. 143).

Many observers report that champions of change can play an extremely important role in the organization. Change can never take flight on its own merits; it has to be energized. Consultants are often brought in not only to help point the way but also to champion change. They can be very useful in that they can bring fresh thinking to old problems and long-established routines. Their usefulness is limited, however, because consultants are widely viewed as temporary help with a limited interest in the long-term health of the organization. "Have a prescription for change, will travel" has become the motto of many consultants who are peddling their magic formulas. If only because of this, many public sector managers consider that their usefulness is limited.

Some government departments and agencies have created a new senior-level position to champion change. The Internal Revenue Service (IRS), for example, established a new Associate Commissioner for Modernization. The incumbent reports directly to the commissioner of the IRS and represents the "single point of accountability for . . . modernization efforts."[4] Other agencies have turned to individuals. This is what the Alaska Native Medical Center did when it asked "Mr. Forbush, a champion with influence in the department, to manage the resistance to change."[5]

Departments and agencies are also reorienting their approaches to staffing. In Canada, the federal government is encouraging departments to hire "adaptive" rank-and-file employees and has promoted a new "manager profile" to guide departments in their staffing. In 1989 the prime minister launched an ambitious public service reform, Public Service 2000, intended to cut red tape, empower employees, and improve public service. Its special report, *Managing Change in the Public Service: A Guide for the Perplexed,* used the management literature to outline the main characteristics of "adaptive people" (Task Force on Workforce Adaptiveness, 1990, p. 25). These people have multiple skills and are versatile, open-minded, able to accommodate ambiguity, unconventional in their ideas, team-oriented, self-confident and resilient, risk-oriented, inclined to look to the future, creative, persistent, self-motivated, interested in relating to people who think differently than they do, and opportunity-focused versus problem-focused.

Whether people possessing such qualities are readily available and willing to work in a government setting is not at all clear. What is clear, however, is that the government is sending out a message that the old public service culture is no longer as valued as it once was. The old culture favored a risk-free approach to administrative rules and regulations that promoted change only at the margins and rarely with regard to policies, programs, or government operations, and that showed a preference for administration rather than management. The report also detailed the attributes of strong managers who promote change and a new culture. Ideal managers should be:

- Team players: they share with others, rather than taking from them.
- Leaders and people developers: they are capable of living with the ambiguity of not being able to control all outcomes.
- Risk takers: they are comfortable working with probabilities as well as certainties.
- Effective communicators: they can express themselves directly and unequivocally.
- Abstract thinkers: they deal effectively with intangibles, integrate information, and generate ideas.
- Good politicians: they respond to external realities, anticipate actions from outside the organization, and cooperate with other organizations on problems over which they may not have complete control.

Central Agencies Must Buy In

Central agencies often like to portray themselves as champions of change. They sit at the apex of the permanent government, often provide the link between politicians and the machinery of government, and usually employ the best and the brightest in government. Given their strategic position, central agencies can often speak not only on behalf of the political leaders but also on behalf of the institutional interests of the civil service. They have all the ingredients to be the true agents of change. In any event, given their position in the machinery of government, one could easily assume that without their support, reform measures will have little chance of success.

Yet many of the measures introduced in recent years would appear to challenge the role of central agencies. Decentralization, empowerment, global budgeting, entrepreneurial management, the establishment of quasi-autonomous organizations to deliver public services—all these suggest that the power of central agencies will be attenuated. How the central agencies deal with this dilemma will invariably have an important impact on the success of many reform measures.

B. Guy Peters writes that "central agencies have been at the centre of the reform process, but they have done little about changing their own structures and behaviours" (Peters, 1992, p. 8). He adds that most central agencies have been busy of late increasing their size and centralizing power, while asking departments and agencies to do the exact opposite. To be sure, like other public institutions, central agencies have been trying to cope as best they can with policy contradictions and conflicting goals—for example, being expected to delegate more authority to departments and agencies to empower front-line employees but also being asked to promote affirmative action in government hiring practices and to identify new areas for cutting spending.

Champions of change are well aware of these contradictions and of the influence that central agencies ultimately have on attempts to reform government operations. By and large, line-department officials view central agencies and their policies as "constraints" or "obstacles" to change that need to be overcome or sidestepped. They argue that central-agency officials will often take the lead in writing reports calling for change, but more often than not, these reports remain silent about the role of central agencies in implementing the reform. The argument goes that, as tigers do not easily part with their stripes, central agencies do not easily part with their policies, guidelines, and rules. Paul Light (1994, p. 65) describes the role of central agencies in "a familiar case" of government reform in this way: "Central staff agencies—personnel, administration, purchasing and so on—would see their role in innovation not as one of facilitation and support, not as one of serving internal customers at all, but as one of monitoring an endless list of prohibitions against the very innovation we sought."

How do champions of change in line departments and agencies overcome or sidestep central agencies in their efforts to make reform stick? Some participants at the Maxwell Symposium reported that they made special and sustained efforts to communicate what they were doing and how they were doing it. Others reported that they hired OMB analysts to work in their departments or agencies. These analysts were in an ideal position to explain central-agency perspectives or government reform measures and also to communicate back to central agencies the concerns of the department or agency.

Still others suggested that too much importance is attached to the role of central agencies. They explained that whenever frontline employees come across administrative regulations or constraints, they automatically assume that they were enacted by central agencies. A closer look, however, often reveals that many administrative constraints were put in place by Congress or at the request of current or past presidents. Some field offices will contact the head office and request that it rid the department or agency of rules and regulations or that it take action quickly on certain fronts, when clearly the request would be better directed to Congress or to the White House.

Still, some line managers have put together a series of "tactics" for dealing with central agencies and for "working around" central-agency rules when introducing change or when attempting to change the organizational culture (Task Force on Workforce Adaptiveness, 1990, pp. 38–39). It is well worth reproducing the list here:

- Know the system as well [as] or better than it knows itself (read the manuals, guidelines, etc.).
- Avoid gratuitous personality conflicts.
- Pick the right staff for the job by designating staff to liaise with the centre and making sure they have the right qualities for the job.
- Ensure that staff understand the importance of their involvement with the centre.

- Build positive attitudes—make sure your shop knows it's in charge.
- Use the "soft" approach (negotiate) when appropriate.
- Use the "hard" approach when necessary:

  Adapt your own budget.

  Be able to prove your case to the centre.

  Build public support for your initiative.

  Make your intentions clear.

  Garner high-level, visible support.
- Bypass, juggle with caution, and document moves and rationale.
- If you can't reason or bypass, escape. Run your initiative outside the overhead systems by:

  (a) Contracting out, but:

    Know precisely what services to buy.

    Specify deliverables.

    Reward subordinates for making the contractors successful.

    Use reporting and monitoring systems.

    Recognize the unique characteristics of different types of contractors.

  (b) Setting up alternate structures to provide:

    Flexibility.

    Less staff turnover.

    Authority to generate revenues.

    Singleness of purpose.

Training and Development

New reform measures need to be conceptually sound and to correspond to the requirements of the departments, and champions of change need to be assembled for the efforts to succeed. But even when these three ingredients exist, it will not be enough. Managers and employees require proper orientation, training, and development opportunities (Task Force on Workforce Adaptiveness, 1990, p. 64). To be sure, senior officials must take specific measures to unfreeze the status quo and to highlight the importance and benefits of change. However, managers and employees may resist change unless they feel confident that they possess the knowledge and the skills to implement the desired change. Without such skills, they will naturally gravitate toward the familiar, toward what existed before. That world will look more comfortable because they know how it works and what is required of them.

A recurring theme in recent government reform measures is that a new "learning culture" should be introduced at all levels of the organization. Change inevitably requires new knowledge, new skills, and a problem-solving capacity that has not been extensively relied on in the past. As one Maxwell Symposium participant pointed out, "overregulation" did not allow staff the opportunities to develop and refine new skills. "Problem identification gained precedence over problem resolution, [and] reviews were replete with findings and timetables for corrective actions, but were woefully anaemic in terms of how the local agencies should go about fixing the problem."[6]

Introducing a successful learning culture is in itself no small achievement. Traditionally, governments have rarely attached a high priority to executive development and training. Indeed, training and development budgets have usually been the first to be cut in rounds of austerity. In addition, training and development have in the past rarely been "taken seriously as a principal means of advancement in the Service" (Canada, 1990, p. 65).

One need look no further than at the much maligned U.S. Federal Executive Institute. The institute is now nearly thirty years old and has had to be reinvented on numerous occasions. With an uncertain mandate, its very existence has been seriously questioned more than once. In the early 1980s, for example, the Reagan administration seriously considered abolishing it, convinced that the institute provided "too much soft management and not enough hard—i.e. too much psychology and not enough business administration" ("Rebuilding a Flagship for Executives," 1987, p. A17).

Governments will have to do much better on this front than in the past if they want to see reform and change take root. They have to commit resources to executive development and training programs and ensure that these resources are protected from austerity measures. They also have to ensure that training and development are fully integrated with career development programs. Last, executive development and training programs should have access to the best development techniques and resources available. The objective is not only to equip public servants with new knowledge and new skills, but also to make executive development and training an important part of the new "carrot" approach to motivating public servants in times of fiscal restraint.

Looking Back

Some ten or twenty years from now, students of public administration will look back to assess the success of the reinvention initiative introduced by President Clinton and Vice President Gore to reshape the administration of the U.S. government. We can already speculate about what they will discover. They will see some genuine success stories, some that were failures, some that showed great promise early on but died on the vine, and some that gave only the appearance of change. In short, they will see a mixed bag.

It is extremely unlikely that they will see a "big answer" successfully applied to all departments and agencies. Changes will have been introduced and some will have lasted. But the changes will neither be fundamental nor apply uniformly to all parts of the government. That would have required some serious changes in the way politicians and their institutions work, and there is no sign that this is forthcoming. They will also be unable to identify a champion of change. Rather, they will be looking at many champions of change, located in obscure administrative units in Washington and probably much more often in field offices. They will see many units that decided to innovate, to change, and to stick it out. They will also discover that there was no magic formula, no all-encompassing model that could be applied everywhere and at all times.

They will see, however, that successes were the result of a number of factors. Some local champions will have dared to be innovative, to look to the history of their own organization for solutions rather than to best practices elsewhere for inspiration. Ian Gow, who has studied administrative innovations in Canadian governments, discovered that emulation and adaptation, rather than innovation, have driven most reform efforts. Yet plenty of available research shows that change has a better chance of taking root when it is tailored to the organization, its purpose, its history, and its needs. Gareth Morgan points out that "too many managers are looking outside themselves for answers to their problems. They are looking for the latest theory and at what successful organizations are doing. They are trying to spot the latest trends. In reality they would be better off engaging in some critical thinking for themselves, recognizing that they and their colleagues already have a vast treasure of insight and experience, which they could and should be using" (Morgan, 1988, p. 218).

Future students will find that the local champions decided very early on that they needed a strong communications plan for all stakeholders. They made certain that the plan included external people, including clients, but also the head office, central agencies, and interested politicians—and, not least, employees. A "no surprise" policy will be found to have permeated the planning and implementation of the communications plan.

History will also likely reveal that successful champions of change started the planning process by asking the question: What does our organization need? We have already learned a thing or two about introducing reform measures in government organizations by studying the ambitious reform efforts launched over the past fifteen years or so. One important lesson learned is that Henry Mintzberg had it right when he wrote that one can "no more prescribe the best way to run all organizations than prescribe one pair of glasses for all people" (1989, p. 93). In many ways, local champions who are able to determine what their organization needs, given its history and current circumstances, are more important than government-wide champions. Local champions are well known to front-line workers and are often able to manage expectations well and to adjust the reform measures as they are implemented.

Local champions will also have made certain that expectations were managed at all times. They will have made it clear that there would be no panacea, no earth-shattering change in the work of the units and, in the end, limited movement on the way oversight bodies go about their work. They will also have explained that the proposed changes would bring benefits, make work more interesting, and provide more flexibility to front-line workers, but that the nature of government and the civil service would not be fundamentally altered. They will have added that change requires time to take root and that above all it requires patience and persistence.

Yet they will never have hesitated to promote debate with front-line employees, having recognized that the single most important resource available to them is their staff.

Local champions will be found to have established goals and deadlines. They will have recognized that if they did not focus the organization on the task at hand with firm objectives, the reforms could be killed by entrenched forces, because inertia is an extremely powerful force in any organization, public or private.

The champions will have made a point of establishing or buying into an executive development or training program. They will have identified resources for the program and dug in their heels against those in the head office or elsewhere who wanted to cut or reduce it. The champions will have recognized that, without such a program, the employees would not have embraced change and would have just carried on as before. They will have known that without the knowledge and skills to make the changes work in practice, the reforms would be certain to be stillborn.

They will also be found to have sought out expertise to assist them either on short-term assignments or in making presentations at special conferences or staff meetings. They will have become champions of change because they never hesitated to admit that they did not have all the answers. They will have shown a willingness to listen to the views of experts and their own employees in leading the organization to a new culture. Finally, they will have been stubborn. They will never have accepted the phrase "They won't let us do that." For one thing, they will have seen that often the rules were their own or could be changed. They will have proved to be extremely tenacious in their dealings with headquarters and central agencies and will have inspired their staff to do the same thing.

Notes

1. Quoted from the transcript of the Maxwell Reinvention Symposium: Wednesday session, morning, Washington, D.C., Sept. 26 and 27, 1995, p. 1.
2. Bob Albicker, director, Office of Business Transition, Internal Revenue Service. Transcript of the Maxwell Reinvention Symposium, Washington, D.C., Sept. 26, 1995, p. 7.
3. Bob Albicker, Maxwell Reinvention Symposium, pp. 7, 10.

4. Bob Albicker, Maxwell Reinvention Symposium, p. 7.
5. Richard Mandsager, director, Alaska Native Medical Centre. Transcript of the Maxwell Reinvention Symposium, Washington, D.C., Sept. 26, 1995, p. 2.
6. Michael B. Janis, general deputy assistant secretary for public and Indian housing, Department of Housing and Indian Housing Reorganization. Transcript of the Maxwell Reinvention Symposium, Washington, D.C., Sept. 26, 1995, p. 2.

References

Berry, F. S., Chackerian, R., and Wechsler, B. "Administrative Reform: Lessons from a State Capital." Paper presented at the American Society for Public Administration National Conference, Atlanta, July 2, 1996.

Canada. *Public Service 2000: The Renewal of the Public Service of Canada.* Ottawa: Minister of Supply and Services, 1990.

Clinton, W. J. "Remarks on the National Performance Review and an Exchange with Reporters." *Public Papers of the Presidents: William J. Clinton,* Vol. 1. Washington, D.C.: U.S. Government Printing Office, 1994.

Gore, A., Jr. *From Red Tape to Results: Creating a Government That Works Better and Costs Less: Status Report, September 1994.* Washington, D.C.: U.S. Government Printing Office, 1994.

Kanter, R. M. *The Change Masters.* New York: Simon & Schuster, 1983.

Levy, A. "Second-Order Planned Change: Definition and Conceptualization." *Organizational Dynamics,* 1987, *16*(2), 5–20.

Light, P. "Creating Government That Encourages Innovation." In P. W. Ingraham and B. S. Romzek (eds.), *New Paradigms for Government: Issues for the Public Service.* San Francisco: Jossey-Bass, 1994.

Metcalfe, L., and Richards, S. *Improving Public Management.* London: Sage, 1987.

Mintzberg, H. *Mintzberg on Management: Inside Our Strange World of Organizations.* New York: Free Press, 1989.

Morgan, G. *Riding the Waves of Change.* Thousand Oaks, Calif.: Sage, 1988.

Perry, W. J. National Performance Review–Department of Defense event transcript, Washington, D.C., Mar. 28, 1994.

Peters, B. G. "Government Reorganization: A Theoretical Analysis." Paper presented at the meeting of the Canadian Political Science Association, Kingston, Ontario, June 1991.

Peters, B. G. "What Works? Lessons from the Canadian and American Experiences in Reform" (mimeo), 1992.

"Rebuilding a Flagship for Executives." *Washington Post,* Oct. 1987, p. 17.

Savoie, D. J. *Thatcher, Reagan, Mulroney: In Search of a New Bureaucracy.* Pittsburgh: University of Pittsburgh Press, 1994.

Task Force on Workforce Adaptiveness, Public Service 2000. *Managing Change in the Public Service: A Guide for the Perplexed.* Ottawa, Canada: Task Force on Workforce Adaptiveness, 1990.

Thomas, P. "Beyond the Buzzwords: Coping with Change in the Public Sector." *International Review of Administrative Sciences,* 1997, *63,* 95–109.

Wilson, J. Q. "Reinventing Public Administration: The 1994 John Gaus Lecture." *PS: Political Science and Politics,* 1994, *27,* 667–673.

Conclusion

Transforming Management, Managing Transformation

Patricia W. Ingraham

The chapters in this book are ample testimony to the fact that something really is happening in efforts to change and manage public organizations at all levels of government. Much of the change is clear, and perhaps inevitable; economic constraints and the decade-long push for smaller, flatter, more flexible government were in clear conflict with old bureaucratic structures and the hierarchical management structures they nurtured. Much of the change has been Yogi Berra–like: when you come to a fork in the road, take it. Behn's "management by groping along" model (1992), while not as purposive as some of the change strategies identified in this book, certainly fits many of the cases and examples discussed in the book's chapters.

On the other hand, there have been numerous efforts by many public managers and by the designers of some reforms to carefully and strategically change patterns and cultures in public organizations and to break the mold of old management practices. One participant at the 1995 Maxwell Symposium could barely contain her enthusiasm: "I can't imagine going back!" These managers have embraced teams, quality management, open communication, and risk taking. They have embraced change in whatever order the "change hooks" became available, and with whatever resources they provided. Some of these efforts have become notable successes. Some survived, or were moderately successful, because they were "out of the line of vision" by virtue of geographic or organizational isolation.

For some change strategies and efforts, success was very much in the eye of the beholder; not surprisingly, those who resided in the old architecture of centralization and hierarchy most often saw the changes as problematic or failures. Still other change managers became pariahs in their organization; they fought the bureaucracy and the bureaucracy won.

Some lessons emerge from these experiences at all levels of government; the fundamental lessons are aptly described by Donald Savoie in Chapter Nine and are also discussed later in this chapter. There are no universal nostrums, however; what is necessary for one organization may not be necessary for another. What works in one may not work in another. In this case, standardization is the problem, not the solution. It is one of the paradoxes of the change efforts described in this book, however, that most of them occurred inside the structures of standardized, hierarchical systems whose architects did not build easy bridges to the future.

In the United States, most public sector efforts to modernize the architecture of organizations and management have done so from the old and still solid foundation of constrained discretion and closely controlled authority. In cases such as that of Florida, where efforts were made to destroy the most obvious old structures—civil service systems—the efforts were never fully realized and most of the basic structures remained (Berry, Chackerian, and Wechsler, 1996). The strategy has not been abandoned, however, as other governments continue to make the effort, with Georgia being the most recent to attempt to start anew.

This may well be the basic conundrum in the transformation of management and managers: the most consistent sources of resistance to change and reform are the structures, rules, and values created by standardized, hierarchical systems and the decision makers who are in positions of authority within them. The rigid foundation they provide and the many barriers they create profoundly affect the capacity to move from the status quo. Change *is* possible in such a setting, but it is much more difficult and requires great persistence—or, as Donald Savoie observes, stubbornness.

Measuring success, or even recognizing it, is also harder in these environments than in organizations and systems whose reform strategy first broke down old walls; then emphasized simplification and clarification of the base budget, financial management, and human resource management processes; and finally added flexibility, discretion, and new ways of creating accountability. Indeed, one of the first things successful change leaders did in the federal reinvention labs analyzed here was to request the waiver of many civil service and budgetary procedures. Even with those waivers, however, old authority structures remained and frequently bumped up against the new systems.

There are other reasons for replacing the old architecture with more flexible and innovative systems. If decision structures are to be integrated with those of service delivery—or if single points of delivery or contact are created, as many current reforms advocate—old structures must also be altered. Aucoin argues that such transformations must move organizations from the traditional hierarchical, pyramidal structure to that of a diamond, providing for multiple agency and organizational participation, but narrowing the focus of contact with citizens (Aucoin, 1995). In Chapter Two, Ronald Sanders argues that the new "structures" are not likely to be that tidy; they will be chaotic, often difficult to discern, and in a state of frequent change themselves.

The role of leadership—or, more accurately, transformed leadership—obviously becomes central. Although political leadership and endorsement of reinvention or similar changes in the federal government and in states such as Florida, Oregon, and Minnesota have been an important component of some of the changes described in these chapters, political commitment continues to be problematic. Enormous political will is required to change or shake the old foundation; more time than many elected officials have or are willing to spend is also necessary. Many examples of this dilemma can be seen both in the United States and abroad. The sweeping changes that Barzelay and Armajani (1992) described in Minnesota did not survive a change in governors; the fundamental changes proposed in Florida were short-circuited by an inability to create adequate political support. The departure of Governor Patricia Roberts Harris in Oregon dramatically changed the level of support for many of the initiatives in that state. In other nations, the same pattern has held, with Australia being the most recent example (Renfrow, Hede, and Lamond, forthcoming; Ingraham, 1996).

How Does It Fit Together? What Is Being Transformed and How?

The lack of clarity with which managers must cope in these settings is notable and has often been described. Kettl (1994) describes "managing off the map"; Sanders and Thompson describe the "principle of ambiguity," arguing that because missions and precise activities are often unclear, "astute managers [can] use this lack of clarity to their own advantage" (Sanders and Thompson, 1996, p. 11). Peters and Savoie speak of "managing incoherence": "Governments increasingly must contend with major forces pulling in diametrically opposite directions. . . . Centripetal forces, unleashed by those wishing to reinvent government, pushing the center of government to decentralize decision making and to empower managers and front line employees; and centrifugal forces calling on the center to strengthen its capacity to coordinate policy development and implementation—and even government operations" (Peters and Savoie, 1996, p. 281).

Of particular significance to managers in these rocky environments is the set of personal skills they must acquire for internal purposes, while simultaneously managing, or successfully avoiding, the external turbulence. The limits to personal authority, the transformed nature of leadership, and the need to create an overarching set of goals around which organizational consensus can be reached and common values coalesced create demands and constraints on managers in the white water of organizational change that cannot safely be predicted. Indeed, Sanders and Thompson conclude that, in the reinvention laboratories described in this book, "The lack of answers [to important questions] is one of the defining elements of the reinvention lab experience" (Sanders and Thompson, 1996, p. 11). In this context, the effective manager-leader necessarily becomes a constant problem solver, an expert balancer of competing demands, and a communicator par excellence. The heat of the kitchen described in Chapter Two's recipe for effective leadership requires enormous commitment to risk taking and a very great tolerance for pain.

The difficulties of fulfilling all of these roles well are exacerbated by the conflicting—often dramatically conflicting—tasks and responsibilities of the transforming manager. An obvious example is the combination of downsizing with employee empowerment and team building. The real agony of managing downsizing is one part of this equation. Managers and other organizational leaders consistently refer to downsizing decisions as among the most difficult they have ever made (Jones and Ingraham, 1997). Part of the agony is maintaining commitment and belief among the employees who will stay, while telling others (often selected for lack of seniority or other civil service–related qualities, rather than for any serious lack of ability) that they are superfluous to the organization's future (Jones, 1995). Further, the need to emphasize downsizing progress can drive out more positive changes and reforms. In Fox's terms, "Costs less defeats works better" (1996, p. 259). In such an environment, the difficulties of building teams, described clearly by Thompson in Chapter One and Frederickson and Perry in Chapter Five, can be daunting.

As this suggests, employees, too, are cast into new and unpredictable roles. While the general rule that if they are not part of the solution they are part of the problem continues to apply, precisely how to be an effective part of the solution is not as clear. Organizational commitment is hard to foster and retain in times of downsizing and other threats. Even in more sanguine reforms, such as quality management and team building, employees face new expectations and substantial instability. Quality management and team efforts are clearly intended to change organizational cultures and to use human resources in different ways. Comfort levels will necessarily be altered and employees know that.

Further, in many change efforts, the introduction of Total Quality Management (TQM) was only a first step in broader and more intensive restructuring reforms. A director of a reinvention lab observed, "I started out calling what I wanted to do TQM. Then it was reinvention. Today, it's reengineering. But it's still all the same changes I wanted to make all along" (Sanders and Thompson, 1996, p. 8). For employees, therefore, changes such as TQM are the first of many. If they get it right, future changes will be both easier and more profound. If they get it wrong, it becomes another obstacle on the road to reform.

The nature and importance of this first step must be clearly recognized. If first steps are too painful or lack direction, this experience will roll over to the steps that follow. Quality management and team building, for example, are not easy first steps, despite their warm and fuzzy appeal: who could possibly be against working together? Too often, these new approaches are important missteps in change activities. In chronicling the experience in Florida, Berry, Chackerian, and Wechsler (1996, p. 20) note that while "most agencies highlighted some TQM processes in their 1991–93 strategic plans" (in keeping with the governor's emphasis on reinvention), a 1995 study "found a low level of TQM activity in most agencies." They observe further that, in the one agency that did successfully implement quality management, sustained leadership, access to additional resources, and persistence in the face of occasional failures and setbacks were critical components of success. In the federal reinvention activities, transplanting team structures and expectations onto the old hierarchies and civil service procedures has created endless difficulty. In this environment, TQM sends one set of signals about employee authority and voice; the old unreformed system and, frequently, some of its managers send another set that is very different. Employees are left to sort them out and to make choices about which is likely to prevail (Ingraham, 1995b). Providing the choice of sitting change out is not likely to nurture its success.

What are the lessons in all of this? Is it possible to sift through the randomness, the complexity, and the apparent chaos to define common threads or patterns that may be linked to successful change in the architecture, management, and behavior of organizations? Will those lessons be different for public organizations? Several such "lists of lessons" are already available; comparing them is a useful starting point.

What We Know About Effective Change Management: Lessons from Practical Experience

In Chapters Five and Nine of this book, Frederickson and Perry and Savoie survey comparative change efforts and the federal reinvention laboratories. Savoie reaches the following set of conclusions about success and the potential for achieving it:

1. Success will not be evident in major, sweeping dimensions. Rather, it will be a series of small, but important, innovations.

2. Leaders of these successful changes will look to the history of their own organization for solutions, rather than to best practices elsewhere.
3. Successful change will depend on a workforce whose skills and competencies match the new demands; this mandates serious commitment to executive and employee training and development.
4. Successful change leaders and managers will be stubborn; they will reject the phrase "They won't let us do that."

Frederickson and Perry supplement the list by focusing on the specific characteristics of change managers. They argue that successful change is based on the following series of strategic processes that are initiated and sustained by the change agent:

1. Articulating a vision of the changed state that appeals to stakeholders and allows them to see opportunities for personal gain
2. Sharing power and control of the design of changes with stakeholders
3. Articulating the consequences of change for each employee
4. Establishing the credibility of the change through a series of small, but early, successes

These conclusions are supplemented and amplified by those drawn from Florida's reform experience by Berry, Chackerian, and Wechsler (1996):

1. Do not set expectations too high, because "the perception of failure will set in early" (p. 26).
2. Similarly, plan not just for the design and for support of that design; plan for and monitor implementation.
3. Provide adequate resources for implementation and provide them consistently. In the Florida case, Berry, Chackerian, and Wechsler argue, budget shortfalls "virtually ensured that expensive reforms would be abandoned . . . or undertaken without much fiscal support" (p. 27).
4. Do not choose symbolic change if substantive change is not possible.
5. Strong, continuous leadership is of central significance.
6. Match professional capability with the demands of reform and the new organizations.

The research of Rainey and Rainey, conducted in a variety of offices of a single federal agency, highlights the following characteristics of success: strong leadership from civil servants; an active, creative staff; and "supportive, but non-interventionist" political overseers (Rainey, 1996). The common themes in all of these analyses are evident. Committed leadership, well-trained and involved employees, and persistence in pursuing reform and change are present across level of government and type of change.

The particularly public quality of some of these lessons is also clear; ensuring adequate resources, providing for careful implementation, and establishing long-term leadership are made more difficult in a political environment and with elected leadership. The window for change is much shorter for elected officials, and the need for "big" successes is greater. John Kamensky's discussion of the implementation of the National Performance Review in Chapter Three clearly identifies the positive role that political leadership can play in major change efforts. At the same time, the changing emphases of reinventing government in its first three years demonstrate that even committed political direction is not necessarily consistent.

The above lessons also demonstrate the tenuous fit between the demands of change and the old structures in which the quest for change must take place. Very few civil service systems have the capacity to adapt quickly, to recruit and develop people for broad and bridging functions and tasks, and to create and sustain rewards for risk and innovation. Civil service systems were created to be stable and standardized and to protect the organization from undue external influence (Ingraham, 1995a). That is what they do well. The demands of the new systems, the new tasks, and the new relationships are completely foreign to civil service systems in most governments. Further, it must be noted that this resistance to change is not always viewed as a liability for people who have a stake in the present structures. These structures and processes serve both political and bureaucratic purposes.

Part of the job of the change manager, therefore, is that of public relations: selling the idea, finding the resources, and holding the appropriate hands when there are bumps along the way. Simultaneously, the manager must avoid being viewed as a "loose cannon," but must create and work within new accountability expectations and mechanisms. As Barbara Romzek notes in Chapter Eight, "The general reform pattern is a shift in emphasis . . . from inputs and processes to outputs and outcomes. This shift to outcomes and outputs presents substantial political, managerial, and methodological challenges."

The Contribution of Theory

Theory should provide some guidance in negotiating the obstacles and tensions described above. In fact, many of the changes now under way in both public and private organizations are in uncharted territory. There have been some guidelines and many more exhortations. With the exception of the state reforms created in New Zealand in the 1980s (Boston, Martin, Pallot, and Walsh, 1996), it is difficult to find reform designs or strategies that are clearly grounded in principle and theory. New Zealand has warmly embraced principal-agent theory as its theoretical foundation; discussions of the intent of the reforms nearly always begin with this point. In this case, a stark alternative to bureaucratic structure and process is firmly established.

The "entrepreneurial" government advocated by the reinventing government initiative (Osborne and Gaebler, 1992) stands in substantial contrast. The compelling quality of its tenets lies in their simplicity and symbolism. The translation of many of Osborne and Gaebler's directives into the language of reinventing government reflects that simplicity: creating commonsense government that "works better and costs less." It is the overlay of that simplicity onto the complexity of public organizations' structures and law that creates the initial set of change problems; many of the necessary levers are elusive or beyond the control of the manager who wishes to initiate change. The same is true of the design espoused by Hammer and Champy's reengineering strategy (1993); the ability to simply eliminate the procedures and processes that hinder performance is assumed. The case of the U.S. Internal Revenue Service demonstrates that, for public organizations at least, that is not true (Thompson and Ingraham, 1996; Chapter Four).

If popular guides to a better future do not provide adequate conceptual clarity and support, what alternatives can be of use? B. Guy Peters, in Chapter Seven, proposes the extraction of three models from existing literature, both practical and theoretical. Arguing that the fundamental models are (1) imposing change from the top down (a hierarchical approach), (2) changing from the bottom up (a total-quality and customer-oriented approach), and (3) imposing changes through external circumstances, Peters concludes that different organizations, different policy settings, and different political and economic environments ensure that no single choice can be the best. Further, evaluations of the consequences and outcomes of each reform design choice are only now emerging on the radar screen of organizational-change managers.

James Thompson and Ronald Sanders (Chapter Four) present yet another set of choices. They rely on Szanton's metaphors of organizational change as gardening or engineering: "Reorganization had best be viewed as a branch of gardening rather than of architecture or engineering. As in gardening, the possibilities are limited by soil and climate, and accomplishment is slow. And like gardening, reorganization is not an act but a process, a continuing job" (Szanton, 1981, p. 24).

While this is a variation on Peters's "top-down" or "bottom-up" theme, the "hybrids" and the amplification of potential strategies that emerge are very useful. The level, or scope, of participation in design and implementation is key. Although the top-down model implies limited participation, that is not necessarily true. It may be possible for a change manager to define broad parameters and objectives for change and to guide and monitor the process carefully, while still creating and encouraging broad participation in the change activities. In fact, the need to set parameters for team and group participation may be one of the most enduring lessons to emerge from reinvention laboratories. Agencies and laboratories that created and "empowered" teams with little thought about how and where their activities and decisions could best be used had, at best, negative outcomes. This suggests that the bottom-up approach cannot achieve its purported benefits in the absence of clear parameters and expectations—that is, in the absence of leadership.

Another modification to the "pure" models is presented by the choice of change levers. The extent to which structural change is a necessary part of the strategy, individual behaviors and expectations for performance are different, patterns and processes of communication must be altered or reinforced, and external influences or demands for change are brought into the process—and how they are—suggests an important set of choices and priorities. The stage at which each lever or set of levers is adopted or emphasized is also significant to the overall outcomes.

The opportunity to choose between components of the top-down or bottom-up models, combined with the wide range of options available for initiating and staging change efforts, obviously creates an extensive set of hybrid or "recombinant" strategies (Beer, Eisenstat, and Spector, 1990). Most current research emphasizes that the hybrids, which combine some level of top-down guidance with extensive bottom-up problem solving, are the most effective strategies, because they permit careful tailoring to the needs and specific culture of the organization in which they are implemented (see Chapter Six for additional discussion of contingent strategy decisions).

It is possible, of course, to derive still different models or different strategies for reform by relying on different literature or different disciplinary perspectives. The New Zealand reforms noted earlier have relied on an economic, market-oriented emphasis; the systems and incentives that the reforms have created—smaller, more independent agencies; performance contracts; and financial incentives—reflect this emphasis. It is assumed in the New Zealand case that performance contracts and related mechanisms are an adequate substitute for the rules and regulations that have traditionally governed public organizations. To date, at least, these reforms have assumed that essentially economic strategies are compatible with a political setting, a conclusion with which some theorists would violently disagree (see Chapter Eight for a discussion of tensions in assessing outcomes).

Following this, it is possible to draw a set of models or reform strategies from the experiences of governments worldwide that have made different choices about the scope and outcomes of reform. The New Zealand model, which essentially blows up the old structures and replaces them with competitive, market-based agencies, represents one end of the continuum that emerges (Ingraham, 1996). The United States and its reinventing government initiatives represent the other; reinventing government has been constructed on an old bureaucratic foundation. No systematic reforms have been implemented that would change the rules of the game. Just as the existing structures and procedures were developed incrementally over a long period of time, it is assumed that change can occur in an incremental way, from an unreformed base.

At this incremental-reform end of the continuum, politics plays an important and continuing, if somewhat directionless, role. New expectations are grafted onto old; the tools for change are primarily symbolic and rhetorical. It has been argued that governments like the United States are able to pursue this rather complacent reform model because they are essentially stable and do not face any external threat or demand that would force more fundamental change (Holmes, 1992). Further, the size and complexity of the government organizations that would require reform render a comprehensive and sweeping strategy much more difficult. Nonetheless, the costs of this strategy are high in both human and organizational terms, and the outcomes are remarkably unclear.

The middle spot on the continuum is occupied by staged-reform strategies. Examples are provided by the national governments of Australia and the United Kingdom, which pursued change strategies that first attacked the complexity and rigidity of the old base systems, then built additional reforms on this simplified base. Both nations, for example, aggressively pursued budgetary and financial management reforms in the early and mid-1980s; other reforms—to personnel systems, leadership structures and incentives, and centralized ministries—proceeded from there. Therefore, although the British Next Steps agencies are very similar to the executive agencies created in New Zealand, the process of reaching them has been much more gradual and more carefully assessed (Ingraham, 1996; U.S. General Accounting Office, 1995).

Which of these strategies is best? Again, it depends on the overall intent and demand for real change. While few would recommend the U.S. experience with reinvention as a tidy and clear approach to public reform, there is no doubt that some very real successes have been achieved in the reinvention laboratories. The question for the labs, and for those who would draw lessons from them, is whether their changes will "take" over the longer term. Can they survive without supportive changes in the fundamental systems on which they must ultimately depend and with the inevitable changes in the political environment?

Questions can also be raised, however, about both the staged and "blow it up" models of reform. The Australian outcomes have been cast into some doubt by the election of John Howard in 1996; far from commending the progress made and the level of performance achieved, the new prime minister delivered a series of blistering attacks on the state of government. As a result, the next stage of reform is not clear.

In New Zealand, on the other hand, there appears to be general satisfaction with most components of the reform (U.S. General Accounting Office, 1995; Boston, Martin, Pallot, and Walsh, 1996), but serious questions are emerging about whether it may have gone too far in ignoring the special responsibilities of public organizations. The question is a variation on the top-down or bottom-up issue, defined in terms of the center. If virtually all of the government's activities and services can be decentralized, privatized, or contracted out, what remains at the center to hold them together? What information and assessment ability does government still need to ensure accountable and effective service delivery? Does it matter?

Conclusion

The examples of change and reform examined in this book do not provide easy answers for those who would draw lessons from them. The process of change is too complex, chaotic, and unpredictable for that to occur. The strategies must depend on circumstance, culture, opportunity, and resources. The outcomes will most likely not be as anticipated—or not as quickly as anticipated—in even the most strategic reforms.

At the same time, however, certain themes and issues run through the "success stories" encountered here and elsewhere; some are obvious, while others are only now emerging. At a minimum, the following should be included:

1. Proceed with change and reform only from the foundation of a thorough understanding of your organization, its culture, and its employees. Although there is a long history of looking to other governments and to private sector organizations for

change ideas and techniques, the lessons must be extracted, evaluated, and tailored carefully. They cannot be simply transplanted.

2. Establish reasonable expectations and revisit them often. The biggest promises are those most easily broken; broken promises and unmet expectations translate into perceptions of failure, decreased motivation and morale, and fewer opportunities for change in the future.
3. Communicate about the need for change, the strategy for change, the expectations for change, the impact of change on employees, and how the change will be evaluated. As one of the directors of the reinvention laboratories noted, "I communicate until I don't think I can stand it any longer, and then I communicate some more." Opportunities for discussion, for debate, and for dissent should be frequent and clear.
4. Plan carefully for implementation and do not make any assumptions about others' behavior and support in the process. (See item 3 above.)
5. Remember that leadership really matters in every change effort. It can be at the top of the organization (and should be in many cases), it can be at lower-level organizational units (as it was in the case of many reinvention laboratories), it can be partnered leadership, and it can be both political and career leadership. Leaders must establish parameters, expectations, and examples for the change effort.
6. Do not overlook any opportunity for change. The variety and multiplicity of change "hooks" described in this book's chapters are remarkable. Although only one change manager described this approach as the "kitchen sink" model of change, virtually everyone analyzed here subscribed to it.
7. Share both problems and solutions with others in similar positions. Managing change does not have to be an isolating activity, although it often feels that way. Find the right channels for support and for learning lessons and use them to maintain a sense of purpose and focus.
8. Finally, don't give up. One of the clearest messages about managing change is that it is hard and takes a long time. It will make people uncomfortable and angry and will often put the change

advocate at substantial professional risk. However, the pressures for change at all levels of government are too intense and consistent to ignore. Stubbornness, as Savoie notes, is a virtue.

References

Aucoin, P. *The New Public Management: Canada in Comparative Perspective.* Montreal: Institute for Research on Public Policy, 1995.

Barzelay, M., and Armajani, B. J. *Breaking Through Bureaucracy.* Berkeley: University of California Press, 1992.

Beer, M., Eisenstat, R. A., and Spector, B. *The Critical Path to Corporate Success.* Boston: Harvard Business School Press, 1990.

Behn, R. *Leadership Counts.* Boston: Harvard University Press, 1992.

Berry, F. S., Chackerian, R., and Wechsler, B. "Administrative Reform: Lessons from a State Capital." Paper presented at the American Society for Public Administration National Conference, Atlanta, July 2, 1996.

Boston, J., Martin, J., Pallot, J., and Walsh, P. *Public Management: The New Zealand Model.* Auckland: Oxford University Press, 1996.

Fox, C. "Reinventing Government as Postmodern Symbolic Politics." *Public Administration Review,* 1996, *56,* 256–262.

Hammer, M., and Champy, J. *Reengineering the Corporation: A Manifesto for Business Revolution.* New York: HarperBusiness, 1993.

Holmes, M. "Public Sector Management Reform: Convergence or Divergence?" *Governance,* 1992, *5,* 472–483.

Ingraham, P. W. *The Foundation of Merit: Public Service in American Democracy.* Baltimore: Johns Hopkins University Press, 1995a.

Ingraham, P. W. "Quality Management in Public Organizations: Pros and Cons." In D. J. Savoie and B. G. Peters (eds.), *Governance in a Changing Environment.* Montreal: McGill University Press, 1995b.

Ingraham, P. W. "Play It Again Sam, It's Still Not Right: Drawing Lessons from Comparative Reform." Paper presented at Dwight Waldo Symposium, Maxwell School, Syracuse University, Syracuse, N.Y., June 1996.

Jones, D. "Management Strategies for Reinvention and Downsizing in the Federal Government." Unpublished Ph.D. dissertation, 1995.

Jones, V. D., and Ingraham, P. W. "The Pain of Organizational Change." In G. Frederickson and J. Johnston (eds.), *Public Administration: Reform and Innovation.* Tuscaloosa: University of Alabama Press, 1997.

Kettl, D. F. *Reinventing Government? Appraising the National Performance Review.* Washington, D.C.: Brookings Institution, 1994.

Osborne, D., and Gaebler, T. *Reinventing Government: How the Entrepreneurial Spirit Is Transforming the Public Sector.* Reading, Mass.: Addison Wesley Longman, 1992.

Peters, B. G., and Savoie, D. J. "Managing Incoherence: The Coordination and Empowerment Conundrum." *Public Administration Review,* 1996, *56,* 281–290.

Rainey, H. G. *Understanding and Managing Public Organizations.* (2nd ed.) San Francisco: Jossey-Bass, 1996.

Renfrow, P., Hede, A., and Lamond, T. "Lessons of the Australian Reforms." *International Journal of Public Administration,* forthcoming.

Sanders, R. P., and Thompson, J. R. "Laboratories of Reinvention." *Government Executive* (Special Supplement), Mar. 1996, pp. 1–12.

Szanton, P. *Federal Reorganization: What Have We Learned?* Chatham, N.J.: Chatham House, 1981.

Thompson, J. R., and Ingraham, P. W. "Organizational Redesign in the Public Sector." In D. F. Kettl and H. B. Milward (eds.), *The State of Public Management.* Baltimore: Johns Hopkins University Press, 1996.

U.S. General Accounting Office. *Transforming the Civil Service: Building the Workforce of the Future.* Washington, D.C.: U.S. Government Printing Office, 1995.

Index

A

Accountability: alignments for, 201–205; aspects of, 193–219; background on, 193–195; conclusion on, 214–216; defining, 195–198; evaluation scope for, 206–210; evaluation standards for, 210–214; and expectations, 199–200; external locus of, 126–127; and governance issues, 198–214; hierarchical, 197–199, 206, 208; ideal, 201–203; legal, 197–199, 206–208; managerial issues of, 213–214; methodological issues of, 214; patterns of, 205–214; political, 198–199, 207–208; political issues of, 212–213; professional, 198–199, 207–208; types of, 197–199; web of, 196–197

Adler, M., 178, 187

Agencies: change vectors in, 97–121; implementation in, 69–71; and institutionalization, 231–234; regulatory, 66

Agency for Health Care Policy and Research (AHCPR), 212–213, 216

Agency for International Development, 74, 83

Agricultural Marketing Service, 20–21

Alaska, team accountability in, 209

Alaska Native Medical Center, 230

Albicker, B., 238–239

Alpern, A., 59, 77, 93

Amberg-Blyskal, P., 13

Americans with Disabilities Act, 8–9

Animal and Plant Health Inspection Service (APHIS), 28: and leadership, 36, 46–47, 52; as learning organization, 24–26; partnering at, 20–21; teaming at, 7–11; virtual organization at, 23–24

Architecture, organizational: and agency restructuring, 110; alternatives in, 5–28; background on, 5–6; concept of, 6; conclusion on, 26–27; flexibility in, 243; information technology in, 17–19; issues of, 27; learning organization for, 24–26; networking in, 19–22; process orientation in, 11–17; teams for, 6–11; virtual organization and, 23–24

Armajani, B. J., 243, 255

Army Chemical and Biological Defense Command, 180

ARNet, 76

Arnold, P. E., 150, 162, 171

Articles of Confederation, 195

Ashforth, B. E., 133, 143

Asquith, S., 178, 187

Astley, W. G., 32, 56

Atlanta, network in, 87

Aucoin, P., 173, 187, 243, 255

Australia, government reform in, 78, 85, 243, 252, 253

Australian Task Force on Management Improvement, 78, 91

B

Ball, R., 159

Baltimore: information technology in, 18–19; power sharing in, 44

Ban, C., 31, 43, 56, 138, 144

Barrett, K., 58, 79, 91

Barzelay, M., 182, 187, 243, 255

Base Realignment and Closure Commission, 133

Bass, B. M., 52, 56

Beard, D. P., 40, 69, 70, 72, 91, 135

Beer, M., 33, 38, 44, 45–46, 48, 53, 56, 99, 100, 101, 103, 105, 114, 118, 120, 251, 255

Behn, R. D., 71, 91, 241, 255

Belgium, government reform in, 72

BenchNet, 76
Berg, D. N., 140, 145
Bernstein, M., 101, 120
Berra, Y., 241
Berry, F. S., 39, 56, 131, 135, 143, 149, 166, 167, 171, 224–225, 239, 242, 246, 247, 255
Bjorkman, J. W., 180, 187
Blair House Papers, 86
Board of Tea Tasters, 82
Boston, J., 249, 253, 255
Bowen, D., 100, 120
Bowsher, C. A., 202, 210, 216
Brady, S., 35
Brand, R., 141, 143
Briggs, J., 45, 56
Broad, M. L., 138, 143
Brookings Institution, 61, 79, 84, 89
Brown, R., 72
Brownlow Commission, 98
Brunsson, N., 178, 187
Bucelato, J., 50–52
Budd, M. L., 138, 143
Budget Officers Advisory Council, 76
Bureaucracy: characteristics of, 12, 26; inadequacies, 1–2; leaders in, 30; machine, 184; work flow in, 14
Burke, J., 196, 216
Burns, J. M., 52, 56
Burns, T., 6, 27, 103–104, 120
Burstein, P., 183, 187
Bush, G., 6, 47

C

Canada: institutionalizing change in, 225, 230, 235, 236, 239; Programme Review in, 184
Carr, N., 45, 46
Chackerian, R., 39, 56, 131, 135, 143, 149, 166, 167, 171, 224–225, 239, 242, 246, 247, 255
Champy, J., 11, 27, 249, 255
Change: active management of, 133–140; alternative approaches to, 173–189, 250; analyzing tactics of, 123–189; background on, 173–174; from bottom up, 178–180, 186; case study of, 157–162; champions of, 230, 232–233, 236–238; conclusions on, 142–143, 186–187; contingencies of, 183–186; employee resistance to, 125–146, 242; evaluating, 186–187; exogenous, 180–182; first-and second-order, 127–128, 222–223; generic, 176–177; goals of, 174, 185; guidelines for, 154–155, 157, 162, 253–255; incremental, 252; institutionalization of, 220–240; large-scale, 153–157, 162–165; lessons for continuing, 191–256; levers for, 103, 105, 113–114, 115, 119, 250–251; modifying, 141–142; objects of, 182–183; overviews on, 123–124, 191–192; paradoxes of, 125–129, 186, 242; recognizing barriers to, 129–133; recombinant strategies for, 251; reinforced, 140–142; staged strategies for, 252; successful, 147–172; tailored, 222–223; from top down, 175–178, 185; urgency of need for, 162–164. *See also* Reinvention
Change vectors: alternative models of, 106–118; analysis of, 97–121; background on, 97–98; compared, 115–118; concept of, 97; conclusion on, 118–120; elements of, 98–99, 102–105; hybrid models of, 104–105; levels in, 102, 105, 115; and participation, 99, 100–102; theories on, 99–100, 114
Chicago, teams in, 138–139
Chief Financial Officers Council, 64, 67, 76
Child, J., 32, 56
Chiles, L., 39, 40, 53, 128, 224–225
Chrétien, J., 184
Cincinnati, power sharing in, 42
Civil Service Commission, 159
Civil Service Reform Act of 1978, 47
Clinton, W. J., 7, 8, 31, 39, 58–62, 64–66, 78–80, 83, 86, 89, 91–92, 106, 148, 152, 164, 169, 171, 211, 221, 224–227, 236, 239
Coch, L., 101, 120
Cohen, A. R., 101, 120
Cohen, S., 141, 143
Collaboration, in change, 100–101
Colorado, team accountability in, 209
Commission on Economy and Effectiveness in Government (Georgia), 170
Communication: and change vectors, 103–104, 105, 109–110, 115; for implementation, 72; for institutionalization, 227–231, 237
Congressional Budget Office, 60

Consortium for Culture Change, 63, 72, 76
Contract with America, 225–226
Corbin, L., 70, 92, 133, 135, 143
Critical-path model, 105, 114
Culture, organizational: of accountability, 195, 199–200, 214–215; and change models, 175, 183, 185; changing, 227–229; of compliance, 48; of disbelief, 226; of government, 193; learning, 235; of partnership, 66; and resistance to change, 140–141; and teams, 9
Cummings, T. G., 100, 120
Customs Modernization Act of 1993, 70

D

Davenport, T. H., 11, 17, 27
Davis, G., 179, 187
de Montricher, N., 174, 187
De Pree, M., 79–80, 92
Dean, J. W., 140, 141, 144
Dear, J., 69, 70–71
Debt Collection Service, 21–22, 43
Defense Mapping Agency (DMA): accountability at, 211; leadership at, 34–35, 42, 45
Defense Personnel Support Center, 132–133
Denver, implementation in, 84
Department of Labor and Employment Security (Florida), 39
Di Iulio, J. J., Jr., 93, 182, 187, 193, 217
Disabled American Veterans, 16
Division of Workers Compensation (Florida), 39
Doig, J. W., 32–33, 56
Downs, G. W., 126, 143
Drucker, P. F., 59, 92
Drug Enforcement Administration, 19
Dubnick, M. J., 195, 197, 199, 201, 218–219
Duncan, R., 102, 121
Dunn, W. N., 101, 120

E

Eisenstat, R. A., 33, 38, 44, 45–46, 48, 53, 56, 99, 100, 101, 105, 114, 118, 120, 251, 255
Employees: ambiguity for, 245–246; and bottom-up change, 178–180, 187; career, support from, 131–132, 142; and contingencies of change, 184; defusing concerns of, 132–133; fears of, 130–131; incentives for, 229–231; job security for, 136–137; participation by, 134, 142; resistance by, 125–146, 242; training for, 137–138
Empowerment: in bottom-up change, 179; and implementation, 71–77, 83, 86–87; and risk taking, 134–135; and teams, 10
Enterprise Board, 151
Environmental Protection Agency, 51, 89
Equal Employment Opportunity Commission, 207
Ericksson, B., 181, 187
Europe, exogenous change in Central, 181
Executive Order 12862, 90

F

Facer, R., 153, 171
Faerman, S. R., 137–138, 144
Federal Acquisition Reform Act of 1994, 98
Federal Aviation Administration, 20
Federal Bureau of Investigation, 19, 83
Federal Communications Commission, 65
Federal Emergency Management Agency, 83
Federal Executive Boards, 76–77
Federal Executive Institute, 235
Federal Quality Institute, 134, 144
Field Servicing Office: leadership at, 36, 47; partnering at, 20–21; teaming at, 7–9
FinanceNet, 76
Finer, H., 196, 217
Finney, M., 100, 120
Finsterbusch, K., 176, 188
Florida: and civil service reform, 128–129, 135, 137, 242, 243, 246, 247; institutionalization in, 224–225; power sharing in, 39; reinvention in, 149, 166
Flyzik, J., 64
Food and Drug Administration, 88
Ford Foundation, 70, 129
Fosler, A., 84, 92
Fox, C., 245, 255
Frederickson, D. G., 123, 125, 174, 245, 246–247

Freeman, G., 183, 188
French, J.R.P., Jr., 101, 120
Friedrich, C. J., 196, 217
Future search process, for learning organization, 26

G

Gaebler, T., 29, 56, 59, 72, 94, 126, 145, 148–149, 166–167, 171, 179, 188, 191, 192, 193, 200, 218, 249, 256
Gardening metaphor, 97, 250
Garvey, G., 195, 201, 217
Gaus, C. R., 212, 217
Geddes, B., 181, 188
General Services Administration (GSA): leadership at, 40, 42, 44, 49; networking at, 19–20; and red tape, 151
Georgia: and privatization, 170; reform effort in, 242; team accountability in, 209
Gerstein, M. S., 6, 19, 28
Gerth, H. H., 201–202, 217
Giacquinta, J. B., 101, 120
Gingrich, N., 225–226
Glick, W. H., 155, 171
Goldberg, F., 116
Goldsmith, S., 136
Golembiewski, R., 178, 188
Goodman, P. S., 140, 141, 144
Goodsell, C., 59, 92
Gore, A., Jr., 37, 38, 40, 52, 53, 56, 59–74, 76–77, 79–81, 83–84, 86–87, 89, 90, 92, 93, 99, 119, 148–150, 152, 163–165, 168–169, 171, 179–180, 182, 188, 191–193, 211, 217, 221, 223–227, 236, 239
Government Information Technology Services Working Group, 63, 67
Government Performance and Results Act of 1992, 47, 64, 80, 81, 82, 85, 88, 98, 210–211
Gow, I., 236
Grace, P., 61, 224
Grace Commission, 60, 61, 152–153, 176–177, 224, 229
Gradick, D., 7–9, 24, 36, 46–47, 52, 54
Grain Inspection, Stockyards and Packers Administration, 20–21
Greene, R., 58, 79, 91
Greer, P., 177, 188
Greiner, L. E., 104–105, 120, 153–155, 157, 162, 171
Gross, N., 101, 120
Gruber, J., 196, 217
Guadagnoli, E., 212, 217
Gurwitt, R., 149, 171

H

Hage, J., 176, 188
Haines, J., 21, 43
Hammer, M., 11, 27, 249, 255
Hammer Awards, 45, 64, 73–74, 83, 90
Hampton, Virginia: accountability in, 204, 209; teams in, 139
Hanna, R. W., 130, 146
Hargrove, E. C., 32–33, 56
Harris, P. R., 243
Harvard University, Kennedy School of Government at, 129
Harwood, J., 1, 3
Health Care Financing Administration, 22, 66
Hede, A., 243, 256
Heifitz, R., 30, 41, 56
Hershey, R. D., 111, 120
Herzberg, F., 159
Hogwood, B. W., 181, 188
Holbek, J., 102, 121
Holmes, M., 252, 255
Hood, C., 72, 93, 176, 188
Hoover, H., 61, 224
Hoover Commission, 61, 98, 126, 224
Horn, S., 78
Horner, C., 171
Houston, network in, 76–77, 87
Howard, J., 253
Huber, G. P., 155, 171
Hughes, S., 16
Human resource practices, alignment of, 140–141
Husock, H., 136–137, 144
Hyde, A. C., 91, 96

I

Idaho, team accountability in, 209
IGNet, 76
Immigration and Naturalization Service, 19
Implementation: in agencies, 69–71; aspects of, 58–96; assessing, 68–69, 77–84; background on, 58–59; and budget cuts, 67–68; and catalyst for change, 62–69; changing environments for, 65–68; conclusion on,

89–90; external champions for, 64; in future, 84–89; issues for, 85–86; problems of, 5–6; recognition in, 64, 73–74; and restructuring, 81–84, 88–89; sustained, 84–86
Increased Ministerial Authority and Accountability (Canada), 225
Indiana Department of Transportation, 141–142
Indianapolis, job security in, 136–137
Information technology: in architecture, 17–19; and exogenous change, 181–182; and process orientation, 17
Information Technology Service, 23–24
Ingraham, P. W., 44, 57, 109, 121, 131, 144, 192, 193, 194, 217, 219, 241, 243, 245, 246, 248, 249, 251, 252, 255, 256
Innovation in Government Award, 70
Inputs, and accountability, 202–203
Installation Excellence Award, 51
Institutionalization of change: and agencies, 231–234; aspects of, 220–240; background on, 220–221; communication for, 227–231, 237; conclusion on, 236–238; and expectations, 221–222, 237–238; political will for, 223–226, 243; training and development for, 234–236
Internal franchising, in networking, 20–21
Internal Revenue Service (IRS): characteristics of, 109–110; culture of, 185; District Organization Study at, 108, 109, 116, 121; implementation at, 74, 82, 88, 249; Information Systems unit at, 107, 109, 115; institutionalization at, 230; Office of Modernization at, 111; Service Center Organization Study at, 108, 116; Tax Systems Modernization (TSM) at, 107, 108, 109, 111, 116–117, 185; top-down change at, 97, 106, 107–111, 115–118
International Personnel Management Association, 209, 217
Interstate Commerce Commission, 81
Ireland, exogenous change in, 181

J

Janis, M. B., 42–43, 239
Jasper, H., 59, 77, 93
Jermier, J. M., 132, 145
Jick, T. D., 5, 27, 100, 120
Johnson, P., 76, 93
Johnson, R., 40
Joint Chiefs of Staff, 35
Jones, D., 245, 255
Jones, V. D., 245, 255
Juran, J., 79

K

Kamarck, E., 119
Kamensky, J. M., 3, 58, 72, 89, 93, 248
Kansas, implementation in, 71
Kanter, R. M., 5, 27, 100, 101, 103–104, 105, 120, 229–230, 239
Kaufman, H., 5, 27, 32, 56
Keep Commission, 58
Kelly, R., 25
Kelman, S., 64
Kettl, D. F., 54, 56, 61, 62, 77, 79, 84, 89, 93, 147, 166, 171, 193, 200, 216, 217, 244, 255
Kickert, W.J.M., 173, 188
Kidd, R., 18, 28
King, L., 24, 25–26
Kochan, T. A., 31, 43, 56
Koonce, R., 65, 94
Koskinen, J., 85, 94
Kotter, J. P., 155–156, 157, 162, 171, 176, 188
Kraemer, K. L., 181, 188

L

Lamond, T., 243, 256
Larkey, P. D., 126, 143
Latin America, exogenous change in, 181
Lawler, E. E., III, 101, 120, 138, 144
Leaders: adaptive, 30; attributes of, 29–57; background on, 29–31; challenge for, 167–170; characteristics of, 30–31; devaluation of, 31–33; entrepreneurial, 33; isolation for, 53; for learning organizations, 54–55; long view held by, 44–46; metaphors for, 52–55; need for, 32–33; political, 243, 248, 252; Pony Express strategy of, 46–48; power sharing by, 38–44; and purpose, 34–38; Pyrrhic victories for, 49–52; ratio of, 31; risk taking by, 48–52; strategic perspective of, 44–48; and systems theory, 31–32; as talk show hosts, 55; transformational, 52
Learning organization: architecture for, 24–26; culture of, 235; leaders for, 54–55

Leavitt, H. J., 125, 138, 144
Lee, R. T., 133, 143
Leemans, A. F., 100, 103, 121
Letts, C. W., 141, 144
Levy, A., 127, 144, 223, 239
Lewin, K., 129, 143, 144
Lewis, R., 11
Light, P. C., 135, 144, 200, 218, 232–233, 239
Likert, R., 159
Lipsky, M., 178, 188
Luke, 222

M

Machiavelli, N., 29, 30, 31, 34, 48, 56
MacKay, B., 128, 224–225
Madison, J., 195, 218
Maine, implementation in, 71
Managers: and accountability, 194, 200, 201–204, 213–214, 215–216; active, 133–140; and ambiguity, 244–246; aspects of change for, 241–256; background on, 241–243; characteristics of ideal, 231; guidelines for, 253–255; and institutionalization, 228–229, 233–234; lessons for, 246–249; and public relations, 248–249; and theory, 249–253
Mandsager, R., 239
Manning, W., 10
March, J. G., 131, 144, 183, 188
Market theory, 251
Marks, M. L., 138, 139, 144
Martin, J., 249, 253, 255
Maryland, team accountability in, 209
Maslow, A., 159
Maxwell Reinvention Symposium, 41, 55*n*, 227, 228, 233, 235, 238–239, 241
McGregor, D., 159
McKenna, H., 159, 160
McNeil, B. J., 212, 217
Merced County (California) Human Services Agency, 18
Merit system, and accountability, 196
Merit Systems Protection Board, 202, 207
Merry, U., 127, 144
Mesch, D. J., 139, 145
Metcalfe, L., 226, 239
Miami: information technology in, 19; teaming in, 9–11
Mills, C. W., 201–202, 217
Milward, H. B., 201, 218
Minneapolis, teaming in, 7–9
Minnesota, reform effort in, 243
Minnesota Trade Office, 213
Mintzberg, H., 222, 237, 239
Mirvis, P. H., 140, 145
Mission to Planet Earth, 22
Moe, R. C., 58, 59, 60, 77, 90, 94, 126, 145, 166, 171, 195, 218
Mohr, L. B., 130, 145
Montana, team accountability in, 209
Morgan, G., 222, 237, 239
Morse, N., 44
Mosher, F. C., 100, 101, 121, 196, 218
Mulroney, B., 225
Murphy, B., 42, 54

N

Nadler, D. A., 6, 19, 28
National Academy of Public Administration, 58, 84, 91, 94, 215, 218
National Acquisition Center, 45
National Aeronautics and Space Administration, 22
National Agriculture Association, 10–11
National Archives and Record Administration, 211
National Association of State Personnel Executives, 209, 218
National Cemetery System, 12, 111
National Commission on the Public Service, 138, 145
National Park Service, 74–75, 83, 88
National Partnership Council: and implementation, 63, 67, 84, 94; and leadership, 31, 43, 51, 56
National Performance Review (NPR): and accountability, 193, 204, 211, 218; as administrative reform, 147–153; and architectural modes, 7, 12, 20, 21, 28; assessing, 68–69, 77–84; as catalyst for change, 62–69; and change models, 175, 179, 181, 187; and change vectors, 98–99, 119; conclusion on, 89–90; cost savings from, 81, 82; and customer service standards, 63–64, 72, 80, 91, 151; described, 59–62; and empowerment, 71–77, 83, 86–87, 151, 168–169; future for, 84–89; implementation of, 58–96, 165, 248; and institutionalization, 221, 223, 225–226; as

large-scale change, 162–165; and leaders, 29, 31, 37–38, 41, 46–47, 53, 57, 69–71, 90, 164, 167–170; limitations of, 165–170; priorities and initiatives of, 150–152; progress of, 149–153; recommendations of, 61, 63–65, 81–84; and resistance to change, 126, 132
National Research Council (NRC), 107, 115
National Rural Development Partnership (NRDP), 200, 209–210, 213
Naval Petroleum Reserve, 81, 82
Networking: in architecture, 19–22; centers of expertise for, 20; for implementation, 63, 72, 75–77, 87–88
New York City: Department of Probation process orientation in, 16–17, 28; implementation in, 73–74; Veterans Health Administration in, 12–16, 111–114
New Zealand: accountability in, 211; reform efforts in, 249, 251, 253
Nietzsche, F. W., 34
Nord, W. R., 132, 145
Nuber, P., 34–35, 42, 45, 54
Nutt, P. C., 101–102, 121

O

Occupational Safety and Health Administration (OSHA): and accountability, 202; change supported at, 132; implementation at, 70–71, 86; and power sharing, 42
Office of Budget and Program Analysis, 25
Office of General Counsel, 25
Ogden, Utah, implementation in, 74, 109
O'Hare, K., 138, 145
Olsen, J. P., 131, 144, 178, 183, 187, 188
Oregon, reform effort in, 243
Organization for Economic Cooperation and Development, 72, 94
Organizations. *See* Architecture, organizational; Culture, organizational; Learning organization; Virtual organizations
Osborne, D., 29, 56, 59, 72, 85, 94, 126, 145, 148–149, 166–167, 171, 179, 188, 191, 192, 193, 200, 218, 249, 256
Outcomes, and accountability, 203–204, 211, 212–213, 214
Outputs, and accountability, 202–204, 211, 213–214

P

Pallot, J., 249, 253, 255
Participation: and change models, 184, 187; and change vectors, 99, 100–102; by employees, 134, 142; in large-scale change, 164; and power sharing, 41–42; for work teams, 159
Partnering: and implementation, 66, 68; in networking, 21–22; and power sharing, 38–44
Pearson, C., 100, 120
Peat, F. D., 45, 56
Pendleton Act of 1883, 196
Performance appraisals: and accountability, 206–208; change of, 113; 360-degree, 207–208
Permission, and power sharing, 38–44
Perry, J. L., 123, 125, 131, 139, 140, 144, 145, 174, 181, 188, 245, 246–247
Perry, W. J., 223–224, 239
Pestka, T., 21–22, 43
Peters, B. G., 124, 131, 145, 146, 163, 171, 173, 179, 181, 184, 188, 189, 193, 218, 220, 232, 239, 244, 249–250, 256
Peters, T., 79, 183, 189
Pew Charitable Trust, 91
Philadelphia, networking in, 20
Pitt, D. C., 183, 189
Plant Protection and Quarantine (PPQ), 7, 9–11, 25
Plastrik, P., 85, 94
Political appointee system, and accountability, 196
Pollitt, C., 173, 189
Porras, J. I., 127–128, 145
Portugal, government reform in, 72
Power: détente in, 42–44; shared, 38–44, 164; trickle-down model of, 40–41
President's Award for Quality and Productivity Improvement, 35
President's Management Council: and implementation, 63, 67, 76, 84, 85; and leadership, 41
President's Private Sector Survey on Cost Control. *See* Grace Commission
Price, R., 22

Principal-agent theory, 249
Process orientation: and accountability, 202–203; in architecture, 11–17; case studies of, 12–17
Public and Indian Housing Administration, 43
Public Health Service, 212
Public Service 2000 (Canada), 225, 230
Purpose: ends and means for, 36–38; and history, 34–35; and leaders, 34–38; and vision, 35–36, 47–48

Q

Quality movement. *See* Total Quality Management

R

Radin, B., 193, 200, 209, 210, 211, 213, 218
Rago, W. V., 145
Railroad Retirement Board, 74
Rainey, G. W., 131, 145, 160, 161*n*, 172, 185, 189, 248
Rainey, H. G., 123–124, 131, 140, 145, 147, 152*n*, 153, 154*n*, 156*n*, 161*n*, 167, 171, 172, 183, 185, 189, 248, 256
Rategan, C. A., 138, 145
Rayner study (United Kingdom), 229
Reagan, R., 6, 152, 176, 235
Recognition, in implementation, 64, 73–74
Reinventing government (REGO) movement, 148–149, 166–167
Reinvention: analyzing tactics for, 123–189; in architecture of organizations, 5–28; aspects of strategic change for, 1–121; change vectors in, 97–121; guidelines for, 253–255; implementation for, 58–96; institutionalizing, 220–240; keeper of torch of, 63–65; leaders for, 29–57; lessons for continuing, 191–256; license for, 38–39; overview on, 1–3. *See also* Change
Reinvention laboratories: and accountability, 194, 208–209; and architecture, 8, 20, 21, 25; and change models, 179–180; and change vectors, 98–99, 114, 119; and implementation, 60, 68–69, 72, 74–75, 87; and leadership, 34, 37, 47; and managers, 244; and resistance to change, 132, 135; and successful change, 152, 163, 165, 169
Renfrow, P., 243, 256
Richards, S., 226, 239
Riley, R., 72
Ripkin, C., 62
Risk taking: by leaders, 48–52; nurtured, 134–136
Robertson, P. J., 127–128, 145
Rogers, E. M., 33, 57, 102, 121
Romzek, B. S., 191, 193, 195, 197, 199, 201, 210, 213, 217, 218–219, 249
Roosevelt, T., 58
Roper Polls, 91, 94
Ruscio, K. P., 215, 219

S

Sanders, R. P., 2, 3, 29, 44, 46, 49–50, 57, 97, 124, 132, 135, 146, 152, 164, 168, 172, 243, 244, 245, 250, 256
Savoie, D. J., 131, 145, 146, 163, 171, 173, 184, 188, 189, 191–192, 193, 218, 220, 224, 225, 229, 240, 242, 244, 246–247, 255, 256
Schein, E. H., 138, 140, 146, 175, 189, 215, 219
Scott, W. R., 185, 189
Senge, P., 24, 28, 54, 57
Shaw, R. B., 6, 19, 28, 138, 139, 144
Shoemaker, F. F., 33, 57, 102, 121
Shoop, T., 69, 76, 94
Siehl, C., 100, 120
Simpson, L., 212, 217
Singleton, A. L., 70, 94
Small Business Administration, 65, 211
Smith, B. C., 183, 189
Social Security Administration: accountability at, 211; and implementation, 66, 82, 185; modules for claims processing at, 157–162
Southern Growth Policies Board, 209, 213, 219
Spector, B., 33, 38, 44, 45–46, 48, 53, 56, 99, 100, 101, 105, 114, 118, 120, 251, 255
Spoils system, and accountability, 196
Stage of change, 102–103, 105, 115, 252
Stalker, G. M., 6, 27, 103–104, 120
States: power sharing in, 39; team accountability in, 209

Stein, B. A., 5, 27, 100, 120
Stern, J., 76, 93
Stone, D., 26
Strategic incrementalism, 44–45
Sweden, exogenous change in, 181
Swierczek, F. W., 101, 120
Szanton, P., 58, 94, 97, 121, 173, 189, 250, 256

T

Tannenbaum, R., 130, 146
Task Force on Workforce Adaptiveness (Canada), 230, 233, 234, 240
Teams: accountability for, 207–210; for architecture, 6–11; case studies of, 7–11; cross-functional, 11; implementation recognition for, 64, 73; importance of, 138–140; and learning organization, 25; and partnering, 21; and power sharing, 42; self-managed work, 15, 36, 47, 112–113; for virtual organization, 23; in work modules, 157–162
Texas, privatization in, 1
Texas Commission for the Blind, 204
Thatcher, M., 176, 177, 224
Thomas, P., 222, 223, 240
Thompson, F. J., 175, 189
Thompson, J., 12–13, 15, 42, 45–46, 47, 49, 54, 73, 112–115, 118
Thompson, J. R., 2, 3, 5, 29*n*, 42, 44, 45, 46, 48, 49, 50, 57, 69, 73, 75, 94, 97, 109, 121, 132, 135, 146, 152, 164, 172, 193, 194, 219, 244, 245, 249, 250, 256
3M Corporation, 7
Total Quality Management (TQM): and accountability, 200, 207; and architectural modes, 5, 7–8, 21; institutionalizing, 224–225; and leadership, 39, 46–47; and managers, 245–246; and resistance to change, 128–129, 137, 141–142; and Tax Systems Modernization, 109
Training: for employees, 137–138; for institutionalization, 234–236
Troanovich, M., 22
Trust, and implementation, 80

U

Unions: and change vectors, 116–117; and implementation, 74; and job security, 136–137; and leaders of change, 31, 43, 50–51; and partnering, 21–22; and teams, 10–11
United Kingdom, government reform in, 72, 80, 85, 176, 177, 224, 229, 252
U.S. Bureau of Customs: and implementation, 69, 70, 82, 83, 86; and partnering, 22
U.S. Bureau of Labor Statistics, 17
U.S. Bureau of Mines, 82
U.S. Bureau of Prisons, 19
U.S. Bureau of Reclamation: and implementation, 69, 70, 86; power sharing at, 40; risk taking at, 135–136
U.S. Bureau of the Census, 17
U.S. Bureau of the Mint, 84
U.S. Department of Agriculture, 28; implementation at, 82; learning organization at, 25; networking at, 20–21; teaming at, 7–11; virtual organization at, 23
U.S. Department of Commerce, 72, 89
U.S. Department of Defense: and implementation, 65, 74, 83; and leadership, 34–35, 50–52; and resistance to change, 132
U.S. Department of Education: implementation in, 72; partnering in, 21–22, 43
U.S. Department of Energy, 83
U.S. Department of Health and Human Services, 22, 212
U.S. Department of Housing and Urban Development, 43, 83
U.S. Department of Justice, 19, 82
U.S. Department of Labor, 70
U.S. Department of the Interior: and implementation, 70, 75; and resistance to change, 135
U.S. Department of the Treasury: and change vectors, 106, 111; and implementation, 64, 70; and institutionalization, 227, 228
U.S. Department of Veterans Affairs: accountability at, 211; and change vectors, 106, 111; and implementation, 73–74, 91; leadership at, 44, 45; and processes, 12
U.S. General Accounting Office (GAO): and accountability, 193–194, 200, 204,

209, 211, 213, 219; and change vectors, 107, 115, 117; and implementation, 58, 60, 73, 75, 78, 79, 87, 90, 95; and institutionalization, 228; and managing reform, 252, 253, 256; and power sharing, 39, 48, 57
U.S. House of Representatives: Appropriations Subcommittee of, 111; Committee on Government Operations of, 58, 95; Committee on Government Reform and Oversight of, 78–79, 84, 95, 210, 214, 216–217; Committee on the Budget of, 58, 95; and implementation, 64, 88–89
U.S. Internal Revenue Service. *See* Internal Revenue Service
U.S. Marshals Service, 19
U.S. National Performance Review. *See* National Performance Review
U.S. Navy, 20
U.S. Office of Management and Budget (OMB): and implementation, 64, 67, 68, 81, 84, 85, 90, 96; and institutionalization, 227, 228, 233; and red tape, 151
U.S. Office of Personnel Management: and accountability, 200, 204, 219; and implementation, 83; and successful change, 159
U.S. Postal Service, 211
U.S. Senate: Committee on Government Affairs of, 64, 96; and implementation, 88–89
Useem, M., 31, 43, 56

V

Vaill, P. B., 54, 57
Van de Ven, A. H., 32, 56
van Vught, F. A., 173, 188
Vectors. *See* Change vectors
Veterans Administration Medical Center, 18–19, 44
Veterans Benefits Administration (VBA): Adjudication unit at, 111–112; bottom-up change at, 97, 106, 111–118; leadership at, 42, 45, 47, 49; processes at, 12–16; Veterans Services at, 112
Veterans Health Administration, 12, 111
Veterinary Services, 7, 8, 25
Virginia, awards in, 51
Virtual organizations: and architecture, 23–24; for implementation, 76
Visalia, California, hotel in, 149
Vision, and purpose, 35–36, 47–48
Vogel, R., 113
Volcker Commission, 193, 219

W

Walsh, P., 249, 253, 255
Walters, J., 193, 214, 219
Walton, R. E., 140, 146
Waterman, R., 183, 189
Weber, M., 201
Wechsler, B., 39, 56, 128, 131, 135, 143, 146, 149, 166, 167, 171, 172, 224–225, 239, 242, 246, 247, 255
Weise, G., 69, 70
Westley, F. R., 130, 146
Wheatley, M., 45, 57
Wilson, J. Q., 106, 121, 221, 240
Winn, M., 16
Winter Commission, 193, 219
Wise, L. R., 134, 146
Wright, H., 16

Y

Yi, H., 91, 96
Yin, R. K., 140, 146

Z

Zaltman, G., 102, 121
Ziegler, J., 40, 41–42, 44, 49, 54
Zifcak, S., 173, 189
Zurita, R., 19

Printed and bound by CPI Group (UK) Ltd, Croydon, CR0 4YY

16/04/2025

14658514-0003